SEABOARD
3048
S E A B O A R D
SOUTHERN
SOUTHERN
24408
SOUTHERN
21397

SEABOARD AIR LINE RAILWAY

The Route Of Courteous Service

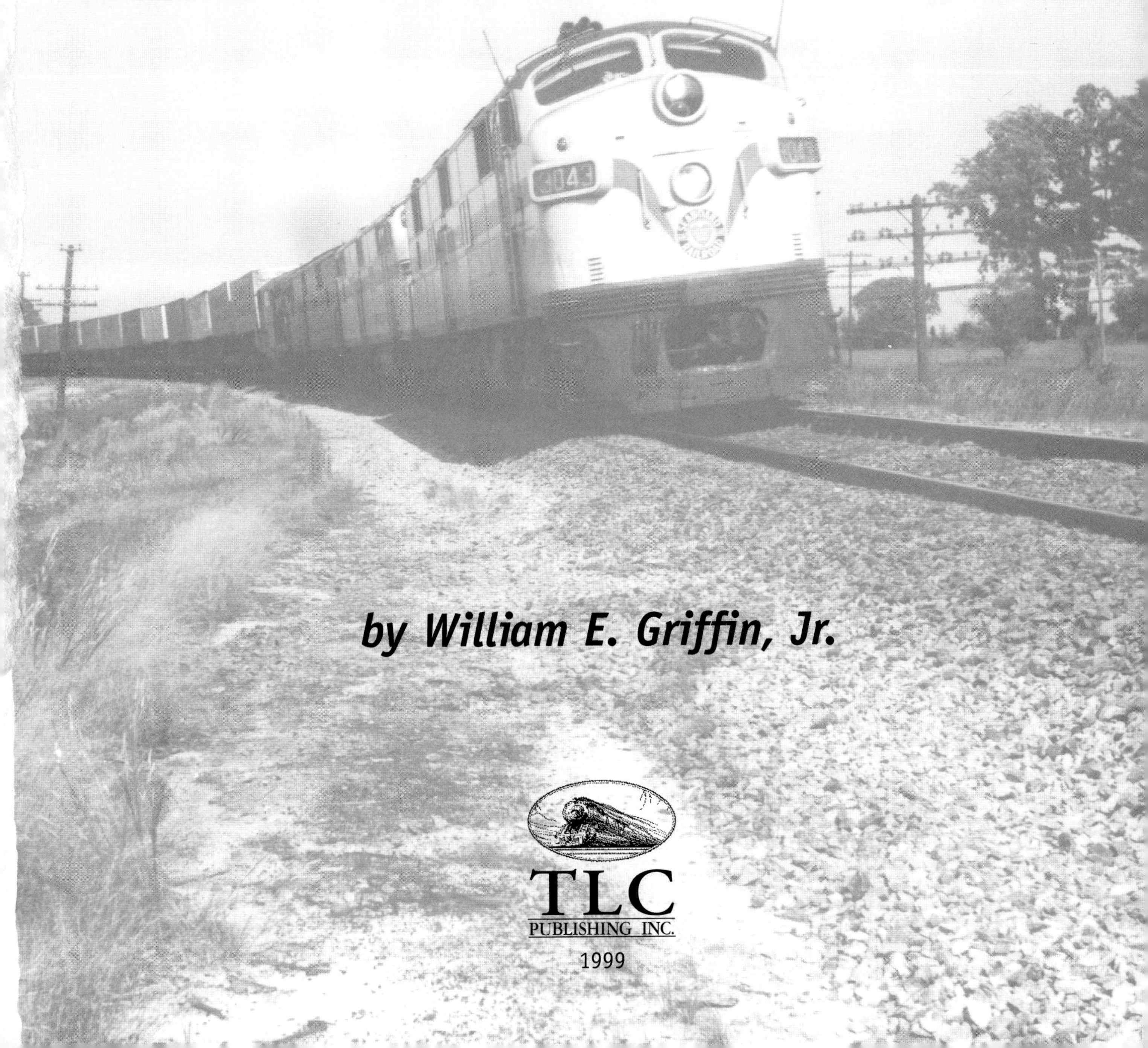

by William E. Griffin, Jr.

TLC PUBLISHING INC.

1999

1999
TLC Publishing, Inc.
1387 Winding Creek Lane
Lynchburg, Virginia, 24503-3776

International Standard Book Number 1-883089-44-1
Library of Congress Catalog Card Number 98-61783

Design, Layout, Type, and Image Assembly by
Kevin J. Holland
type&DESIGN
Burlington, Ontario

Color Image Assembly, Separations, and Printing by
Walsworth Publishing Company
Marceline, Missouri, 64658

Produced on the MacOS™

Cover –
In a classic SAL publicity pose, E7 number 3030 leads one of the Seaboard's "Silver Fleet" through a Florida orange grove.
(SAL Photo)

Title Page –
Trailer-on-flatcar (TOFC) business was first handled on the SAL in 1959. Soon, some of the SAL's fastest trains were the solid TOFC freights, such as TT-23, *The Razorback*, operating between Hialeah, Florida, and Kearney, N.J., in conjunction with the Pennsylvania Railroad. This 75-car TT-23 is rolling through Gill, N.C., in May 1962 behind three E7As and a GP9.
(Curt Tillotson, Jr.)

Table of Contents

SEABOARD

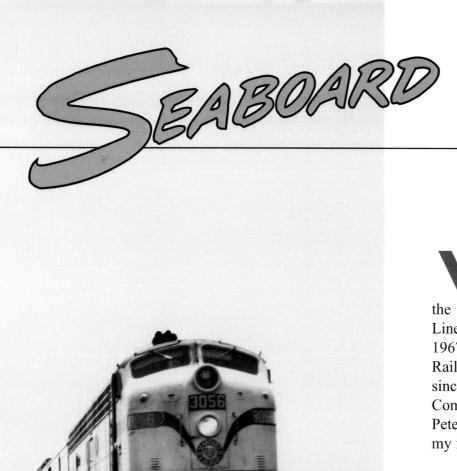

While this book was being completed, it occurred to me that it has been over thirty years since the corporate identity of the Seaboard Air Line Railway came to an end as a result of its 1967 merger with the Atlantic Coast Line Railroad. Could so many years have passed since that day when I drove over to the SAL's Commerce Street Station in my hometown of Petersburg, Virginia, to witness the last run of my favorite passenger trains?

No, my favorite trains weren't members of the Seaboard's grand "Silver Fleet" of streamliners. Rather, they were the Passenger, Mail and Express trains – Nos. 3 and 4. Unlike most of the streamliners that passed through the Old Dominion at night, Locals 3 and 4 operated during daylight hours. Southbound No. 3 was scheduled in Petersburg at 1:00 pm and passed near my grandmother's home at Alberta, Virginia, about an hour later. Northbound No. 4 passed through Alberta at about 11:00 am and reached Petersburg before noon. They were great trains to watch and – as long as you were only traveling the forty miles between Petersburg and Alberta – they were great trains to ride. Besides, they were the only Seaboard trains that stopped in Alberta.

So on Friday morning, June 30, 1967, I drove over to the Commerce Street Station to say goodbye to my old friends. They arrived, conducted their business, and then left town – never again to return under the flag of the Seaboard Air Line Railway. At 12:01 am the following morning the new Seaboard Coast Line Railroad came into existence. Later that

Introduction and Acknowledgments

day, SCL logo decals were applied to the noses of the SAL and ACL diesels. The new Company was still named "Seaboard," but things would never be the same again. The SCL discontinued the operation of Nos. 3 and 4 in April the following year. The old Commerce Street station was taken out of service in 1972 and the building was sold in 1977. Ten years later, the SCL's successor company – CSX Transportation – abandoned much of the SAL's old Virginia Division, including the trackage between Petersburg and Alberta.

There was very little fanfare to herald the demise of the Seaboard Air Line. Press coverage at the time tended to focus on the new company that had been created by the merger. I doubt that there were very many of us at trackside that fateful day in 1967 when the Seaboard passed into history.

However, in the years that have ensued, the SAL's admirers have grown in both number and enthusiasm – including many who never personally observed the railroad in operation. This book is for those Seaboard enthusiasts. For those of you who knew the Seaboard, I hope that it will help you to remember the glory of days past. For future generations, I hope that it will pique your interest and make you want to learn even more about this remarkable and innovative railroad.

This book would not have been possible without the assistance of many people. One of the real joys of doing a book such as this is the association with old friends and the opportunity to make new ones along the way. The following photographers and collectors have graciously shared photographs from their collections of prints and/or original negatives: August A. Thieme, William J. Husa, Jr., Harold K. Vollrath, Mac B. Connery, Anthony L. Dementi, Beaufort S. Ragland, L.W. Rice, Jr., D. Wallace Johnson, L. D. Moore, Jr., H. Reid, R. B. Carneal, Frank E. Ardrey, Jr., J. R. Quinn, H. L. Kitchen, James B. Harris, Wiley M. Bryan, Thomas G. Wicker, Hugh M. Comer, James F. Byrne, Richard E. Prince, Paul E. Parrish, Jay Williams, Lloyd D. Lewis, Thomas W. Dixon, Jr., Bruce Lewis, Robert K. Durham, R. D. Sharpless, J. A. Sargeant, Bob's Photos, M. D. McCarter, Don Hensley, W. J. Rivers, Walter Gay, Curt Tillotson, Jr., Charles Conniff, James H. Wade, Jr., Warren Calloway, Robert G. Lewis, Tom G. King, H.H. Harwood, C. K. Marsh, Jr., David W. Salter, J.E. Jones, Mallory Hope Ferrell, Homer R. Hill, C. L. Goolsby, H. Allan Paul, Howard W. Ameling, John C. LaRue, Jr., O.W. Kimsey, Jr., D. Ray Sturges, Richard J. Short, Ralph Coleman, Robert S. Crockett, Railroad Avenue Enterprises, and John P. Stith.

I also wish to express my appreciation to Richard E. Bussard and Gary T. Sease of the Corporation Communications Department of CSX Transportation, Inc., Mark J. Cedeck of the John W. Barriger III National Railroad Library, the St. Louis Mercantile Library, the Virginia Historical Society, the Denver Public Library (Western History Department), and the Smithsonian Institution.

William E. Griffin, Jr.
Orange Park, Florida
July 1998

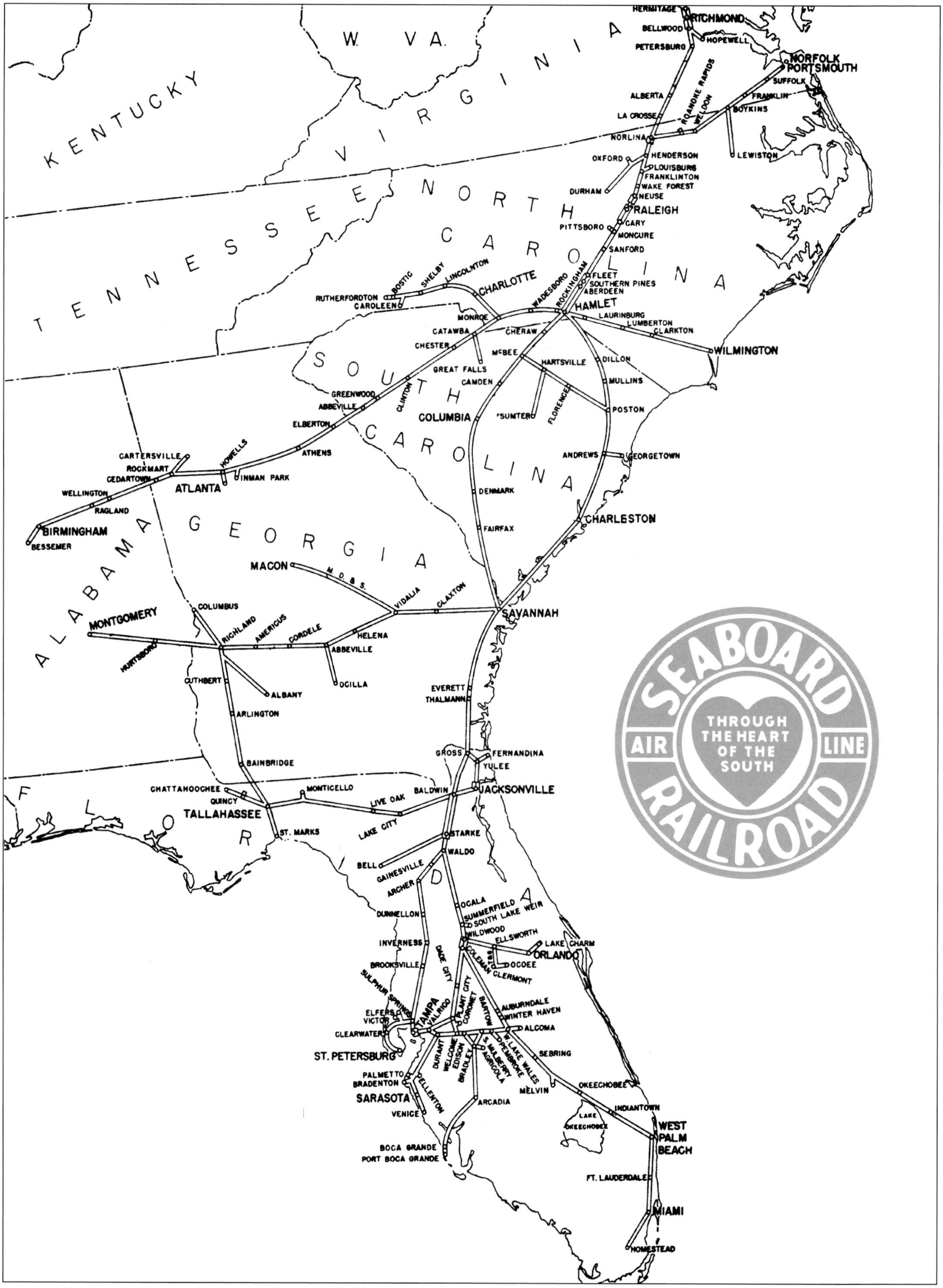
KENTUCKY
W. VA.
VIRGINIA
TENNESSEE
NORTH CAROLINA
SOUTH CAROLINA
GEORGIA
ALABAMA
FLORIDA
HERMITAGE
RICHMOND
BELLWOOD
PETERSBURG
HOPEWELL
NORFOLK
PORTSMOUTH
SUFFOLK
FRANKLIN
BOYKINS
ALBERTA
ROANOKE RAPIDS
WELDON
LA CROSSE
NORLINA
LEWISTON
OXFORD
HENDERSON
LOUISBURG
FRANKLINTON
WAKE FOREST
DURHAM
NEUSE
RALEIGH
PITTSBORO
CARY
MONCURE
SANFORD
FLEET
SOUTHERN PINES
ABERDEEN
WADESBORO
ROCKINGHAM
HAMLET
LAURINBURG
LUMBERTON
CLARKTON
WILMINGTON
BOSTIC
SHELBY
LINCOLNTON
CHARLOTTE
RUTHERFORDTON
CAROLEEN
MONROE
CATAWBA
CHERAW
CHESTER
McBEE
HARTSVILLE
DILLON
GREAT FALLS
CAMDEN
MULLINS
GREENWOOD
CLINTON
ABBEVILLE
FLORENCE
COLUMBIA
SUMTER
POSTON
ELBERTON
ANDREWS
GEORGETOWN
CARTERSVILLE
HOWELLS
ATHENS
ROCKMART
CEDARTOWN
INMAN PARK
ATLANTA
WELLINGTON
RAGLAND
DENMARK
BIRMINGHAM
BESSEMER
CHARLESTON
FAIRFAX
MACON
M. D. & S.
VIDALIA
CLAXTON
SAVANNAH
COLUMBUS
MONTGOMERY
RICHLAND
AMERICUS
CORDELE
HELENA
ABBEVILLE
HURTSBORO
CUTHBERT
ALBANY
OCILLA
EVERETT
THALMANN
ARLINGTON
BAINBRIDGE
GROSS
FERNANDINA
YULEE
CHATTAHOOCHEE
MONTICELLO
BALDWIN
JACKSONVILLE
QUINCY
LIVE OAK
TALLAHASSEE
LAKE CITY
ST. MARKS
STARKE
WALDO
BELL
GAINESVILLE
ARCHER
OCALA
SUMMERFIELD
SOUTH LAKE WEIR
DUNNELLON
WILDWOOD
ELLSWORTH
LAKE CHARM
INVERNESS
ORLANDO
OCOEE
DADE CITY
COLEMAN
CLERMONT
BROOKSVILLE
SULPHUR SPRINGS
PLANT CITY
CORONET
BARTOW
AUBURNDALE
WINTER HAVEN
ELFERS
VICTOR
TAMPA
VALRICO
CLEARWATER
ALCOMA
ST. PETERSBURG
DURANT
WELCOME
EDISON
BRADLEY
MULBERRY
AGRICOLA
PEMBROKE
LAKE WALES
SEBRING
PALMETTO
BRADENTON
ELLENTON
MELVIN
OKEECHOBEE
SARASOTA
ARCADIA
INDIANTOWN
VENICE
LAKE OKEECHOBEE
WEST PALM BEACH
BOCA GRANDE
PORT BOCA GRANDE
FT. LAUDERDALE
MIAMI
HOMESTEAD
SEABOARD AIR LINE RAILROAD
THROUGH THE HEART OF THE SOUTH

SEABOARD Chapter

A brief history of the Seaboard Air Line

The Seaboard Air Line Railway was assembled under the direction of Richmond, Virginia, banker John Skelton Williams over a five-year period between 1895 and 1900. During that period, Mr. Williams and his banking associates acquired through the process of stock control a number of separately organized railroads then operating in the Southeastern United States from Virginia to Florida and Alabama. Some of these SAL predecessor companies were among the earliest railroads incorporated in America.

The earliest of the predecessor companies was the Portsmouth and Roanoke Railroad, an enterprise chartered in 1832 to build 79 miles of railroad between Portsmouth, Virginia, and Weldon, North Carolina, on the falls of the Roanoke River. The Portsmouth and Roanoke commenced construction in 1833. The first track consisted of long wooden stringers with a strip of strap rail nailed to the top. By July of 1834, the line had been extended from Portsmouth through the western edge of the Great Dismal Swamp to Suffolk. In the absence of locomotives, operations commenced with horse-drawn coaches making two daily trips to Suffolk. The ride cost $1 each way or $1.50 if the round trip was made the same day.

On September 4, 1834, the first steam locomotive arrived in Portsmouth aboard the packet schooner *Hand*. Named the *John Barnett*, this five-ton locomotive was soon handling trains between Portsmouth and Suffolk in an hour and fifteen minutes at the unheard of speed of 15 mph. Despite occasional bitter opposition, the line was completed to Weldon by 1836. Some members of the public considered the steam railroads to be diabolical contraptions that set fire to their barns and frightened their livestock. The line was also poorly constructed and by 1843 this first Seaboard predecessor was sold at public auction on behalf of its creditors.

A successor company – the Seaboard & Roanoke Railroad – was incorporated in 1846 and rebuilt the railroad from Portsmouth to the Virginia-Carolina state line. Another company, the Roanoke Railroad, rebuilt the 18 miles of line from the Virginia-Carolina state line, near Margaretville, to Weldon, North Carolina. This line was absorbed by the Seaboard & Roanoke in 1849, and in 1851 the entire line from

Portsmouth to Weldon was rebuilt, with the hazardous strap rail replaced by "T" iron rail imported from England.

During this same period, another early SAL predecessor became one of the first major rail companies to be chartered in the State of North Carolina. The Raleigh and Gaston Railroad was incorporated in 1835 to build an 85-mile railroad from Raleigh to Gaston (now known as Thelma), all in North Carolina. The line was completed in 1840 and when the first train operated into Raleigh on March 21st, it set off a three-day celebration. Unfortunately, this line also soon floundered financially and in 1845 the railroad was sold to the State of North Carolina. The line was returned to private ownership in 1851 and two years later it extended its line from Gaston to Weldon where connection was made with the line of the Seaboard & Roanoke.

(above left) The locomotive "Raleigh" was built in England in 1836 for the Raleigh and Gaston Railroad. Delivered to the Petersburg Railroad, it was used during construction of the R&G. This full-size model was built by Seaboard shop craft employees in 1927, and was later donated to the state. It is now on display at the National Railroad Museum in Hamlet, N.C.
(SAL Photo/CSX Transportation)

(left) The first locomotive to arrive in Raleigh over the new Raleigh and Gaston was the "Tornado." This replica of the engine was built by the Seaboard in the Raleigh shops in 1892.
(W. E. Griffin, Jr. Collection)

(below) The Orlando and Winter Park Railway 0-4-2T No. 1, the "F. B. Knowles" was photographed at Orlando, Florida, circa 1890. The O&WP operated from 1889-1891 and later became a part of the Seaboard.
(M. B. Connery Collection)

Portsmouth & Roanoke

RAIL ROAD.

Cars and Carriages, for the Transportation of Produce, Merchandize, and passengers, on the *Rail Road* between *Portsmouth* and *Suffolk*, are now running twice a day.

The connection at Weldon established the first unbroken rail line for the conveyance of North Carolina products directly to the markets in Europe, New York, and Baltimore via the ports of Norfolk and Portsmouth. Shallow water, sand bars, and dangerous capes along the Carolina coast forced that state's freight to go to Norfolk in preference to its own ports. Establishment of the connection set off a rollicking four-day celebration that was marked by glittering dinners and a two-train excursion over the new route.

The Weldon connection was also significant for another reason, though it is unlikely that any of the celebrants in 1853 could have foretold such a result. This connection also marked the first expansion of the Seaboard & Roanoke Railroad into what became the Seaboard Air Line Railway, a company that drew together more than 140 separate railroad corporations into a rail system of over 4,000 miles operating in six Southeastern states.

Further expansion was deferred during the 1860s as the nation endured the War Between the States. In the final days of the conflict, a retreating Confederate army burned the important railroad bridges at Weldon and Gaston. When the little railroads resumed operation of their properties after the war, they were required to use a barge to ferry traffic across the Roanoke River until a new bridge could be completed at Weldon in 1867. With the lines reopened and traffic beginning to flow again, the Raleigh and Gaston extended its reach in 1871 by acquiring control of the Raleigh and Augusta Air-Line Railroad (formerly the Chatham Railroad), a company that was in the process of building a 98-mile railroad south of Raleigh to Hamlet, North Carolina. The company's rail line reached Hamlet in 1877 where connection was made with the Carolina Central Railway, a 267-mile railroad running from Wilmington, North Carolina, via Charlotte to Rutherfordton, North Carolina.

During this period, the president of the Seaboard & Roanoke was John Moncure Robinson, a member of the powerful Philadelphia family that had been instrumental in the construction of a number of railroads in Virginia and North Carolina. Robinson was also President of the Richmond, Fredericksburg & Potomac Railroad and during the depression years of the mid-1870s he also acquired control of the Raleigh and Gaston and its subsidiary companies.

Control of the Carolina Central was achieved in 1883. Atlanta was reached in 1892 with construction of the Georgia, Carolina and Northern Railway. This railroad built 265 miles of railroad from Monroe, North Carolina (located on the line between Hamlet and Charlotte) to Atlanta, Georgia, with another 45 miles of line extending from Monroe to Charleston, South Carolina. On July 1, 1889, it was jointly and perpetually leased to the Seaboard and Roanoke and the Raleigh and Gaston railroads.

On August 1, 1893, the five railroad companies whose tracks extended from Portsmouth through the Carolinas to Atlanta formed an unincorporated association which they called the "Seaboard Air-Line System." The five companies were the Seaboard & Roanoke, the Raleigh and Gaston, the Raleigh and Augusta Air-Line, the Carolina Central, and the Georgia, Carolina and Northern. This "Seaboard Air-Line System" of 1893 was purely an operating association and the legal status of the associated companies and their leased lines were not affected in any manner. The association set traffic policies and directed the solicitation of freight and passenger business by the member roads.

The Seaboard Air-Line System also operated the fleet of steamboats owned by the Baltimore Steam Packet Company that plied the waters between Baltimore, Norfolk, Portsmouth, and Old Point Comfort. The Seaboard & Roanoke also held a large interest in the Old Dominion Steamship Company, whose steamboats supplied the Seaboard Air-Line System with a connection to the port of New York.

The Seaboard Air-Line System, and the future Seaboard Air Line Railway, inherited the "Seaboard" in their names from their predecessor, the Seaboard & Roanoke Railroad.

The words "Air Line" also came into the Seaboard's name through one of its predecessor companies. In 1871, the North Carolina Legislature changed the name of the Chatham Railroad to the Raleigh and Augusta Air-Line Railroad. It was the first recorded application of the words to a railroad. During that period, the words "air line" were used to signify the shortest distance between two points and may have derived from the expression "as the crow flies." In any event, the use of the words in the name of the Raleigh and Augusta Air-Line Railroad predated the Wright brothers' first engine-powered heavier-than-air flight from Kitty Hawk, North Carolina, by 32 years.

John M. Robinson passed away in 1893, shortly after the establishment of the Seaboard Air-Line System. It was John Skelton Williams who would complete the expansion of that rail system to form the Seaboard Air Line Railway. John Skelton Williams was born in Powhatan County, Virginia, a few months after General Robert E. Lee surrendered the Army of Northern Virginia to General Ulysses S. Grant at Appomattox Court House, Virginia, to end the War Between the States. Both of Williams' parents came from prominent Virginia families. His father, John Langborne Williams, was a noted Richmond banker and was descended on his mother's side of the family from Judge Bartholomew Dandridge, the brother of George Washington's wife Martha. Through his mother, Maria Ward Skelton, Williams was descended from the Skeltons and Randolphs, two of the finest "First Families of Virginia."

He was educated in Richmond private schools and studied law at the University of Virginia. Leaving the University, he joined his father's banking firm and at the age of eighteen published a pamphlet that became a popular guide for financial investors. The notoriety of the pamphlet brought much favorable attention to John Skelton Williams and to the Williams banking firm.

After successfully financing a number of electric street car companies and banking institutions in Virginia and South Carolina, the Williams firm entered the field of railroad banking in 1895. Working in concert with the Middendorf Banking Firm of Baltimore, the Williams group gained control of the Savannah, Americus and Montgomery Railroad and reorganized this 263-mile railroad then operating between Montgomery, Alabama, and Lyons, Georgia, to form the Georgia and Alabama Railway. At the age of 30, Williams was elected President of the new railroad and by 1896 he had extended its line eastward to Savannah, Georgia.

Williams gained entry into Savannah for the G&A by leasing a 17-mile section of railroad between Lyons and Meldrim, Georgia, from the Central of Georgia Railway. The Central had been reluctant to lease the line but relented when Williams threatened to build a parallel line. The G&A was given a long-term lease of the Lyons-Meldrim line and trackage rights to Savannah. It was a strategy that Williams would use again.

Williams' successful handling of the Georgia and Alabama attracted the attention of other railroad entrepreneurs, among them DeWitt Smith. In June 1897, Smith came to Williams for financial assistance to build the Richmond, Petersburg and Carolina Railroad. The RP&C was a successor to the franchise of the Virginia and Carolina Railroad, a company that had been incorporated in 1882 to build a railroad from Richmond, Virginia, to a connection with the Raleigh and Gaston at Ridgeway Junction, North Carolina (now known as Norlina). The City of Petersburg, Virginia, held a financial interest in this enterprise and when the company failed in 1892 without laying a single mile of track, the city purchased the franchise under a sale of foreclosure.

Seaboard and Roanoke locomotive "Ajax" was built by Taunton in 1883 and became Seaboard Air Line No. 22.
(Harold K. Vollrath Collection)

After five years without activity on this project, the City of Petersburg contracted with DeWitt Smith on June 10, 1897, to build the railroad and conveyed to him the entire capital stock, property, and franchise of the RP&C. Smith obtained the financial backing of John Skelton Williams and the 20 miles of road between Petersburg and DeWitt, Virginia, were finally opened for service in 1898. By December of that year, the Williams and Middendorf banking groups had acquired both the RP&C and a controlling interest in the Seaboard Air-Line System.

Two months later, they also purchased a majority of the shares of the Florida Central and Peninsula Railroad, a 940-mile line operating in the states of Florida and Georgia. Like other early rail systems, the FC&P was made up of many predecessor railroads. The earliest of its ancestors was the Tallahassee Railroad, a company chartered in 1834 to build a 22-mile line from Tallahassee to Port Leon on the Gulf of Mexico. When a tidal wave completely destroyed the town of Port Leon in 1843, the entire line was reconstructed between 1855-1856 with a new terminus at St. Marks.

Larger portions of the FC&P were acquired from the Florida Railway and Navigation Company and the Tavares, Orlando and Atlantic Railroad. The Florida Railway and Navigation Company operated three main lines, one from Jacksonville to River Junction, one from Fernandina to Cedar Key, and the other from Waldo to Plant City, all in the state of Florida. The Tavares, Orlando and Atlantic operated a main line from Tavares to Orlando. In 1893, the FC&P extended its line from Yulee, Florida, to Savannah, Georgia, where it made connection with the South Bound Railroad to Columbia, South Carolina. The FC&P first leased and then purchased the South Bound Railroad

Hence, the FC&P acquired by the Williams group had main lines extending from Columbia (Cayce), South Carolina, via Savannah, Georgia, to Jacksonville, Florida; Fernandina to Cedar Key, Florida; Waldo to Tampa, Florida; and, Jacksonville to River Junction, Florida. It also operated eight branch lines, the most notable being the branch that extended from Wildwood to Lake Charm, Florida.

By October of 1899, the Williams and Middendorf groups had acquired control through capital stock purchase of a 2,600-mile rail system comprised of 18 separate railroads that had previously been operated in three groups and under separate managements as the Seaboard Air-Line System, the Georgia and Alabama Railway, and the Florida Central and Peninsula Railroad. About 200 miles of railroad was then built to complete and link the three systems. To connect the line between Hamlet, North Carolina, and Savannah, Georgia, via Columbia, South Carolina, an extension was built from Cheraw, South Carolina, on the Georgia and Alabama Railway to Camden, South Carolina, and thence to Columbia via Cayce by the Chesterfield and Kershaw and the South Bound railroads to connect with the existing South Bound line from Savannah.

While the new Seaboard had tied together a 2,600-mile rail system from Richmond to Tampa, John Skelton Williams realized that direct rail service through the Washington, D.C., gateway to the Northeast would be essential if his company was to successfully compete with the Atlantic Coast Line Railroad and the Southern Railway. Of course, the ACL had no intention of allowing the Seaboard to gain access to its traffic in the Northeast. The Richmond, Fredericksburg and Potomac Railroad, at that time controlled by the ACL, initially refused to work out satisfactory arrangements to handle Seaboard traffic north of Richmond. Those companies felt quite secure in their position account the long-time provisions contained in the RF&P's charter which provided that the General Assembly would not permit another railroad to be built parallel to the RF&P.

However, both the RF&P and the ACL underestimated Williams' influence in the Commonwealth of Virginia. Using the same tactic that he had employed with the Central of Georgia when he sought entry into Savannah, Williams threatened to extend the trackage of the Seaboard through Richmond to Washington. When Williams was granted a charter by act of the Virginia General Assembly on March 3, 1900, to build a new railroad between Richmond and Washington and the Legislature coupled to this franchise the condition that the incorporators of the new railroad could purchase the State's interest in the RF&P's common stock, the RF&P and the ACL quickly acquiesced in an agreement for the interchange of SAL traffic at Richmond. The agreement between the RF&P and SAL provided that the RF&P's facilities at Acca Yard would be enlarged to accommodate the SAL traffic and that its traffic would be handled by the RF&P on the same terms and conditions that applied to the traffic of the ACL.

On April 10, 1900, the name of the Richmond, Petersburg and Carolina was changed to the Seaboard Air Line Railway. By the end of that month, the line extension was completed between Cheraw and Camden, South Carolina, and the line of the former RP&C was completed between DeWitt, Virginia, and Norlina, North Carolina. By the end of May, the Appomattox and James Rivers had been bridged and SAL tracks extended from Petersburg through the City of Richmond to a connection with the RF&P at a point called Hermitage.

On May 30, 1900, two special trains departed Richmond over the newly completed Seaboard Air Line Railway, destined for Tampa, Florida. They were filled with businessmen, public officials, newspapermen, and railroad executives who had been invited as guests to make an inspection tour of the new railroad.

The parties returned to Richmond on June 2nd for a "Golden Spike Ceremony" celebrating the birth of the Seaboard. At that time, Main Street Station was still under construction in Richmond by the Chesapeake & Ohio Railway for joint use by that company and the new Seaboard. Hence, the ceremonies were held at 17th Street just south of Broad Street and north of the new depot then being constructed at Main Street.

The "Golden Spike Ceremony" was unquestionably a large event for the city. Thousands of Richmonders gathered at the foot of Broad and Main streets to watch the arrival of the first through train from Tampa. A select group of dignitaries stood on the viaduct between Broad and Franklin streets. In that group was a three-year old boy dressed in a sailor's suit – John Skelton Williams, Jr. – the son of the Seaboard's founder. As the first train approached Richmond at 4:30 pm, a spike made of gold and a hammer of silver were quickly placed in the little boy's hands. Then, as one of his young uncles held the spike in place in a pre-drilled hole, John, Jr. tapped it on its head with the silver hammer. The spike clicked against a telegraph key and all along the route of the new railroad the signal of completion was received. Flags were hoisted over every agency on the new system to celebrate the occasion.

Disembarking from the two Tampa trains, the inspection party and special guests were taxied to the nearby Virginia State Capitol Building. From the south portico of Capitol Square, they heard speeches by various dignitaries. That evening, a banquet was held for over 400 guests at the elegant Hotel Jefferson. Tables were decorated with fruits grown along the route from Richmond to Tampa. Twelve courses were served and ten speeches were made, sandwiched between musical selections. History does not record how long the banquet lasted.

If John Skelton Williams felt pleased with himself and his new railroad that evening, one could hardly blame him. He had not only created a new railroad, he had a property that possessed routes which were 75 to 100 miles shorter than his competitors. It was no mean achievement, especially when considered in light of the financial condition of the South during that period. It was a time when, according to David St. Clair, a financial writer of the day, "there was little reliable information to be had on the subject of Southern securities, and some southern states had not recovered their credit from Reconstruction politics." Williams had been raised during the Reconstruction era and as an adult he vowed that the South would not be a colony of Wall Street. He saw the Seaboard Air Line Railway as a means to promote and foster Southern industry without the backing of Northern money. Williams often referred with pride to the fact that the Seaboard was owned in the South with not one cent owed to a financial institution north of Baltimore. He neglected to mention that seven of the Seaboard's nine directors were from the North.

The Seaboard's connection with the RF&P at Hermitage was opened and interchange of freight traffic between the two roads began on July 1, 1901. On July 31, 1901, and agreement was reached between the Baltimore & Ohio Railroad, Pennsylvania Railroad, Atlantic Coast Line Railroad, Southern Railway, Chesapeake & Ohio Railway, and Seaboard Air Line Railway for formation of the Richmond-Washington Company, a New Jersey corporation, in which each of the six railroads would have an equal interest. The Richmond-Washington Company acquired all stock of the Washington Southern Railway and a majority of the voting stock of the RF&P. The RF&P and Washington Southern were to provide the necessary additional facilities and would be operated as a unit called the "Richmond-Washington Line." The traffic of the six railroads would be handled over the RF&P and the Washington Southern with equal promptness and upon equal terms.

The first two decades of the Seaboard's corporate existence were highlighted by the expansion of the rail system and the Company's first receivership and reorganization. It was also during this period that John Skelton Williams lost control of the railroad.

Expanding its rail system enabled the SAL to not only increase its base of originated freight traffic but also to capture new interline shipments through the creation of favorable routes and interchanges with other railroads. The SAL reached the heart of the Alabama iron ore and coal fields by extending its line from Atlanta to Birmingham in 1904. This gave the SAL access to coal for the industries located on its lines and a long haul on iron ore over the shortest route to the various ports along the Atlantic coast. At Birmingham, the SAL also established an important connection with the St. Louis-San Francisco Railway (Frisco Line), enabling the two railroads to create the shortest and most direct route for the movement of grain from the Midwest to the Eastern Seaboard.

The SAL was able to extend its line to Birmingham by purchasing and then rebuilding the East and West Railroad that operated a rail line between Cartersville, Georgia, and Pell City, Alabama. The SAL then organized the Birmingham & Atlanta Air Line Railway to construct a railroad from Birmingham to a connection with the East & West Railroad at Coal City, Alabama.

During this period, the SAL also expanded its lines in the state of North Carolina and improved its line between Bostic and Monroe enabling it to handle shipments of coal that originated on the Clinchfield Railroad. The four-mile Oxford & Coast Line Railroad was built in 1903 from Dickerson to Oxford and was operated as a branch of the Henderson-Durham line.

However, one of the most significant developments during this era was the expansion of SAL system in Florida. In 1903, the SAL entered into a traffic contract with the Florida West Shore Railway to become that company's preferred connection. The Florida West Shore had recently expanded its line from the Manatee River to Sarasota, Fruitville, and Bradenton, thus giving the SAL access to much new traffic in the shipment of the early fruits and vegetables grown in that area. The Florida West Shore was merged into the SAL in 1909 and later extensions of the line were built to Venice, Early Bird, Hernando, and Inverness.

During this period, the SAL also gained access to the various phosphate mines of south Florida by purchasing a number of short line railroads, including the Plant City, Arcadia & Gulf and the Charlotte Harbor and Northern railroads. Initially, phosphate was loaded onto ships from SAL trains via an elevator located at Fernandina. In 1909, the SAL built a port at Tampa, with extensive facilities for the handling of lumber and coal as well as phosphate.

To fund his expansion program, John Skelton Williams was required to find a source of capital. In 1903, for reasons that have always puzzled students of SAL history, he elected to borrow a portion of the capital needed to finance construction of the Birmingham line from Thomas Fortune Ryan. This enabled Ryan, a major stockholder of the old Seaboard and Roanoke who had opposed the formation of the SAL, to gain a voice in management of the new railroad. Within months, Ryan and his associates had wrestled control of the SAL from Williams and removed him as president of the company. The following year Williams and Middendorf sold their stock in the Seaboard and resigned from the board of directors. The embittered Williams would remain a staunch antagonist of the SAL's new management for the rest of his life.

Following John Skelton Williams' departure, the SAL's management went through an unsettled period, changing presidents three times within a twelve-month period. Much to Williams' delight, the railroad failed to prosper under its new management and in 1908 it was forced to apply for receivership. When one of Williams' brothers was appointed a receiver, there was even speculation that the Williams group might regain control of the Seaboard. However, the Ryan group was equally determined to retain its dominion over the affairs of the railroad.

Under the direction of S. Davies Warfield, who served as chairman of the receivers, a plan was quickly devised to reduce the railroad's operating ratio and resolve the issues of control. By 1909 the SAL was discharged from bankruptcy, the receivers having successfully averted both a foreclosure sale and a reorganization of the company.

A native of Maryland, Warfield had assisted John Skelton Williams in the formation of the SAL. A businessman and financier, he served as chairman of the company's receivers from 1908-1909 and, in 1912, became the chairman of the board of directors and representative of the principal owners of the Seaboard. He also served as the SAL's president from 1918 until his death in 1927. Under his leadership, the Seaboard weathered the trying period of federal control during World War I and continued an aggressive policy of expansion. The eventual physical property of the modern day Seaboard was shaped during Warfield's administration.

Further expansion of the SAL in South Carolina provided the vehicle for the voluntary reorganization of the railroad to form the Seaboard Air Line Railway Company. Through a series of mergers beginning in 1901, a group of small railroads in eastern South Carolina (known as the Charleston Northern, the South Carolina Western and the South Carolina Western Extension) had been merged to form a company known as the North and South Carolina Railway. In 1914, that company's name was changed to the Carolina, Atlantic and Western Railway and was then operating a main line railroad from Gibson, North Carolina, to Charleston, South Carolina, with branch lines to McBee, Sumter, and Timmonsville. It also operated a transverse line from Lanes to Georgetown, South Carolina, and connected with the Seaboard via trackage rights over the SAL line from Hamlet Junction to Gibson. In 1915, the Seaboard Air Line Railway and the

Carolina, Atlantic and Western Railway were merged to create the Seaboard Air Line Railway Company.

Under the provisions of the merger, the first issue of Seaboard Air Line Railway Company First and Consolidated Mortgage six per cent bonds were offered in December 1915. The mortgage was made broad enough to cover the refunding of all the bonds of the subsidiary companies and underlying bonds and the proceeds of the first sale were applied to the construction of a low-grade extension of the line from Charleston to Savannah, Georgia, where connection was made with the old main line. The extension of the line to Savannah, as well as an upgrade of the line between Hamlet and Charleston, was completed just as the Federal Government was beginning to take over the operation of the railroads during the World War I.

Hence, the SAL now had two separate and distinct main lines between Hamlet and Savannah. The new line, which would come to be known as the East Carolina Line, had been built in six segments by seven different companies and had a ruling grade of five-tenths percent in both directions between Hamlet and Jacksonville. On the new portion of the line there was a maximum three-tenths percent grade between Charleston and Savannah in both directions. This enabled the SAL to realize substantial savings in the operating costs of traffic handled over this route. It also permitted the SAL to increase the tonnage per train that could be handled over this route as compared to that which could be handled over the Hamlet to Savannah route via Columbia. As a result, the East Carolina route was principally used as a freight line, over which "perishable" trains from Florida and other high-speed and tonnage freights were operated. The shorter route via Columbia was reserved for the operation of the SAL's fleet of passenger trains.

However, even with its superior routes and expanding base of originated traffic, the Seaboard was still in no position to effectively compete for traffic with its well-established rivals, the Atlantic Coast Line and the Southern. The Seaboard was running its railroad with inadequate and outmoded equipment resulting in high operating costs. It was also burdened with high funded debt as a consequence of its expansion program. To make matters worse, the SAL's management was unable to reach agreement with the Federal Government as to the proper reimbursement for the use of its facilities during the period of government control. It filed claims against the government for what it considered to be inadequate compensation but ultimately accepted the government's settlement.

As the decade of the 1920s began, S. Davies Warfield was firmly of the opinion that the only way the Seaboard could gain a competitive edge on its rivals was to further expand its position in the State of Florida. And time was of the essence. If the Seaboard was allowed to struggle along with poor credit and only gradual improvements to its lines and equipment, Warfield feared that the great opportunities to be gained through the development of the State of Florida might be lost. Boldly, he proposed that the Seaboard use such credit as it could muster to build a cross-state railroad connecting the East and West Coasts of Florida.

Beginning in 1924, the SAL built a 204-mile extension from its Jacksonville-Tampa main line at Coleman to West Palm Beach. When opened on January 21, 1925, it gave Florida its first cross-state railroad. The following year, the SAL extended the main line from West Palm Beach to Miami on the East Coast and to St. Petersburg, the Pinellas Peninsula, Fort Myers and Naples on the West Coast. This gave the Seaboard not only two main lines, one down the East Coast to Miami and one down the West Coast to Tampa and Fort Myers, but also a line of railroad across the state connecting those magical cities. In January 1927, these lines were officially opened by dignitaries who were transported over the line by five sections of the Seaboard's famous train, the *Orange Blossom Special*.

The SAL would only have a brief period of time to bask in the glory of this achievement. Scarcely had the extension of its lines in Florida been completed when a hurricane roared in to devastate the state and collapse the land boom. Among the most severely devalued areas of real estate were those into which the SAL had expanded. Then, in

October of 1927, the dynamic S. Davies Warfield passed away.

Leadership of the company was passed to Legh Richmond Powell, Jr., who – at 43 years of age – was the youngest president of any major railroad in the country. With the Florida land boom shattered, the South's economy in recession, and the SAL's finances in disarray, Powell faced a daunting task. He proved to be uniquely qualified to meet the challenge.

Powell was 18 years of age when he joined the Seaboard in 1902 as a clerk in his hometown of Portsmouth, Virginia. His hard work and abilities were quickly recognized and he was promoted to positions of steadily increasing importance. In 1918 he became the assistant to the comptroller. Two years later he was made comptroller of the line. In his will, S. Davies Warfield designated Legh Powell to be his successor as president of the Seaboard. He was formally elected to that position by the Company's board of directors in 1927. Powell's intimate knowledge of the Seaboard, especially of its finances, enabled him to pilot the company through difficult times and groom it into one of the most efficiently operated railroads in the country.

Powell continued Warfield's policy of expansion in Florida and in 1928 the SAL opened a new gateway for western traffic moving over its line between the Florida panhandle and Montgomery, Alabama, by leasing the Georgia, Florida and Alabama Railway. The GF&A's mainline extended from Richland, Georgia, on the SAL's Savannah, Georgia, to Montgomery, Alabama, line through Tallahassee, Florida, on the Seaboard's Jacksonville-River Junction line to the town of Carrabelle, Florida, on the Gulf Coast.

However, by 1928 the SAL was overextended and approaching a financial crisis. Faced with high fixed charges because of its expansionist policies and shrinking revenues as a result of the Florida real estate collapse and fierce competition from its transportation rivals, the SAL submitted a voluntary reorganization plan to its stockholders and investors.

(facing page) An exterior view of the SAL's freight car repair yard in Jacksonville as it appeared in January 1947.
(SAL photo by William Rittase/John B. Corns Collection)

(above) The SAL took delivery in 1937 of five new R-2 class simple articulated 2-6-6-4 type locomotives, numbered 2505-2509, and staged this christening in Richmond to publicize the event. For the christening, the locomotives were named *Miss Virginia, Miss Carolina, Miss Georgia, Miss Alabama,* and *Miss Florida* for the states served by the SAL, and were christened simultaneously by young ladies from each of the named states.
(SAL Photo/CSX Transportation)

The Seaboard's timing for a financial crisis could not have been worse. On October 29, 1929, the stock market crashed to begin the Great Depression that would grip the country during the decade of the 1930s. The company's proposed plan of readjustment quickly proved inadequate to permit the SAL to meet its financial obligations and, on December 23, 1930, the Seaboard was forced into receivership. Legh Powell, the SAL's president, and Ethelbert W. Smith, a Pennsylvania Railroad vice president, were appointed to serve as receivers. Three years later, Smith was replaced by Henry W. Anderson, a Richmond attorney. For the next 16-1/2 years the Seaboard was operated as a ward of the United States District Court for the Eastern District of Virginia. Powell and Anderson served as the company's receivers from 1933 until the end of receivership in 1946.

The depressed economic condition of the country during the 1930s certainly contributed to the long duration of the SAL's receivership. Wisely, the SAL's management used this period to ready the railroad for the future. They correctly reasoned that if the Seaboard's heavy debt structure could be lightened and money found to upgrade the physical property and rolling stock, the railroad stood an excellent chance of being operated profitably when the country's economy recovered.

To reduce costs, Seaboard management initiated various economies. Gas-electric passenger trains were purchased to replace the more costly steam-powered locals and some runs were curtailed altogether. Contraction of the system also became a company strategy. While the SAL did build a 16-mile branch line via a subsidiary company to serve the large complex of chemical plants located at Hopewell, Virginia, over 400 miles of unprofitable branch lines were abandoned during the receivership.

However, the economies effected by the receivers were insufficient to discharge the claims of its creditors and in 1932 the receivers were authorized by the Interstate Commerce Commission to secure a loan from the Reconstruction Finance Corporation for this purpose. The SAL also borrowed from the Federal Emergency Administration of Public Works to begin a rolling stock and physical plant modernization program.

In 1933 the SAL introduced its first use of air-conditioning on the passenger equipment operated on the *Orange Blossom Special.* In 1938 the Seaboard put into service the first diesel-electric locomotives in the Southeast with the delivery from Electro-Motive of nine E4s for service on the *Orange Blossom Special.*

In 1939 the SAL commenced operation of the *Silver Meteor*, the first lightweight streamlined train to operate in regular service between New York and Florida. The

409

Seaboard also improved its roadway, laying heavier rail, ballast, treated ties, and installing longer passing sidings and automatic block signals.

As the nation's economy began to recover in the late 1930s, the Seaboard's improved physical plant and rolling stock enabled it to not only reduce its operating costs but also to handle more business, thereby boosting revenues. In testimony before the ICC during a 1951 proceeding involving the railroad's request for increased freight rates, Atlantic Coast Line Railroad President Champion M. Davis opined that the SAL, supported by federal loans, had been able during the 1930s to make expenditures for improvements to its physical property while the ACL and other solvent roads were at times pressed to find money just to pay bond interest. Hence, the Seaboard was able to commence the rehabilitation of its property some ten or more years earlier than the ACL.

(facing page) The Seaboard never missed an opportunity to pose attractive young ladies with its trains to commemorate significant events, such as the arrival of the first air-conditioned *Orange Blossom Special* in Miami on January 3, 1934. Note that the motive power was provided by Q-3 class Mikado No. 409.

(right) These Florida bathing beauties posed with E4 No. 3000 during a stop of the SAL's Diesel Exhibition Tour Train in November, 1938.

(Both, W. E. Griffin, Jr. Collection)

(below) When the SAL received its first E4 passenger diesels, it operated a Diesel Exhibition Tour Train over the main routes of its system to show off the new diesels and promote the *Orange Blossom Special.* The E4 diesel set of 3000-3100-3001 and their train are being inspected by the public at Main Street Station in Richmond, Virginia, on November 1, 1938.

(Beaufort Selden Ragland)

(above) During World War II soldiers went to war and returned home again on the American railroads. Joyous families welcomed home their sons and husbands as a Seaboard troop train arrives at West Palm Beach, Florida.

(SAL Photo)

(below) This painting, once displayed at the SAL's Division Office Building at Raleigh, N.C., commemorated the installation of Centralized Traffic Control between Richmond, Va., and Hamlet, N.C., at the time the longest stretch of CTC in the world.

(M. B. Connery Collection)

The Seaboard also was helped out of receivership by the increased traffic and earnings generated by the Second World War. Most of the great military camps of World War I were rebuilt and enlarged and many new training centers were opened in the South Atlantic States. The movement of men and equipment between the various training centers resulted in passenger trains that were so crowded the government had to urge the public to discontinue all non-essential travel. The increase in freight traffic was even more dramatic. The movement of military equipment to our own forces as well as to our Allies under the "Lend-Lease Act," the mammoth shipbuilding programs along the Atlantic and Gulf Coasts, and the diversion of steamship traffic to the railroads because of the threat of German submarines, brought enormous freight tonnage to the Seaboard during the war years.

Seaboard's receivers, faced with an operational bottleneck in the early traffic-heavy months of World War II, gambled on electronic dispatching methods in preference to double track and installed the Southeastern United States' first centralized traffic control system on the Richmond Subdivision. CTC, directed from the Dispatcher's Office at Raleigh, was superimposed on the existing automatic signal system on the 63 miles of track from south of the James River Bridge in Richmond to Alberta, Virginia. Installation of the CTC system was completed on Christmas Day, 1941.

CTC didn't arrive any too soon for even though the increased traffic was improving the Seaboard's financial position it was creating operational problems that would have taxed the old train order system of operation beyond its capacity. By the end of the war, CTC also had been extended to Raleigh on the Norlina Subdivision, on the important section of main line between Savannah and Thalmann, Georgia, and, between Alabama Junction and Blossom, Georgia.

During the early war years, the Seaboard prospered for the first time in its history. And this prosperity was not solely due to the men and munitions that the railroad was transporting to support the war effort. The economy of the South was finally recovering from the devastation of the War Between the States, the years of Reconstruction and the Great Depression. For the first time since the beginning of receivership, the management of the Seaboard saw an opportunity for the Company to be reorganized. In 1944 a plan of reorganization was approved by the federal courts and application was filed with the ICC to end the receivership.

Pursuant to the approval of the plan by the courts, the properties of the Seaboard Air Line Railway Company were sold under foreclosure at public auction on the passenger platform of the Portsmouth station on May 31, 1945. The railroad was purchased for $52,000,500 by the Seaboard Air Line Railway Company Reorganization Committee. The committee was the only bidder.

On June 28, 1946, the ICC approved the issuance of securities provided for under the reorganization plan and approved the acquisition by a new company – the Seaboard Air Line Railroad Company – of the properties of the old Seaboard Air Line Railway. The receivership was terminated and operation of the new company began at 12:01 a.m. on August 1, 1946.

Directors of the new company elected Legh Powell to remain as the president of the railroad. His co-receiver, Henry Anderson, was elected to serve as chairman of the board. In a statement issued to the press after the first directors' meeting, Powell pledged that the new Seaboard would continue to purchase new equipment such as diesel locomotives, lightweight modern coaches and sleeping cars, and that the property would be improved with the laying of heavier rail, more ballast, improved bridge structures, and installation of improved signaling devices.

In fact, the Seaboard emerged from the receivership with its physical properties in the best condition in the history of the railroad. Moreover, the relatively high war earnings allowed the receivers to accumulate substantial funds which were turned over to the reorganized Seaboard in the form of reserves of various kinds. One such reserve was turned over to the new company for purpose of overcoming deferred maintenance. Another reserve, which had been set aside for

(above) In later years, the major repair work on SAL steam engines was performed at the company's shops in Savannah, Jacksonville, and Howells, Georgia. This group photo of Seaboard shop craft employees at Jacksonville was taken circa 1930.
(SAL Photo/CSX Transportation)

(facing page, top) Interior view of the SAL's diesel shop at Hialeah Yard in Miami. The two-tiered work walkways and service pits are to the right with the service platform to the left. Overhead cranes could deliver heavy items anywhere inside the building.
(SAL photo)

(facing page, bottom) This aerial view of SAL's West Jacksonville locomotive shops was taken in 1949.
(SAL photo)

claims against the receivers, was found not to be needed for that purpose and over $12 million of that reserve was used for the cash purchase of 112 new diesel locomotives. Hence, the managers of the new Seaboard came into possession not only of a railroad in an improved condition but also one with the resources to further upgrade its properties and rolling stock.

In the post-war years, the Seaboard finally fulfilled the dreams of John Skelton Williams and S. Davies Warfield to become one of the premier railroads in the Southeastern section of the country. It enjoyed a particularly outstanding reputation for the excellence of its passenger service, especially for the service and accommodations on its famous silver fleet of streamliners.

In 1952, Legh Powell retired as president of the Seaboard after 50 years of service to the company. During his tenure the Seaboard had become the first railroad in the South to introduce air-conditioned trains, the first in the South to use diesel-electric locomotives, the first in the South to operate a lightweight streamlined train in regular service and the first in the South to use lightweight stainless steel passenger coaches.

Powell was succeeded by John W. Smith, who was the last president of the Seaboard Air Line. Like S. Davies Warfield, Smith was a native of Baltimore and he joined the Seaboard's engineering department in 1924 following his graduation from the University of Maryland. Like Legh Powell, he had worked his way up the ranks of the company's management, serving in both the engineering and operating departments. Prior to his election as Seaboard president in 1952, he held the position of administrative vice-president.

Smith continued his predecessor's program to modernize the SAL, investing in automatic block signals, new stations and shops and a radio communications system between yard locomotives and fixed base stations at Richmond, Savannah, and Howells (Atlanta) that expedited terminal switching. By 1953 the SAL had completed dieselization of its motive power fleet and CTC would eventually be extended to cover most of the system.

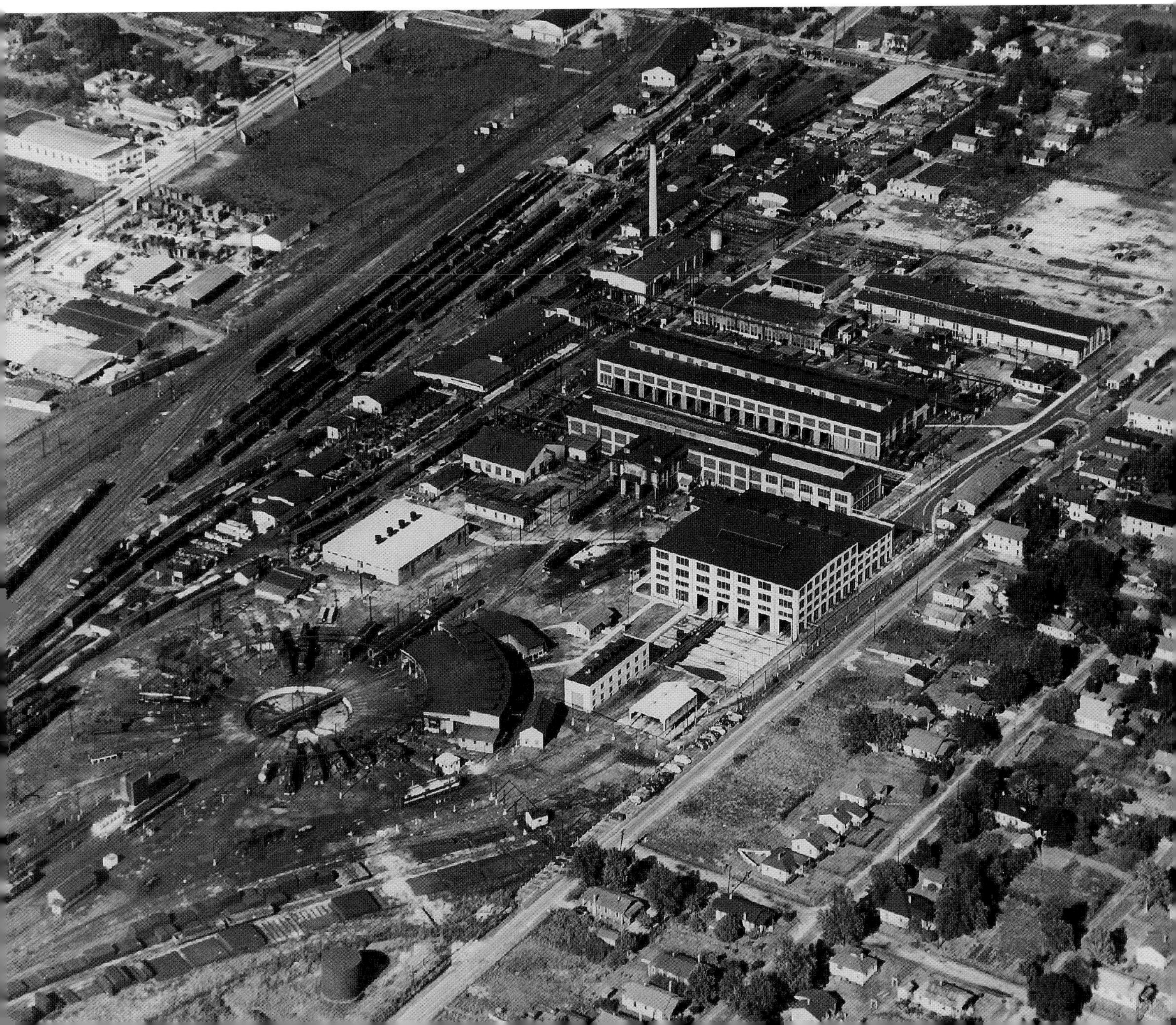

In 1953 the SAL commenced construction of a new $7.5 million retarder-equipped, 58-track hump classification yard at Hamlet, North Carolina, that was the first of its kind on the railroad. Five of Seaboard's main lines converged at that point and by concentrating much of its classification work at Hamlet the SAL was able to relieve a number of its other terminals from having to perform that function. Supporting facilities included a new diesel repair shop and service tracks to maintain the fleet of new motive power. The new yard was opened on November 29, 1954, and enabled the Seaboard to substantially reduce its operating costs by conserving yard switching power, increasing the utilization of freight rolling stock and expediting the flow of traffic.

During the 1950s, the Seaboard acquired its final new lines. In 1958 it absorbed the Macon, Dublin and Savannah Railroad, a 90-mile short line that it had controlled since 1905. It also acquired all of the stock of the 42-mile Gainesville Midland Railroad in 1959, bringing SAL mileage to over 4,100.

(below) This aerial view shows the construction as of January 27, 1954, of the SAL's new automatic retarder-equipped classification yard at Hamlet, N.C. The $8.5 million yard and diesel shop were completed in 1955.

(W. E. Griffin, Jr. Collection)

(bottom) SAL switcher No. 1465 and boxcars are posed with the new Hamlet hump tower for this November 1964 view.

(SAL photo)

(facing page) The SAL gambled on electronic dispatching methods and installed the Southeastern United States' first Centralized Traffic Control system, beginning in late 1941.

(SAL photo)

The Seaboard also made some significant facility changes in the late 1950s. For many years the company's general offices had been spread about the Norfolk-Portsmouth, Virginia, area in four separate buildings. To consolidate its corporate offices in one location, the Seaboard announced in 1956 that it was removing its offices from Norfolk and Portsmouth to a new general office building to be built in Richmond, Virginia. The new office building faced 420 feet along West Broad Street and contained 315,000 square feet of floor space for over 800 employees. When opened in August of 1958, it was the largest office building in Richmond. The following year, the Seaboard also relocated its passenger train operations in Richmond from Main Street Station to Broad Street Station of the Richmond Terminal Railway Company. The capital stock of this terminal company was jointly owned by the ACL and RF&P railroads and to gain access to the station and its terminal facilities, the SAL was required to enter into an agreement to acquire a one-third interest in the company.

However, the most significant event of 1958 was the announcement that the Seaboard and the ACL were studying the possible advantages of merging their two rail systems. At special meetings held on August 18, 1960, the stockholders of the two companies approved the proposed plan of merger, subject to the required authorization by the ICC. However, the road to merger was not a smooth one. Even though the ICC approved the merger in 1963, its consummation was delayed as opponents (principally the Florida East Coast Railway, the Southern Railway, and railroad labor unions) first sought reconsideration by the ICC and then pressed litigation opposing the merger through the federal court system.

While the merger proceedings were pending, the SAL continued to modernize the railroad and offered new and innovative services to its customers. In 1959, the SAL began to install continuous welded rail and, the following year, it began the installation of hot box detectors at strategic locations along the railroad. In 1959, the Seaboard also inaugurated the first through trailer-on-flatcar (TOFC) service between the Southeast and Eastern cities. This TOFC, or "piggyback" service as it was popularly called, quickly grew to be an

important source of the Seaboard's revenues and was handled in "hot shot" unit trains that operated on some of the fastest freight schedules in the United States. By 1965, TOFC and multi-level car traffic accounted for 52,500 carloads and over $12 million of the railroad's revenues.

The SAL's revenues from passenger service began to sag during this period as a result of the general malaise affecting the nation's rail passenger service and the diversion of mail and express traffic to trucks. Nevertheless, to the end of its corporate existence, the SAL's Florida trains offered a passenger serivce that was as splendid as any in the country.

Finally, in 1967, the challenges to the SAL-ACL merger were set aside at both the ICC and the federal courts. On July 1, 1967, the two roads were officially merged to create the Seaboard Coast Line Railroad. John W. Smith, SAL's president, was named chairman

The Seaboard's distinctive passenger station at Portsmouth, Virginia, also served until 1958 as the Company's general office building for the accounting department. The structure was built in 1894, rebuilt after a fire in 1905, and topped by a fourth and fifth story in 1915. The passenger station was located on the first floor with the corporate offices located on the upper floors.

(SAL photo)

of the board and W. Thomas Rice, ACL's president, was named president of the new railroad.

The Seaboard Coast Line was created by the merger of two roads with parallel routes and 75 common points. Since the majority of the economies were to be achieved by the consolidation of functions and elimination of duplicate routes, it was inevitable that this merger would result in some substantial retirements on the former properties. Unfortunately for admirers of the Seaboard, the majority of lines and facilities abandoned happened to be on the former SAL. In the years since 1967, either all or substantial portions of the former SAL lines between Richmond and Raleigh, Atlanta and Birmingham, Savannah and Jacksonville, Charleston and Savannah, and the Chattahoochee River and Montgomery have been retired and taken up for scrap.

But if the Seaboard is gone, it certainly is not forgotten.

Its legacy lives on in those segments of the road that still form a vital part of the CSX Transportation system and in its many innovations that endure as an ingredient of today's modern railroads. And it still lives on in the hearts of those admirers who came to know that "The Route of Courteous Service" was more than just another company slogan. It really was the way the Seaboard Air Line did business.

This building, located at the corner of Plume and Granby streets in Norfolk, Va., served as the general office headquarters for the executive department of the Seaboard from 1934 until 1958.
(SAL photo)

When it opened on August 22, 1958, the Seaboard's new consolidated general office building was the largest office building in Richmond, Va., with a frontage of 420 feet on West Broad Street and 315,000 square feet of floor space.
(Anthony L. Dementi)

Chapter 2

The Glory Days of Seaboard Steam

The Seaboard took a conventional approach in the selection of its steam locomotives, matching traditional motive power types to the diverse terrain traversed by its trains. The terrain of the SAL's more inland route twisted back and forth over an undulating profile until the line reached the coastal plain south of Columbia, South Carolina, thus dictating that the Seaboard employ a heavier locomotive than its rival, the Atlantic Coast Line. Between Richmond and Florida, the ACL's flat coastal topography allowed for the operation of dual purpose 4-6-2s for much of the steam era. With the introduction of steel passenger cars and the growth of its freight tonnage, the SAL was required to use 4-8-2s and 2-8-2s to power its fast passenger and freight trains. Santa Fe (2-10-2 type) locomotives were assigned to the North Carolina Division and Georgia Division between Atlanta and Birmingham where the grades and tonnage were even more demanding.

Burnished would not have been an adjective used to describe the SAL's steam power. There was no fancy striping, delicate lettering, or buffed cylinder heads. Unlike the rival Southern Railway that had a reputation for keeping its motive power lustrously clean, the Seaboard's locomotives were "no nonsense" workhorses.

But for a few notable exceptions, nor would the SAL locomotives have been characterized as modern steam power. The majority were acquired in the 1910s and 1920s. The SAL's long period of receivership as well as its early decision to dieselize meant that the Seaboard would never own any locomotives with the so-called Super-Power features that were introduced in the 1930s. However, while many of the SAL's locomotives were delivered without such features as feedwater heaters or stokers and none were equipped with roller bearings or cast-steel frames with integral cylinders, the company was able to

SAL engineers remembered that the road's articulateds were dirtier engines to operate because the longer boiler gave the cinders and smoke time to come out of the smoke stack and then back into the cab. Goggles were a must for the engine crew to keep the cinders out of their eyes. This SAL publicity photo shows an engineer at the throttle of a stationary R1 locomotive.
(SAL Photo/CSX Transportation)

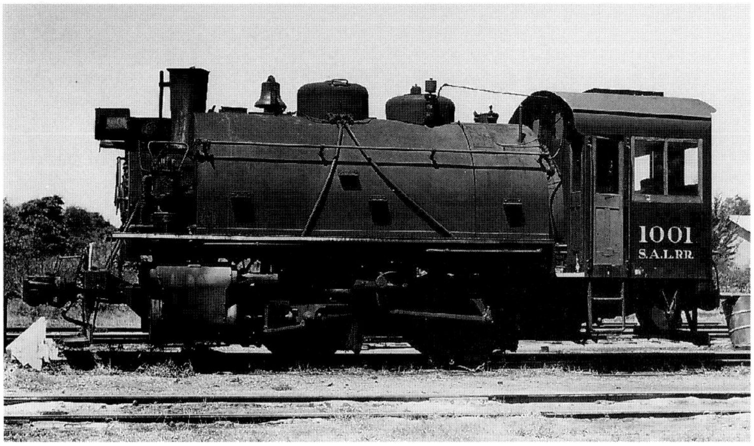

(top) The SAL began operations in 1900 with locomotives inherited from the many roads that were joined to form the new rail system. 0-4-0 switcher No. 23 was built in 1885 by Taunton for the Seaboard and Roanoke. It was retired and scrapped at Portsmouth, Virginia, by the SAL in 1912.
(SAL Photo/CSX Transportation)

(above) Fifty-five-ton saddle tank 0-4-0T No. 1001 had four drive wheels and a self-contained fuel and water reservoir. Built by Baldwin in 1936, it was the last steam locomotive purchased by the SAL and was designed to negotiate the tight curves encountered while switching in the city streets of Columbus, Ga. It remained in operation until 1958 when it was donated to the city and put on display at Holiday Park.
(L. D. Moore, Jr. Collection)

(below) F2 class 0-6-0 switcher No. 1020 was built at the Rhode Island Locomotive Works in 1900 as No. 575. The locomotive is at Savannah, Georgia, in May of 1924.
(H. K. Vollrath Collection)

produce a fleet of highly efficient locomotives by wisely investing its available resources in extensive upgrade and maintenance programs.

Many of the locomotives were improved. Disc-type main drivers were installed on the Georgia Division 2-10-2s to correct their counterbalance problems. Berkley stokers were installed on the early Q-class 2-8-2s and their cylinders were rebushed to provide for better steaming conditions. The P-1 class Pacifics were rebuilt to create the dual purpose P-2 class 4-6-2 with 69-inch drivers and 23" x 28" cylinders. Substantial improvements were made to the SAL's Mountains. Stokers were eventually applied to all 4-8-2s and in the mid 1930s, fifteen M-2 class engines received feedwater heaters and large six-wheel-truck Vanderbilt tenders with increased capacity for coal and water. After World War II, feedwater heaters were installed on additional Mountains and six M-2 class 4-8-2s, as well as three Q-3 Mikes and five P-2 Pacifics, were converted to burn fuel oil.

The SAL established superior steam locomotive maintenance facilities at Portsmouth, Va., Savannah and Howells (Atlanta), Ga., and Jacksonville, Fla. One of the most modern back shops in the country was established at Portsmouth in 1916 and it served as the primary SAL maintenance facility until the locomotive shops were relocated to Jacksonville in 1936. A modern locomotive erecting shop was located at Howells and in the later years the shops at Savannah, Jacksonville, and

Howells performed the majority of the steam locomotive back shop work. Heavy locomotive repairs were also performed at the major roundhouses, located around the system at Hermitage (Richmond), Virginia, Hamlet, Monroe, and Raleigh, N.C., Abbeville, S.C., Bainbridge, Ga., Birmingham, Alabama, and Wildwood, Tampa, and Hialeah (Miami), Fla.

When the SAL began operations in 1900, its motive power primarily consisted of locomotives in the 0-4-0, 4-4-0, and 4-6-0 wheel arrangements which had been in service on the railroads that made up the new Seaboard Air Line System. The first locomotives to be purchased by the SAL were the class L 2-8-0s in 1900. Numbered in the series 508-515 and 520-523, they were renumbered in the 900 series in 1916 and scrapped after the First World War.

By 1911, many old 4-4-0s had been retired and 4-6-0s had become the SAL's primary passenger and freight locomotive. In that year, SAL acquired the H-1 class Consolidations and the superheated P class Pacifics. The twenty H-1 Consolidations were the heaviest 2-8-0s ever owned by the SAL and were the most powerful engine on the railroad until the arrival of the Mikados in 1914. Designed for power with 56-inch drive wheels, they were assigned to slow heavy tonnage trains and remained on the roster until

(top) L5 class 0-6-0 switcher No. 1038 at Durham, N.C., on January 23, 1952.
(R. B. Carneal Photo)

(middle) L5 No. 1057 with a cut of cars at Portsmouth, Va., on January 24, 1942. Built by Baldwin between 1907-1913, the L5 switchers had 51-inch drivers and 32,000 lbs of tractive effort.
(H. Reid)

(bottom) The SAL F5 class 0-6-0s were numbered 1090-1099 and were built by Alco in 1918. No. 1091 is at Jacksonville in 1946.
(L. D. Moore, Jr.)

(above) The SAL F7 class switchers were nationally recognized as one of the most efficient and economical 0-6-0 type switchers ever designed by American locomotive builders. Built by Baldwin, Nos. 1101-1125 were delivered in 1927; Nos. 1126-1150 were delivered in 1928. No. 1119 is at Petersburg, Va., in July 1951.
(H. K. Vollrath Collection)

(left) L. D. Moore, Jr. photographed his father, L. D. Moore, Sr., at the throttle of F7 No. 1134 at Portsmouth, Va., on May 8, 1952.
(L. D. Moore, Jr.)

(below) F7 0-6-0 No. 1130 is at Birmingham, Alabama, in 1948.
(F. E. Ardrey, Jr. Photo/J. R. Quinn Collection)

(above) In an extremely rare photograph, August Thieme captured one of the SAL F9 class 0-8-0s in action. No. 1179 is just getting under way from RF&P's Acca Yard in Richmond, Virginia, with a transfer cut of perishable cars en route to SAL's Hermitage Yard in April 1944.

(August A. Thieme)

(right) During the heavy traffic of World War II, the SAL acquired five 0-8-0 switchers from the Elgin, Joliet and Eastern Railway. Designated as SAL class F9, these locomotives were originally 2-8-0s that the EJ&E had converted to switchers. F9 class 0-8-0 No. 1179 is at Hermitage Yard in Richmond, Virginia, on March 9, 1945.

(August A. Thieme)

retired in the late 1940s. The P class Pacifics were delivered with 72-inch drive wheels and along with the L-4 class Tenwheelers were assigned to the fast freight and perishable trains. The Pacifics were also bumped from main line freight service by the Mikados and 31 4-6-2s were rebuilt as the P-2 class with larger drive wheels for use strictly in passenger service.

The Seaboard took delivery of its first Mikados in 1914. Nineteen hand-fired Q class 2-8-2s were delivered new to the SAL from the Richmond Works of the American Locomotive Company. Numbered in the series 300-318, they were equipped with the Vanderbilt tender that became the most distinguishing characteristic of Seaboard steam power. These tenders consisted of a boxlike coal bunker set before a cylindrical water tank and drew their name from a design that had been specified for locomotives on railroads of the Vanderbilt group in the early part of the century. These locomotives, as well as fifteen duplicates that were designated the Q-2 class and numbered in the series 319-333, performed service on all of the SAL until retired in the early 1950s. Ten standard USRA Mikados were assigned to the SAL by the United States Government in 1918. These locomotives were primarily operated on the Virginia, North Carolina, and Georgia Divisions.

The locomotives that became the SAL's standard heavy and fast freight engines joined the

(left) The first 2-8-0 type locomotives owned by the Seaboard were the 500-series Consolidations built by Baldwin in the 1890s. They were designated the L-class, were renumbered 956-966 in 1916 and were scrapped during World War I. No. 512 is shown in as-delivered condition.

(SAL Photo/CSX Transportation)

(below) The H1 class 2-8-0s were numbered in the series 900-918 and were built by Baldwin in 1911. Superheaters were later installed by the SAL.

(H. K. Vollrath Collection)

(bottom) H1 class 2-8-0 No. 900 switches a train of perishable traffic at Richmond, Virginia, in March 1946.

(H. K. Vollrath Collection)

(above) H2 class 2-8-0 No. 933 was the former Chicago and North Western Railway locomotive No. 1744. The SAL purchased five such locomotives from the C&NW during World War II and they were rated the most powerful of the SAL Consolidations.
(H. L.. Kitchen Photo/James B. Harris Collection)

(right) L3 class 2-8-0s in the number series 970-999 were built in 1902-1904 and were all retired in the late 1930s. No. 987 is at Savannah, Georgia, on May 18, 1924.
(Joseph Lavelle Photo/L. D. Moore, Jr. Collection)

(below) SAL H1 class 2-8-0 No. 922 was former Georgia, Florida and Alabama Railway No. 202 and was acquired by the SAL in 1929. It is at Cordele, Georgia, in September 1938.
(H. K. Vollrath Collection)

roster in 1923 when the American Locomotive Company's Schenectady Works delivered twenty-three Q-3 class Mikados. Of 170 Mikados owned by the SAL, 117 were of the Q-3 design as delivered by both the American and Baldwin Locomotive Works between 1923 and 1926. A personal favorite of the author, the Q-3 engines were essentially a modified version of the USRA light Mikado, equipped with Vanderbilt tenders, stokers, and a trailing truck booster that increased their tractive effort to 65,200 lbs. However, the feature that distinguished the Q-3 from all other locomotives operating on Southeastern railroads was the placement of their cross-compound air pumps on the front of the smokebox, over their headlight that had been lowered below center. The Q-3 engines were in general use over most of the SAL system and were often found doubleheading on fast freight trains. When finally bumped from Red Ball and heavy freight service by the new FT diesels, footboards were installed on their pilots and they were used extensively on the Seaboard's many road switcher assignments until finally retired in the early 1950s.

The locomotives that became the SAL's standard passenger engines also first joined the roster in 1914. In that year the Richmond Works of the American Locomotive Company delivered ten M class 4-8-2s in the number series 200-209. With their 69-inch drive wheels they immediately satisfied the SAL's need for a locomotive to handle fast heavy passenger trains and even fast freight service. The SAL was one of the earliest railroads to adopt the "Mountain" (or 4-8-2) wheel arrangement and these locomotives proved to be well-suited for the Seaboard's terrain and tonnage. Eventually, the SAL's fleet of Mountains grew to 61 locomotives with the delivery of additional M and new M-1 and M-2 classes.

The SAL's requirement for an even higher-speed passenger locomotive was met with delivery of the thirty-six M-2 class Mountains. These locomotives came with 72-inch drive wheels and Delta trailer truck boosters. As did all of the SAL's Mountains, the M-2's came with heavy tenders and eventually were equipped with stokers. Several

(below) The first Mikados came to the SAL in 1914 with the delivery of nineteen new 2-8-2s from Alco's Richmond Locomotive Works. Designated the Q class and numbered 300-318, they were delivered as hand-fired engines and equipped with the distinctive Vanderbilt tender. They were later modified with the application of Berkley stokers. No. 302 is at Richmond, Virginia, in August 1949.

(H. K. Vollrath Collection)

(above) Q1 class 2-8-2s in the number series 490-499 were standard USRA Mikados assigned to the SAL by the United States Railroad Administration during World War I. No. 491 was photographed on a train near Raleigh, N.C., in 1948.
(H. L. Kitchen Photo/James B. Harris Collection)

(right) Fifteen duplicates of the Q class Mikados were acquired in 1922 by the SAL from Alco's Schenectady Works. Numbered 319-331, they were designated the Q2 class. No. 319 is at Hermitage Yard in Richmond, Virginia, in September 1946.
(D. Wallace Johnson Photo/H. K. Vollrath Collection)

(below) Q1 class Mikado No. 494 arrives Petersburg, Virginia, with a northbound freight train on November 11, 1948.
(H. Reid)

(above) The Q3 Mikados had 63-inch drivers and exerted 54,700 lbs tractive effort. They were also equipped with a Franklin booster that exerted additional tractive effort for starting heavy trains or pulling hills. No. 373 is at Abbeville, S.C., on March 16, 1947.

(Hugh M. Comer)

(below) The Q3 2-8-2s also sported Vanderbilt tenders holding 9600 gallons of water and 17 tons of coal. Q3 No. 427 is at Raleigh, N.C.

(T. G. Wicker Collection)

(facing page) Unique among steam locomotives operating in the South, the Q3s' air pumps were mounted on the front of the smokebox, directly above the headlight that was lowered below center. The distinctive front of Q3 No. 355, stenciled for the Virginia Operating Division, was captured by Wiley Bryan at Raleigh, N.C.

(Wiley M. Bryan Photo/M. B. Connery Collection)

355
VA.
KEEP
OFF
VA.
KEEP
OFF

(above) Bumped from the through freight jobs by the new diesels, the Q3s were equipped with footboards and spent their final years on the SAL's many road switcher assignments. No. 357 is southbound from Richmond, Va., with the Bellwood Switcher on September 11, 1949.

(D. Wallace Johnson)

(left) The SAL acquired its first Q3 class Mikado from Alco's Schenectady Works in 1923. These locomotives were so successful that they soon became the standard SAL freight locomotive and the most numerous class of locomotive on the railroad. This view of Q3 No. 446 in as-delivered condition was taken at Richmond in 1925.

(Virginia Historical Society Collection)

M-2s were modified to burn fuel oil, and in 1936 six were equipped with 16,000-gallon heavy tenders that the SAL purchased from Baldwin to eliminate expensive trains stops for water and to shorten train schedules. With their clean lines, the Mountains were certainly the most handsome locomotives in the Seaboard's fleet.

Perhaps the most unorthodox wheel arrangement on the SAL was that of the Decapod, or 2-10-0 type locomotive. The SAL's first Decapods were assigned to the Company by the United States Railroad Administration in 1918. The 2-10-0 had been a popular wheel arrangement for European locomotives, and in 1917 the Czarist regime in Russia placed a large order for such locomotives with American builders. However, when the Czar was overthrown in the Russian Revolution, Baldwin and the American Locomotive Works were stuck with over 200 of these Decapods. The USRA allotted the undeliverable locomotives among the American railroads. The SAL received twenty and designated them the D class in number series 500-520. Fortunately for the SAL, the relatively light axle loadings of the Decapods made them ideal for operation over the light rail and bridge loadings on many of its branch lines. The SAL was so pleased with the 2-10-0 wheel arrangement that it eventually owned 51 of them. Only the D-3 class engines in number series 529-536 were custom built for the SAL. The balance of the SAL Decapods were either purchased second-hand from other railroads or were acquired from the Georgia, Florida and Alabama Railway when the Seaboard absorbed that company into its system in 1928.

Another locomotive that came to Seaboard during the First World War was the Class B Santa Fe, or 2-10-2 type. The SAL had acquired ten of the Class B 2-10-2s in the number series 400-409 from Baldwin in 1918. Fifteen additional locomotives of this type, designated the B-1 class and numbered 485-499, were assigned to the Seaboard by the USRA during the period of Federal control. These locomotives were renumbered in the 2000-series, becoming 2400-2409 and 2485-2499 when additional Mikados were acquired in 1925. They were upgraded with disc-type main drivers to solve counterbalancing problems and eventually served the SAL well, handling tonnage trains over the Georgia and North Carolina Divisions.

(above) The SAL was assigned 20 Decapod locomotives by the USRA when they could not be delivered to Russia because of the Communist Revolution in 1918. The SAL found them suitable for its operations and purchased several from other railroads. One of the SAL's original "Russian" Decapods, D class No. 504, is at Raleigh, N.C., on June 7, 1937.
(James F. Byrne Photo/T. W. Dixon, Jr. Collection)

(below) D4 class Decapod No. 545 was acquired by the SAL from the Detroit, Toledo and Ironton Railroad. It is seen at Boykins, Va., in operation on the Lewiston Branch.
(D. Wallace Johnson)

(bottom) D2 class Decapod No. 525 was built for the Georgia, Florida and Alabama Railway. The locomotive is at Durham, N.C.
(R. B. Carneal Photo/H. Reid Collection)

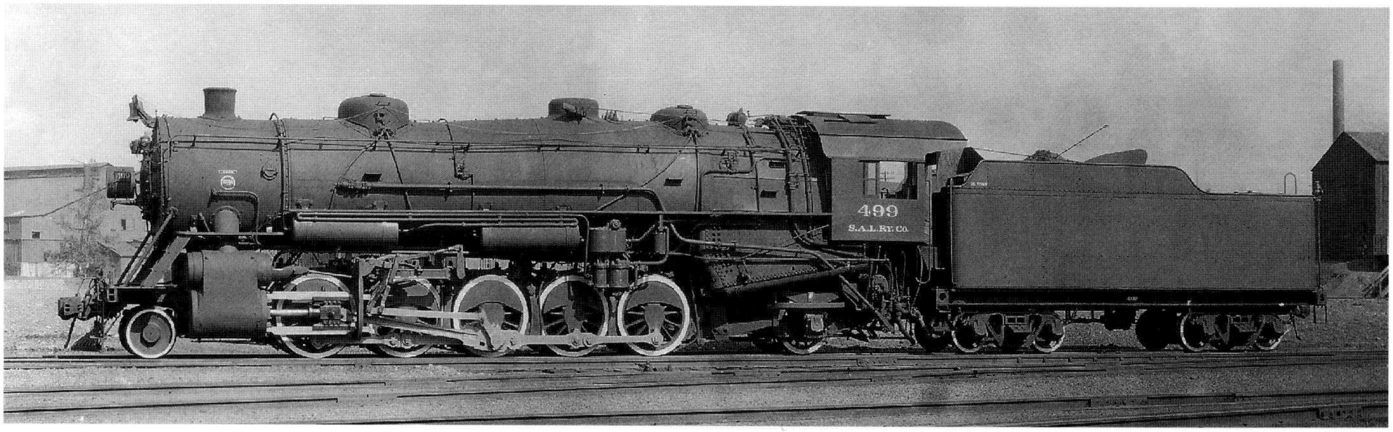

(top) Ten heavy 2-10-2s were delivered to the SAL by Baldwin during World War I. Designated the B class, they were originally numbered 400-409, later renumbered 2400-2409.
(Baldwin Photo/W. E. Griffin, Jr. Collection)

(above) B class 2-10-2 is being serviced for its next assignment at Charlotte in 1932.
(Paul E. Parrish/W. E. Griffin, Jr. Collection)

(below) Until modified with counterbalanced disc-type main drivers, the B1 class 2-10-2s rode so rough and damaged so much track that their speed had to be restricted to 25 mph. With the improved drivers they were found to be well suited for the heavy ore and coal trains operating between Atlanta and Birmingham. B1 No. 2489 is at Birmingham on July 19, 1940.
(Jay Williams Collection)

The SAL briefly experimented with Mallet compound locomotives when sixteen 2-8-8-2 engines were purchased from Richmond Locomotive Works in 1917. Numbered in the series 500-515, the locomotives were not delivered until the beginning of Federal control of the railroads in 1918. Nine of these locomotives when delivered had been used by the Director General on other lines and were turned over to the SAL at the termination of Federal control in used condition. The locomotives were determined to be too heavy for use on the SAL and they were sold in 1920 to the Baltimore & Ohio Railroad.

However, the SAL did not give up on the articulated type of steam locomotive. Between 1935 and 1937, ten single-expansion articulated 2-6-6-4 locomotives were purchased from Baldwin. The Class R-1 engines were numbered 2500-2504; Class R-2 in the series 2505-2509. These giants were 110 feet long, 16 feet high, weighed close to 400 tons and developed 4,000 horsepower. At the time they were the largest locomotives in service in the Southeastern states and embodied the latest developments then available in steam locomotive design. Equipped with superheaters, stokers, feedwater heaters, and thermic syphons, they were as close as the Seaboard got to owning a "modern steam locomotive." Affectionately referred to as "Twin Pacifics" by Seaboard employees, they proved to be extremely successful in high-speed freight service and were touted as the first successful application of articulated locomotives for such service. When bumped from these runs by the new FT diesels, all of the SAL's 2-6-6-4 articulateds were sold to the Baltimore & Ohio Railroad in 1947.

(above) The SAL purchased sixteen 2-8-8-2 Mallet Compound locomotives from Alco's Richmond Works in 1918. Designated the A class, they were numbered 500-515. They were quickly determined to be too heavy for the SAL's light rail and were sold to the Baltimore and Ohio Railroad in 1920. This builders view of No. 515 was taken at Richmond in March 1918.
(H. K. Vollrath Collection)

(below) Designated the R1 class, Nos. 2500-2504 were delivered by Baldwin in 1935. These locomotives were put into fast freight service between Richmond, Va., and Hamlet, N.C. No. 2503 is departing Raleigh with a northbound *Red Ball* perishable train.
(H. L. Kitchen)

(left) Blasting out of Raleigh, N.C., with a southbound perishable train in 1936 is R1 2-6-6-4 No. 2500.
(Bruce Lewis/Robert K. Durham Collection)

(below) The R1s were so successful the SAL purchased five more compound articulateds in 1937. Designated as the R2 class, they were numbered 2505-2509. The unusual angle of this photograph conveys the massive size of these magnificent locomotives. R2 No. 2505 is at Richmond, Va., in 1937.
(SAL Photo/W. E. Griffin, Jr. Collection)

(facing page, top) The SAL's R class 2-6-6-4s were nationally recognized as the first articulateds to be successfully operated in fast freight service and were the closest thing the SAL owned to modern steam power. The crew proudly poses with R1 No. 2502 at Charlotte, N.C., on September 5, 1937.
(F. E. Ardrey, Jr. Collection)

(facing page, middle) Steaming through Raleigh, N.C,. in splendid form with a coal train is R1 No. 2-6-6-4 No. 2504.
(H. L. Kitchen)

(facing page, bottom) With the addition of the R2s, the SAL began to operate its articulateds from Hamlet to Portsmouth, Va., and to Monroe and Charlotte, N.C. The articulateds were eventually bumped from the fast freight assignments by the FT diesels and in 1947 all of these locomotives, such as R2 No. 2506 pictured here, were sold to the Baltimore and Ohio Railroad.
(Jay Williams Collection)

2502

2504

2506
2506

(left) The SAL owned many 4-4-0 type locomotives inherited from its predecessor roads. Other locomotives of this type were built for the SAL or its newly acquired roads between 1900 and 1913. No. 25 was originally built for the Seaboard and Roanoke.

(below left) Sporty 4-4-0 No. 503 was originally owned by the Georgia, Carolina and Northern Railway.

(facing page, top) The first Tenwheeler, or 4-6-0, was acquired by SAL predecessor roads in 1890. They were used in both freight and passenger service and some were still on the SAL's roster in the 1950s. Tenwheeler No. 43 was built by Baldwin in 1910 and subsequently renumbered the second No. 662 in 1918.
(Three SAL Photos/CSX Transportation)

(facing page, second row) 4-6-0 No. 557 was built for the SAL in 1896 at the Pittsburgh Locomotive Works and was renumbered 1557 in 1918.
(SAL Photo)

The standard SAL Tenwheelers for use in the freight service were the L4 class, such as No. 789, shown here with an extra freight.
(Jay Williams Collection)

(facing page, bottom) A number of the former K class Tenwheelers were modified for passenger service and reclassified a L2-S. However, the 659 retained its older 20" x 28" cylinders along with its Baker valve gear. The sporty engine is at Hamlet, N.C., in June 1938 in this classic view.
(H. K. Vollrath Collection)

Another Seaboard locomotive that achieved nationwide acclaim was the F-7 class 0-6-0 switcher. Baldwin delivered 50 of these locomotives in 1927 and 1928 in number series 1101-1150. Equipped with 51-inch drive wheels and a front end throttle, various railroad publications praised the locomotives' cut-off valve gear which provided for maximum work output as well as efficient and economical operation. It was acclaimed the most outstanding 0-6-0 type switcher ever built in this country. They were used all over the SAL system until retired in 1952-53.

In addition to the Decapods previously mentioned, the Seaboard purchased a number of locomotives second-hand from other railroads. Notable among these purchases were the ten P-4 class Pacifics from the Western Maryland (numbered 871-880); the six H-2 class Consolidations from the Chicago and North Western (numbered 933-937); the eight Q-4 Mikados from the Wabash (numbered 480-487); and the five F-9 class 0-8-0 switchers from the Elgin, Joliet and Eastern (numbered 1175-1179). The F-9s were the only 0-8-0s ever owned by the SAL and they were used at various points around the system during the late 1940s.

With the end of the Second World War, the Seaboard rapidly completed the dieselization of its motive power fleet that had begun in the 1930s. By the end of 1949, the Seaboard reported to its stockholders that the railroad owned 207 diesel locomotives (112 freight, 57 passenger, and 38 switchers) and that orders had been placed for an additional 62 diesel locomotives. At the beginning of 1950, diesel power handled 75 per cent of the freight gross ton miles, 80 per cent of the passenger train miles, and 46 per cent of the yard switching assignments. In early 1950, the South Florida Division became the first operating division to be completely dieselized.

The majority of the Seaboard's steam power was retired and sold for scrap during the period 1950-53. Due to the Korean War, a few of the locomotives were held in reserve against the possibility of an all-out national emergency. For example, seventeen Q-3 Mikados were stored during this period at Raleigh, N.C. Skeleton coaling and watering facilities were also retained along the line in the event it became necessary to use the steam locomotives. With the end of the Korean conflict, the stored Seaboard steam locomotives were soon consigned to the scrap yards.

The last steam locomotive to be operated by the Seaboard was No. 1001, an 0-4-0T Saddle Tank switcher that had been purchased in 1936 to handle switching assignments on the city streets of Columbus, Georgia. It remained in service until 1958 and was then donated to the city of Columbus for display in that city's Holiday Park.

In the early 1900s, the Tenwheelers were the principal SAL freight and passenger locomotive. The first L2 class engines were delivered in 1901 and eventually the SAL owned forty-nine such locomotives. L2 class 4-6-0 No. 617 is at Hamlet, N.C., in June 1938. (J. R. Quinn Collection)

(above) American Locomotive's Richmond Works delivered ten 4-6-2 type locomotives to the SAL in 1911 for fast passenger service. Designated P class and numbered in the series 90-99, the superheated locomotives were so successful that ten more were ordered. In 1929 they were renumbered 851-870. P class Pacific No. 867 is stopped at the 32nd Street Yard Office, Birmingham, Alabama, for orders eastbound in 1939.

(F. E. Ardrey, Jr. Collection)

(left) P class Pacific No. 861 makes a station stop at Franklin, Virginia, with Train No. 13 on October 10, 1948.

(H. Reid)

(below) In 1940, P class 4-6-2s No. 865, 867, and 868 were provided with streamlined shrouding for service on the *West Coast Silver Meteor* between Wildwood and St. Petersburg, Fla. The freshly painted portrait of No. 868 was taken on May 25, 1940.

(SAL Photo)

(right) During 1912-1913, the SAL acquired fifty P1 type Pacifics, with the construction orders handled by both Baldwin and the American Locomotive Works. Numbered in the series 800-849, they replaced the L4 Tenwheelers as the fast freight locomotives. P1 No. 807 is at Miami, Florida, in December 1938.

(below) After the Mikados replaced the Pacifics as the standard fast freight locomotive, certain of the P1 class 4-6-2s were rebuilt for both passenger and freight service and reclassified as P2s. The numbers of the reclassified locomotives, 815-831 and 833-849, were unchanged. This classic portrait of P2 No. 819 was taken at South Boca Grande, Florida, in March 1937.

(Both, H. K. Vollrath Collection)

To meet the increased need for passenger locomotives during World War II, the SAL acquired ten Pacifics from the Western Maryland Railway. These locomotives were classified as P4s and were numbered 871-880. P4 No. 876 is at Hamlet, N.C., in August 1950.

(H. K. Vollrath Collection)

(above) P4 4-6-2 No. 872 is running light with two cabooses at Raleigh, N.C., in 1950.

(H. L. Kitchen Photo/James B. Harris Collection)

(left) P-2 Pacific No. 836 sports brass flag holders and a fancy *Orange Blossom Special* name plate.

(SAL Photo/W. E. Griffin, Jr. Collection)

(below) The SAL acquired its first "Mountains," or 4-8-2 type steam locomotives, in 1914 from the Richmond Locomotive Works. Designated the M class, these ten locomotives were numbered 200-209 and with their 69-inch driving wheels, they were used in heavy passenger service. No. 200 is at Jacksonville, Fla., in June 1938.

(H. K. Vollrath Collection)

(right) The engineer of M class 4-8-2 No. 203 has decorated the front of his locomotive by placing a brass eagle in front of the locomotive's smokestack. No. 203 was photographed at Birmingham, Alabama, in July 1940.

(H. K. Vollrath Collection)

(below) The initial Mountains performed so well that the SAL purchased ten more from Alco's Schenectady Works in 1922. Designated as the M-2 class and numbered 215-224, they were also identical to the M class locomotives. M-1 No. 215 is at Wilmington, N.C., in May 1937.

(H. K. Vollrath Collection)

(bottom) As delivered by Baldwin, the M-2s were hand-fired engines. They were all eventually equipped with stokers. M-2 Mountain No. 245 departs Raleigh, N.C., in 1938 with the Johnson Street coal chute in the background.

(Wiley M. Bryan)

(above) To meet the need for motive power for high speed passenger service, the SAL purchased thirty-six M-2 class 4-8-2s from Baldwin between 1924-1926. Numbered 235-270, these locomotives had 72-inch driving wheels and increased boiler pressure of 200 lbs. M-2 No. 238 is at Columbia, S.C. on July 18, 1937.

(M. B. Connery Collection)

(left) M-2 4-8-2 No. 259 and F-7 0-6-0 No. 1138 at Howells (Atlanta), Georgia, on September 2, 1951.

(Bob's Photo Collection)

(below) The SAL spared no efforts in decorating M-2 class 4-8-2 No. 264 for a Jacksonville, Florida, to Toronto, Canada, *Shrine Special.*

(SAL Photo/W. E. Griffin, Jr. Collection)

Seaboard Air Line Steam Locomotives

	Numbers	Class	Cylinders	Drivers	Weight	Builder	Date
0-4-0	1001	ODD	16x24	42	108,000	Baldwin (BLW)	1936
	1004	ODD	10x24	50	86,500	BLW	1913
0-6-0	1030-1059	L-5	19x28	51	144,280	BLW	1907-1913
	1090-1099	F-5	21x28	51	165,000	Alco	1919
	1101-1125	F-7	23x28	51	180,000	BLW	1927
	1126-1150	F-7	23x28	51	180,000	BLW	1928
0-8-0	1175	F-9	22x28	51	184,500	Alco	1904
	1176-1179	F-9	22x28	51	187,900	Alco	1905
2-8-0	900-918	H-1	23x30	56	217,000	BLW	1911
	919	H-1	25x30	56	214,700	BLW	1911
	920-924	GF&A	20x26	56	147,800	BLW	1906-1913
	927-928	CH&N	20x26	54	164,500	Alco	1913
	929-932	CH&N	21x28	54	177,000	BLW	1920
	933-937	H-2	25x32	61	243,500	Alco	1910-1912
	956-966	L	20x24	50	117,000	BLW	1890-1891
	967-969	L-1	20x24	50	124,600	Alco	1892
	970-989	L-3	20x28	57	145,200	Alco	1902-1903
2-8-2	300-318	Q	26x30	63	282,000	Alco	1914
	319-333	Q-2	26x30	63	283,000	Alco	1922
	334-356	Q-3	26x30	63	300,000	Alco	1923
	357-376	Q-3	26x30	63	300,000	BLW	1924
	377-396	Q-3	26x30	63	300,000	Alco	1925
	397-410	Q-3	26x30	63	300,000	BLW	1925
	411-450	Q-3	26x30	63	300,000	BLW	1926
	451	Q-3	26x30	63	300,000	SAL	1931
	480-481	Q-4	26x30	64	266,840	Alco	1912
	482-487	Q-4	26x30	64	266,840	BLW	1912
	490-499	Q-1	26x30	63	292,000	Alco	1918
2-10-0	500-520	D	25x28	52	207,000	Alco	1918
	521-522	D-1	25x28	52	207,000	BLW	1918
	523-528	D-2	24x28	56	212,000	BLW	1924-1926
	529-536	D-3	24x28	56	212,000	BLW	1930
	537-546	D-4	25x28	52	207,700	Alco	1917-1918
	547-550	D-5	25x28	52	207,700	Alco/BLW	1918
2-10-2	2401-2408	B	27x32	63	336,000	BLW	1918
	2485-2499	B-1	27x32	57	352,000	BLW	1919
2-6-6-4	2500-2504	R-1	22x30	69	480,000	BLW	1935
	2505-2509	R-2	22x30	69	480,000	BLW	1937
2-8-8-2	500-515	A	26x42x32	63	497,000	Alco	1917-1918
4-6-0	600-609	L-2	20x28	67	152,500	Alco	1902
	610-618	L-2	20x28	67	165,090	BLW	1903-1907
	620-629	L-2	20x28	67	165,090	Alco	1905
	630-644	L-2	20x28	67	165,090	BLW	1906
	645-649	L-2	20x28	67	165,090	BLW	1907
	650-651	L-4S	19x28	60	172,000	BLW	1910
	652-654	L-2S	19x28	67	176,130	BLW	1910
	655-657	L-4S	19x28	60	172,000	BLW	1910
	658	K	21x28	72	173,700	BLW	1910
	659	L-2S	19x28	67	176,130	BLW	1910
	660-664	L-4S	19x28	60	172,000	BLW	1910
	671-680	I-12	18x26	57	128,800	BLW	1909-1912
	681-683	I-13	19x26	62	139,200	BLW	1915
	700-796	L-4	19x28	60	161,050	BLW/Alco	1903-07
4-6-2	800-814	P-1	22x28	63	220,000	BLW	1912
	815-849	P-2	23x28	69	230,600	Alco	1913
	851-870	P	23x28	72	223,000	BLW/Alco	1911-1913
	871-880	P-4	23x28	68	201,700	BLW	1909-1911
4-8-2	200-209	M	27x28	69	316,000	Alco	1914
	210-214	M	27x28	69	316,000	Alco	1917
	215-219	M-1	27x28	69	315,000	Alco	1922
	221-224	M-1	27x28	69	315,000	Alco	1922
	235-270	M-2	27x28	72	320,000	BLW	1924-1926

Chapter 3

The Diesel Era

Further encounters with snow will be rare for this EMD F-unit. In 1948, the SAL added eleven F3A units to its roster of freight locomotives. This front view of No. 4024 was taken at EMD's La Grange, Illinos, factory in March 1948.
(SAL Photo/CSX Transportation)

When the steam era came to an end on the Seaboard Air Line, the railroad's steam locomotives were replaced by a fleet of diesels that were as colorful and diverse as any in the country. If there was ever an equal opportunity purchaser of diesel locomotives, it had to be the Seaboard. The railroad's roster of diesels consisted of thirty-eight different models, including ten different models of switchers, from four different builders. And while the more popular models were the mainstay of the SAL's diesel roster, the railroad did experiment with a number of distinctive locomotives.

The Seaboard first explored the use of other than steam power as early as 1917 when it purchased two gas-electric motor cars (Nos. 2000-2001) for service on local passenger trains. These two cars, built by GE/Watson, were the first of many motor rail cars owned by the Seaboard. While one of these cars was retired in 1923, the other car (No. 2000) remained in SAL service until 1932.

As was the case with its diesels, the SAL owned a diverse fleet of rail cars. In addition to the two original GE/Watson cars, the SAL also owned motor cars built by Brill, American Car and Foundry, and EMC/St. Louis Car Company.

The first Brill car, No. 2012, was acquired in 1922 and consisted of a motor car with a 68-horsepower gasoline engine and trailer car. It proved so successful that by 1928, the Seaboard had in service sixteen motor cars (eleven from Brill, four from EMC, and one from GE/Watson) and thirteen trailer cars. These later Brill motor cars (Nos. 2013-2021) were equipped with 275-horsepower Hall-Scott engines and successfully supplanted steam power on light density passenger routes throughout the system. Three AC&F motor cars (Nos. 2024-2026), powered by

4024
4024
SEABOARD
AIR
LINE
RAILROAD
THROUGH THE HEART OF THE SOUTH

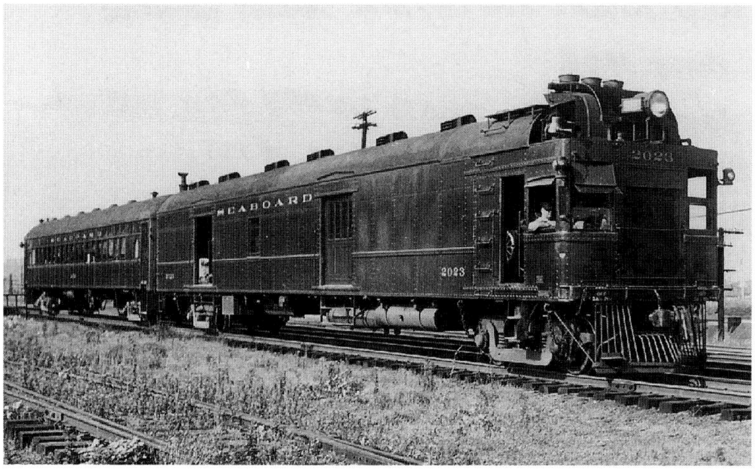

(above) The SAL was an early purchaser of gas-electric motor cars. The earliest cars were acquired in 1917 and by the close of 1928 the SAL had in operation 16 gas-electric motor cars and 13 trailer cars which had supplanted steam trains on runs that could be more economically operated with motor cars. One of the earliest was car No. 2011, seen here at Tampa, Fla., on August 16, 1923.
(Don Hensley Collection)

(left) Two St. Louis Car Co./EMC rail cars, numbered 2022 and 2023, were purchased in 1928. This is a view of the 2023 at Winder, Georgia, on July 5, 1936.
(W. J. Rivers Photo/M. B. Connery Collection)

(below) Gas-electric No. 2017 was built by Brill in 1927. In this view the motor car is seen at Raleigh, N.C., on January 9, 1936.
(H. L. Kitchen)

176-horsepower Hall-Scott engines and painted in a cream and light blue paint scheme, were delivered in 1935 for local passenger train service on the lines between Richmond-Raleigh; Jacksonville-Tampa; and Jacksonville-Tallahassee-River Junction.

The final SAL motor cars (Nos. 2027-2028) were acquired from St. Louis Car/EMC in 1936. They were equipped with a 600-horsepower eight-cylinder, two-cycle diesel engine and were the first SAL motor cars that could pull standard passenger coaches. They were even used for many years on the *Silver Meteor's* Tampa-Sarasota-Venice connection and one of these cars (No. 2028) survived the SAL-ACL merger, being retired in 1971.

(above) Gas-electric No. 2025 came to the SAL from AC&F in 1935. Henry Kitchen recorded this station stop at McKenney, Virginia, on January 18, 1936.

(H. L. Kitchen)

(left and above) Perhaps the most noted of the SAL rail cars were St. Louis Car Co./EMC car Nos. 2027 and 2028. Purchased in 1936, they were the last rail cars purchased by the SAL and the 2028 lasted until the ACL/SAL merger in 1967. Shown here in its original paint scheme, the 2027 was divided into three compartments, the first being the motor and engineer's position, and the second and third devoted to mail and baggage respectively. Passengers were transported in trailer cars.

(SAL Photos)

The Seaboard acquired its first diesel-electric locomotives in 1938 to power the *Orange Blossom Special*. These 2000-horsepower E4 diesels were built by the Electro-Motive Corporation at La Grange, Illinois, and had two 1000-horsepower "V" type, two cycle, 12-cylinder engines, two EMC-type 600-volt main generators, and four EMC 600-volt traction motors. Each unit had two 6-wheel trucks with 36-inch diameter wheels. The units were delivered in three A-B-A sets and the main parts of all units were interchangeable. The "A" units could operate as a complete locomotive and carried complete control equipment for independent operation or for operation in conjunction with other "A" or "B" units.

The six "A" units were numbered 3000-3005 and the three "B", or booster units, were numbered 3100-3102. All of these units were painted in a new "citrus" paint scheme of dark green, orange and yellow, with silver pilots and running gear. They were the first diesels to be operated in the Southeast and to promote the new motive power, the Seaboard operated a special "Diesel Exhibition Tour Train" over the main routes of the system between Virginia and Florida in November 1938. With completion of the tour, the train was christened at New York's Penn Station on December 15, 1938, and the new *Orange Blossom Specials* began a new winter season and a new era of passenger service.

These new diesels were initially used during the 1938-1939 winter tourist season between Washington and Miami on the SAL's East Coast *Orange Blossom Special* which operated between New York and Miami. The East Coast *Blossom* generally consisted of 16 cars and was assigned two "A" units with a "B" unit between forming one 6000-horsepower locomotive manned by an engineer, fireman,

(left) Seaboard's September 4, 1938, public timetable contained this ad for the road's new diesel passenger locomotives.

(below) The SAL lined up five of its new EMD E4 diesels for this 1941 publicity shot.

(Both, W. E. Griffin Collection)

and diesel attendant. The diesel attendant positions were equally divided between machinists and electricians. The West Coast *Blossom* generally consisted of 12 cars and was assigned one "A" and one "B" or two "A" units and was also manned by an engineer, fireman, and diesel attendant.

Since the new diesels operated over the Richmond, Fredericksburg & Potomac Railroad between Richmond, Virginia, and Washington, DC, each "A" unit was equipped with Union Switch and Signal Company's two-speed, three-color indicating, continuous inductive automatic train control and train stop.

In operation on northbound trips, the train control device on the leading "A" unit was cut in on the SAL main line track leading to the RF&P tracks at "AY" Tower in Richmond. On southbound trips, the train control device was cut out when passing the RF&P territory at South "Y" junction. To eliminate train delays occasioned by the stops at RF&P's Acca Yard, train control test circuits were installed at Main Street Station in December 1939.

(above) In 1938, SAL acquired three A-B-A sets of E4 diesels to power its *Orange Blossom Special*. They were painted in a Pullman green, orange, and yellow scheme that was referred to as the "Citrus Scheme." E4A Nos. 3000-3006 were delivered in 1938, and Nos. 3007-3013 came in 1939.
(Below, L. W. Rice Photo/Both, T. W. Dixon Jr. Collection)

SEABOARD
3006
3006
SILVER METEOR

SEABOARD

(facing page, top) Located under the first set of side windows, the E4As carried train assignment plates that identified the train to which the locomotive was assigned. E4A No. 3006 was assigned to the *Silver Meteor* when photographed at the Ivy City locomotive facility at Washington Terminal.

(Jay Williams Collection)

(facing page, bottom) E4A No. 3006 was assigned to the *Orange Blossom Special* when photographed at Washington Terminal on April 30, 1939.

(Bob's Photo Collection)

(above) Seaboard locomotives were not the only ones to display train identification. In this photo taken at Ivy City, C&O F-17 Class 4-6-2 No. 470 exhibits a *George Washington* cameo, while SAL E4 No. 3013 has its *Silver Meteor* name plate.

(L. W. Rice Photo/ T. W. Dixon, Jr. Collection)

(below) A classic scene at Washington Terminal in the District of Columbia. A set of SAL EMD E4 A-B-A diesels holds the outside track as a steam-powered passenger train pulls alongside. On the far tracks, a Pennsylvania Railroad GG-1 electric completes this 1939 scene of diesel, steam, and electric power.

(Jay Williams Collection)

(above) In the later years, the E4s were repainted in SAL's light green and red stripe scheme. E4A Nos. 3008 and 3006 were nearing the end of their career with Mail and Express Train No. 3 at Manson, N.C., in April 1964.

(Curt Tillotson, Jr.)

(left) E4B No. 3102 was one of five 2000-horsepower "B" units in the series 3100-3104. Raleigh, N.C., June 12, 1963.

(James H. Wade, Jr.)

The SAL's E4s were an immediate success and when the *Orange Blossom Specials* were not operating, the diesels replaced steam power on other passenger trains, such as the *Southern States Special*. The SAL received additional E4s in 1939 and placed them in service on its new streamlined passenger train, the *Silver Meteor*. During its initial year of operation, the *Silver Meteor* generally consisted of one "A" unit and seven streamlined lightweight coaches.

Eventually, the Seaboard owned fourteen E4 "A" units (Nos. 3000-3013) and five E4 "B" units (Nos. 3100-3104). They made continuous runs between Washington, DC, and Miami, Fla., a distance of 1,162 miles, in just under 21 hours on the *Silver Meteor*. They made the trip between Washington, DC, and St. Petersburg, Fla., a distance of 1,021 miles, in 21 hours and 40 minutes on the *Orange Blossom Special*. The units were fueled at Washington, DC, and on southbound trips made eight minute stops at Hamlet, N.C., and Wildwood, Fla., for fuel, boiler water, icing the diners and inspection.

Following the E4s, the Seaboard continued to purchase streamlined diesels from EMD for its passenger trains. Three E6 "A" units (Nos. 3014-3016) were acquired in 1940 and 1941 and, along with the E4s, served the SAL until 1964. EMD delivered thirty-two E7 "A" units (Nos. 3017-3048) and three E7 "B" units (Nos. 3105-3107) between 1945 and 1949 and eleven E-8 "A" units (Nos. 3049-3059) between 1950 and 1952. The SAL also owned one E9 "A" unit (No 3060), which was built in 1963. Except for the E9, all E-units were delivered in the "citrus" paint scheme and were repainted in 1954 with light green carbodies and red lettering and striping.

(above) E6A No. 3016 with Train No. 6, the northbound *Cotton Blossom* near Atlanta, Georgia, on November 27, 1949.
(Hugh M. Comer Photo/F. E. Ardrey, Jr. Collection)

(below) The SAL owned three 2000-horsepower EMD E6A passenger diesels that were acquired in 1940-41. They were numbered 3014-3016 and in this photo, E6 No. 3014 with E4A and E4B units lead southbound Train No. 21, the *Silver Star*, across the James River after departing Main Street Station at Richmond, Va., in February 1956.
(H. H. Harwood)

SEABOARD
3031
SEABOARD
19177

SEABOARD
3027
3027
SEABOARD
RAILWAY

(left) Between 1945 and 1949, the SAL added thirty-two 2000-h.p. EMD E7A diesels for high-speed passenger service. E7A Nos. 3031 and 3032 are at Waldo, Fla., with a southbound passenger train on November 12, 1949.

(William J. Husa, Jr.)

(facing page bottom) E7A No. 3027, with its nose door headlight, is typical of the Phase Ia carbody design units that were numbered in Seaboard series 3021-3030.

(below) The Phase III carbody E7A featured 45-degree angle mounted number boards and louvered air intakes. No. 3038 represents the SAL's Phase III units in the number series 3036-3048.

(Both, T. W. Dixon Jr. Collection)

(right) Seaboard's E-units featured retractable front couplers, which were concealed by different styles of pilot doors. This cross-section is from an EMD E7A Operating Manual.

(Kevin J. Holland Collection)

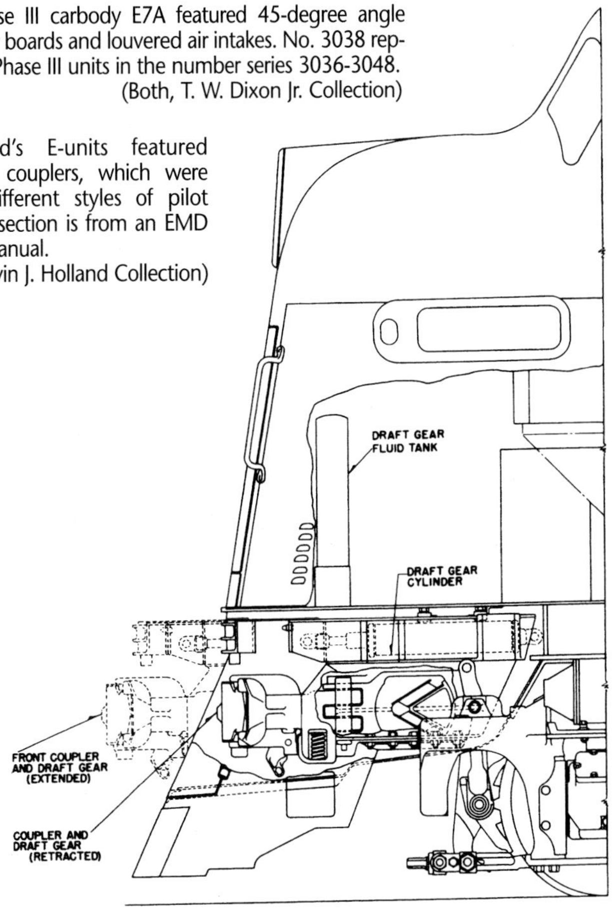

In the later years, the SAL assigned its E7As in both passenger and fast freight service. In this photo, three E7As – led by No. 3043 – are rolling south of Greystone, N.C., with a 65- car Train TT-23, *The Razorback*, in July 1962.

(Curt Tillotson, Jr.)

(above) E7A No. 3037 leads a passenger train at Miami, Fla., on March 16, 1958.

(Walter Gay Collection)

(below) Seaboard's earliest E7As, the Phase I units numbered 3017-3020, were delivered with single headlights. Later the SAL modified these units with the addition of Pyle two-bulb sealed beam headlights mounted on the nose door. No. 3017 heads up Train No. 3 at Wake Forest, N.C., in August 1965.

(Curt Tillotson, Jr.)

EMD delivered 2250-horsepower E8A diesels to the SAL between 1950-52. Numbered 3049-3059, E8A No. 3054 is at Hamlet, N.C., in October 1950.

(M. B. Connery)

(below) E8A No. 3059 pauses at the Greenwood, S.C., passenger station on August 1, 1963.

(Conniff Railroadiana Collection)

(facing page top) Seaboard No. 3060 was one of a kind. The only E9A on the roster, the 2400-horsepower unit was delivered by EMD in 1963. It is at Raleigh, N.C. on October 24, 1964.

(Warren Calloway)

Coming straight at you, E8A No. 3052 is about to pass under U.S. Route 1 with Train No. 3 at Gill, N.C., in May 1965.
(Curt Tillotson, Jr.)

(above) The SAL's first freight diesel, FTA No. 4000, has its freight train in the side track to permit the passage of a passenger train with one of the SAL's first passenger diesels, E4A No. 3001. Both the freight and passenger diesels are in second-generation paint schemes.

(SAL Photo)

The Seaboard's first road freight diesels were acquired in June 1942 with the delivery by EMD of six semi-permanently coupled A-B sets of FTs. Six additional sets of A-B-B-A FTs were delivered in 1943 followed by ten A-B sets in 1944. All FTs were delivered in a modified version of the "citrus" paint scheme applied to the passenger units. Between 1948 and 1949, they were repainted in what became the standard SAL freight paint scheme of Pullman Green carbodies with a wide yellow center stripe bordered by orange pinstripes. With 1350 horsepower each, theFT "A" units were numbered 4000-4021; the FT "B" in the series 4100-4121. Since they were semi-permanently coupled, the FTs were initially operated in sets of A-B or A-B-B-A. In 1948 the SAL purchased eleven F3 "A" units (Nos. 4022-4032) to augment the FTs and other freight diesels.

(above) The 1350-horsepower FTA and FTB units were the SAL's first freight diesel locomotives. Numbered 4000-4021, the FTAs were delivered by EMD between 1942-1944 in a modified version of the color scheme used on the passenger units. This A-B-B-A set is led by FTA No. 4010.

(SAL Photo)

(right) Steam-powered Local Freight No. 97 is in the siding with Q-3 Mike No. 397 at Henderson, N.C., for a northbound perishable train behind FTA No. 4019 and one FTB unit.

(Wiley M. Bryan)

(below) FTB No. 4120 is at Greenwood, S.C., on December 23, 1962.

(James H. Wade Jr. Photo/F. E. Ardrey, Jr. Collection)

(above) FTA No. 4017 and an FTB unit handle a northbound perishable train at Kingsland, Georgia, on January 31, 1950.
(William J. Husa, Jr.)

(below) The FTs that were delivered by EMD in 1942 came in six semi-permanently coupled A-B sets. One of the 1942 FTAs – No. 4001 – hustles this southbound freight through Alberta, Va., in May 1951.
(Robert G. Lewis)

(left) In a rare view of an F3 in passenger service, F3A No. 4030 leads E7As 3038 and 3043 with a 16-car Mail, Passenger and Express Train No. 3 at Manson, N.C., in September 1964.
(Curt Tillotson, Jr.)

(left) The F3s were rated at 1500 h.p. and were used in consists of multiple freight locomotives, as seen in this train passing through Raleigh, N.C.
(Warren Calloway)

(below) F3A No. 4024 in a classic builder's photo view at the EMD factory in March 1948.
(T. W. Dixon, Jr. Collection)

(above) The SAL also purchased freight cab units from Alco, with three FA1-FB1 sets acquired in 1948. FA1 No. 4200 is shown with an FB1 unit in this view.

(T. W. Dixon, Jr. Collection)

(left) FB1 No. 4300 is at Savannah, Ga., on July 26, 1964.

(James H. Wade Jr. Photo/F. E. Ardrey, Jr. Collection)

(below) FA1 No. 4202 and FB1 No. 4302 are southbound with freight train at Waldo, Fla., on June 15, 1952.

(William J. Husa, Jr.)

In addition to the FTs, the SAL also purchased three sets of Alco freight cab units in 1948. These 1500-horsepower FA1s (Nos. 4200-4202) and FB1s (Nos. 4300-4302) were originally assigned between Richmond and Birmingham but spent most of their service years in Florida.

The Seaboard's first road switchers (designed for both yard and road service) were four Alco 1500-horsepower RSC2s (Nos. 1500-1503) equipped with A-1-A trucks. These units arrived in 1947 and were immediately put in service on the SAL's light rail lines in Georgia. The first road switchers equipped with B-B trucks were the Alco RS2s that arrived in 1949. Seaboard was a major purchaser of Alco road switchers, eventually rostering thirty-seven RSC2s, seven RSC3s, thirty-two RS2s, and sixty RS3s. The majority of these diesels were retired in 1974 after primary service on the Georgia and Florida Divisions. A small group of the RSCs were assigned to Hamlet and were used on the light rail lines in North Carolina, particularly the branch line between Durham and Henderson.

(above) Alco RSC2 No. 1526 was purchased by the SAL in 1949. These 1500-horsepower units were geared for a maximum speed of 65 mph.

(SAL Photo)

RSC2 No. 1525 gets an assist from GP7 No. 1707 as it handles a train of pine tree stumps at Wildwood, Fla. on May 6, 1950.

(William J. Husa, Jr.)

(above) Alco RSC3 Nos. 1538 and 1541 and their short train are parked in front of the Henderson, N.C. passenger station. After completing their round trip from Henderson to Norlina and return, the local freight's crew has parked the train to take lunch. (Curt Tillotson, Jr.)

(left) The SAL rostered a large group of Alco RS3s in the number series 1629-1691. They operated throughout the SAL lines in Georgia and Florida. RS3 No. 1648 is at Hialeah, Fla. (James H. Wade, Jr.)

(below) The SAL owned 32 Alco RS2 class road switchers. Nos. 1600-1628 were purchased by the SAL in 1949-50. RS2 Nos. 1685-1687 were originally MD&S diesels built in 1949. The 1607 is at Bainbridge, Georgia, on October 23, 1967. (Conniff Railroadiana Collection)

(above) Alco RS11 No. 104 parked beside a switcher at Baldwin, Florida, on November 20, 1965.
(Conniff Railroadiana Collection)

(below) Alco RS11 No. 104 is at Jacksonville, Fla. The SAL received ten of this class locomotive from Alco in 1960.
(Walter Gay Collection)

(above) Alco C420 No. 110 was the first of 27 such units in the number series 110-136. This portrait of the 110 was taken at Starke, Florida, in May 1967.

(H. K. Vollrath Collection)

While the Seaboard purchased a few late-model Alco road switchers (ten RS11s and twenty-seven C420s), it looked to EMD as its preferred provider of road switchers. The SAL acquired 123 of the 1500-horsepower GP7s (Nos. 1700-1822) between 1950 and 1953, then ordered eighty 1750-horsepower GP9s between 1955 and 1959. The fleet of SAL EMD road switchers grew with the acquisition of ten 1800-horsepower GP18s (Nos. 400-409) in 1960; thirty-five 2250-horsepower GP30s in 1962-63; ten 2500-horsepower GP35s in 1965; twenty 2500-horsepower dual purpose SDP35s in 1964; and fifty-one 3,000-horsepower GP40s in 1966-67. With the exception of the SDP35s, all EMD road switchers were used throughout the SAL system on local, road switcher, and through freight assignments. Whenever possible, the Seaboard operated its diesel consists with the later GP diesels in the lead because they were equipped with the more modern 24-RL and 26-RL brake control systems.

The GP40s were only in service for a short time prior to the 1967 SAL/ACL merger but they attracted much attention because of their paint scheme. They arrived from EMD with a light green carbody and a broad yellow carbody band trimmed by an orange pinstripe that separated the yellow band and green carbody. Railroaders and railfans alike referred to the new diesels as "The Jolly Green Giants." The paint scheme was also applied to some of the older diesels and to the 15 new GE U30Bs, the only General Electric diesels purchased by SAL.

This southbound freight has an all-Alco consist with C420 No. 118, RS11 No. 101, C420 No. 133, and RS11 No. 103. The train is at Maxville, Florida, on April 2, 1967.

(William J. Husa, Jr.)

Having just cleared the double track crossover, Train No. 75 – the southbound *Merchandiser* – is picking up speed at Manson, N.C., on this clear January 1962 afternoon. Up front are two GP9s, Nos. 1978 and 1911, followed by two FTs and two F3s.

(Curt Tillotson, Jr.)

(above) First acquired in 1950, the EMD GP7s were versatile diesels that could handle both road freight and yard switching assignments with ease. Units 1700-1755 were delivered in 1950. Units 1756-1822 came between 1951-1952. No. 1745, shown here at Birmingham, Alabama, on October 15, 1964, was equipped with a steam generator.

(left) This view shows the long hood end of 1500-horsepower GP7 No. 1752 at Raleigh, N.C.

(Both, Walter Gay Collection)

(below) Brand new GP9 Nos. 1926 and 1927 pose for this SAL publicity photograph. The 1750-horsepower GP9s were delivered to SAL by EMD between 1955-1959.

(SAL Photo)

(above) Rolling by at 60+ mph, SAL Train TT-23, the *Razorback*, glides through Manson, N.C., in January 1963. Led by GP18 No. 406, GP9 No. 1901, and F3 No. 4023, the engineer will have no trouble making time with his 53-car train.

(Curt Tillotson, Jr.)

(below) SAL Train No. 75, the southbound *Merchandiser*, rounds the curve at Gill, N.C., in February 1962. GP9 Nos. 1964 and 1924 and four F-units propel the 144-car train.

(Curt Tillotson, Jr.)

513
513
SEABOARD
513
516
SEABOARD
SEABOARD

514
SEABOARD

(left) Three GP30s, Nos. 513, 516, and 517, head up this freight train at Lilesville, N.C. on June 9, 1963.

(William J. Husa, Jr.)

(facing page bottom) It's early afternoon in December 1965 as four GP30s and one GP18 roll through Norlina, N.C., with a 130-car Train No. 75, *The Merchandiser*.

(Curt Tillotson, Jr.)

(below) Numbered in the series 500-534, the GP30s generated 2250 h.p. and quickly took over the freight assignments on the northend of the railroad. GP30 No. 534 was an ex-EMD demonstrator unit built in March 1962. It was the only SAL GP30 to have an extra cab horn and short cab.

(Warren Calloway)

The SAL began to replace its first generation diesels in the 1960s and the first of the second generation power to arrive were the EMD GP30s. Four of the new units are posed for this SAL publicity shot in 1962.

(SAL Photo)

538
SEABOARD
538

605
632

(facing page, top) The SAL rostered a small group of 2500 h.p. EMD GP35s in the series 535-544. GP35 No. 538 leads a GP30, GP9, and F3A with a 133 car Train No. 27, *The Capital*, at Henderson, N.C., in January 1963.

(Curt Tillotson, Jr.)

(facing page, bottom) The SAL treated its employees and fans to a new paint scheme with the delivery in 1966 of the EMD GP40s. Numbered 600-650, these 3000-horsepower diesels kept the striping and lettering used on the earlier GP35s, but the body was painted a lime green color. The SAL railroaders promptly named them "The Jolly Green Giants." In this view, three new GP40s are passing through the campus of North Carolina State University and Pullen Park with Train No. 75, *The Merchandiser*, in April 1967.

(Curt Tillotson, Jr.)

(right) A front view of GP40 No. 627.

(Warren Calloway)

(below) The SAL GE U30Bs, represented by No. 810 at Jacksonville, Florida, on July 8, 1967, were also painted in the lime green scheme that was applied to the GP40s. The SAL purchased 15 of these 3000-h.p. units and numbered them 800-814.

(Ed Mims Photo/Tom King Collection)

Perhaps the most unique EMD diesels on the SAL roster were the twenty SDP35 dual-purpose road switchers acquired in 1964. With passenger business in decline and the SAL's fleet of E-units nearing retirement, the SDP35 was intended as a diesel that could handle both passenger and high-speed freight trains. They were frequently utilized on Mail, Passenger and Express Trains 3 and 4, the *Palmland* and the *Silver Comet*. Their high gear ratio also made them suitable for use on time-sensitive TOFC trains such as the TT23.

Certainly, the most unusual of all SAL diesels were the 14 freight and three passenger cab units built by Baldwin. At a time when EMD and Alco freight cab units could only generate 1,350 and 1,500 horsepower, one Baldwin DR-12-8-3000 delivered 3,000 horsepower from two supercharged four-cycle, eight-cylinder engines and was geared to attain a maximum speed of 90 mph. These diesels had two four-wheel engine trucks and two articulated drive wheel trucks. With wheels running the length of their carbody, they were commonly referred to as the "Centipedes."

The Seaboard envisioned that these units could be used in fast freight service, especially on its perishable trains. After experimenting with one of the Baldwin Centipedes in 1945, the SAL purchased thirteen additional units between 1947 and 1948. Numbered 4500-4513, they were initially placed in service on through freight runs from Richmond to Atlanta and Jacksonville. They were eventually assigned to service in Florida and were retired in 1957.

SAL's Baldwin passenger cab units were every bit as rare as the freight cab DR-12-8-3000s. In fact, the Seaboard was one of only two railroads to purchase one of Baldwin's entry into the passenger cab unit market. Designated as DR6-4-1500s, Baldwin intended the diesels for use in light-duty passenger service. SAL acquired three of these 1500-horsepower locomotives (Nos. 2700-2702) in 1947-48 and after an initial assignment on trains out of Hamlet, they spent most of their career on light-duty passenger runs in Florida.

In 1964, the SAL acquired twenty SDP35 diesels from EMD in the series 1100-1119. With their higher speed gearing, the units were dual-purpose locomotives, equally suited for high speed passenger or TOFC freight service. Flying extra flags, SDP35 No. 1107 heads up a piggyback train.

(W. E. Griffin, Jr. Collection)

True to its dual-purpose capabilities, SDP35 No. 1115 rolls the northbound Mail and Express Train No. 4 toward Norlina, N.C., in October 1965.

(Curt Tillotson, Jr.)

Passenger, Mail and Express Train No. 6, with SDP35 No. 1107, rolls across the Pumpkin Vine Creek trestle, west of Dallas, Ga. This photo of the Birmingham Sub-Division local was taken on November 4, 1965.

(David W. Salter)

(above) Perhaps the most unusual of the SAL's diesels were the freight cab units acquired from Baldwin between 1945-47. Called the "Centipedes" because of their wheel arrangements which comprised two four-wheel engine trucks and two articulated drive wheel trucks, these 3000-horsepower units were numbered 4500-4513. No. 4500 is at Jacksonville, Florida, in January 1946.

(H. K. Vollrath Collection)

(facing page) Designated the DR12-8-3000, this is a head-on view of No. 4500, the initial member of the class.

(below) The Centipedes were occasionally used in passenger service, as evidenced by this view of the 4500.

(Both, SAL Photos)

4500
SEABOARD
AIR
LINE
RAILROAD
THROUGH THE HEART OF THE SOUTH

(above) The SAL's Centipedes were painted in the more simple freight color scheme and were initially assigned to mainline freights north from both Atlanta and Jacksonville to Richmond. In this photo, we see Centipede No. 4506 rolling a freight train through Mt. Holly, N.C., on June 24, 1947.

(W. E. Griffin, Jr. Collection)

(above) The Baldwin Centipedes were intended for use in freight service such as in this view of No. 4504 with a northbound perishable train at Waldo, Florida, on March 26, 1950.

(William J. Husa, Jr.)

(below) "Babyface" Baldwin DR6-4-1500 No. 2702 is in the "citrus" passenger paint scheme at St. Petersburg, Florida, in 1949.

(C. K. Marsh, Jr. Collection)

(below) The most unusual passenger diesels on the SAL's roster were the three Baldwin DR6-4-1500 class units delivered in 1947. Numbered in series 2700-2702, these 1500-horsepower diesels spent most of their service years on passenger runs in Florida. The 2700 is shown in a builder's photograph.
(T. W. Dixon, Jr. Collection)

(above) SAL owned only one EMD SW1, the 1200. It was purchased in 1939 and served until 1966. The 1200 pauses in its switching chores at Miami, Florida, in May 1962.
(W. E. Griffin, Jr. Collection)

When it came to switchers, the Seaboard experimented with a variety of different models before selecting Baldwin as its preferred builder. The SAL's first switcher was No. 1200, a 600-horsepower SW1 built by GM-EMC in 1939. Originally assigned to Greenwood, South Carolina, it remained on the roster until retired in 1966. The SAL also acquired one S1 (No. 1201) from Alco-GE and one VO-660 (No. 1202) from Baldwin in 1941. Eventually, the Seaboard acquired fifty-three switchers from Baldwin; twenty-four from Alco; and eight from EMD. All SAL switchers were painted with black carbodies, Chinese Red trim, and aluminum lettering and striping.

To service the diesel fleet, shop facilities were located at strategic points on the system and, in 1946, the Seaboard began construction of a new maintenance and repair shop at Jacksonville, Florida. Costing approximately $815,000, it opened in 1947 equipped with the most modern machinery and technology available for the maintenance of diesel locomotives. The facility had over 43,000 square feet of floor space and contained a unique 300-ton transfer table that was used to place diesels on the five tracks within the main shop. A new diesel locomotive research and testing laboratory was also opened at Jacksonville in 1954.

(below) SAL switcher No. 1411 was an EMD NW2 built in 1942.
(SAL Photo/CSX Transportation)

(above) The SAL owned 13 Alco S2 switchers numbered 1403-1405, 1425-1434. This is a builder's view of the 1403.

(T. W. Dixon, Jr. Collection)

(below) Baldwin-built No. 1202 was another one-of-a-kind – the only VO-660 on the SAL roster. It was built in 1941 and is seen here at Durham, N.C., on April 4, 1949.

(T. G. Wicker Collection)

(bottom) No. 1416 was one of eight Baldwin-built VO-1000 diesel switchers owned by the SAL. The unit is at Baldwin, Florida, on April 13, 1963.

(Walter Gay Collection)

(above) Another Baldwin switcher, DS4-4-1000 number 1461, heads south past Main Street Station in Richmond, Virginia, with a cut of freight cars.

(below) No. 1438 was one of the 1417-1461 number series DS4-4-1000 class switchers built for the SAL by Baldwin between 1946-51. The diesel is at Rusboro, Ga. on April 12, 1963.
(Both, Walter Gay Collection)

(bottom) Baldwin RS12 No. 1475 is at Hermitage Yard in Richmond, Virginia, in July 1957. The SAL owned ten of this class of switchers, all built in 1952-53.
(W. E. Griffin, Jr. Collection)

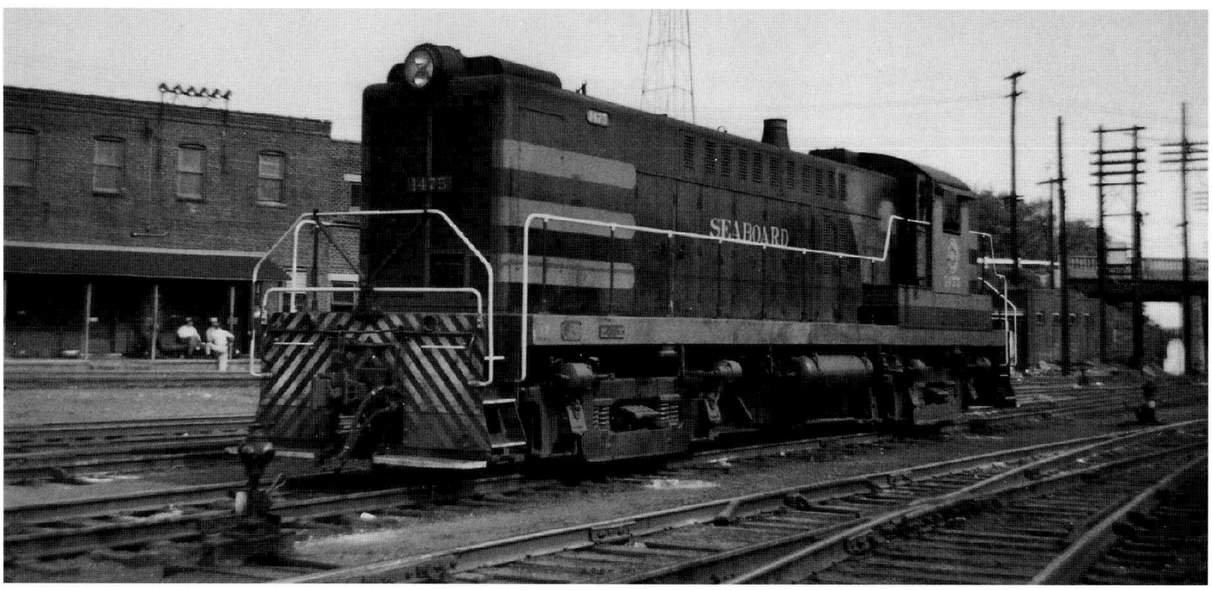

Seaboard Air Line Diesel Locomotives

Road Number	Model	Builder	Date	HP
100-109	RS11	Alco	1960	1800
110-135	C420	Alco	1965	2000
136	C420	Alco	1966	2000
400-409	GP18	EMD	1960	1800
500-509	GP30	EMD	1962	2250
510-533	GP30	EMD	1963	2250
534	GP30	EMD	1962	2250
535-544	GP35	EMD	1965	2500
600-629	GP40	EMD	1966	3000
630-650	GP40	EMD	1967	3000
800-814	U30B	GE	1967	3000
1100-1119	SDP35	EMD	1964	2500
1200	SW1	EMC	1939	600
1201	S1	Alco-GE	1941	660
1202	VO-660	Baldwin	1941	660
1400-1402	VO-1000	Baldwin	1941	1000
1403-1405	S2	Alco-GE	1942	1000
1406-1412	NW2	EMD	1942	1000
1413-1416	VO-1000	Baldwin	1944	1000
1417-1424	DS4-4-1000	BLW	1946	1000
1425-1431	S2	Alco-GE	1946	1000
1432-1434	S2	Alco-GE	1948	1000
1435-1458	DS4-4-1000	BLW	1950	1000
1459-1461	DS4-4-1000	BLH	1951	1000
1462-1465	S12	BLH	1952	1200
1466-1471	RS12	BLH	1952	1200
1472-1475	RS12	BLH	1953	1200
1476-1481	S12	BLH	1953	1200
1482-1491	S4	Alco	1953	1000
1492	VO-1000	Baldwin	1942	1000
1500-1503	RSC2	Alco	1947	1500
1504-1531	RSC2	Alco	1949	1500
1532-1536	RSC2	Alco	1950	1600
1537-1540	RSC3	Alco	1950	1600
1541-1543	RSC3	Alco	1951	1600
1600-1604	RS2	Alco	1949	1500
1605-1628	RS2	Alco	1950	1600
1629-1653	RS3	Alco	1950	1600
1654-1667	RS3	Alco	1951	1600
1670	RS3	Alco	1951	1600
1669-1669	RS3	Alco	1952	1600
1671-1684	RS3	Alco	1952	1600
1685-1687	RS2	Alco	1949	1500
1688	RS3	Alco	1951	1600
1689-1690	RS3	Alco	1950	1600
1691	RS3	Alco	1956	1600
1700-1752	GP7	EMD	1950	1500
1753-1782	GP7	EMD	1951	1500
1783-1822	GP7	EMD	1952	1500
1900-1921	GP9	EMD	1955	1750
1922-1925	GP9	EMD	1957	1750
1926-1929	GP9	EMD	1957	1750
1954-1978	GP9	EMD	1956	1750
1979	GP9	EMD	1959	1750
2700-2702	DR6-4-1500	BLW	1947	1500
3000-3005	E4A	EMC	1938	2000
3006-3013	E4A	EMC	1939	2000
3014	E6A	EMD	1940	2000
3015-3016	E6A	EMD	1941	2000
3017-3030	E7A	EMD	1945	2000
3031-3035	E7A	EMD	1946	2000
3036-3044	E7A	EMD	1948	2000
3045-3048	E7A	EMD	1949	2000
3049-3054	E8A	EMD	1950	2250
3055-3059	E8A	EMD	1952	2250
3060	E9A	EMD	1963	2400
3100-3102	E4B	EMC	1938	2000
3103-3104	E4B	EMC	1939	2000
3105-3107	E7B	EMD	1948	2000
4000-4005	FTA	EMD	1942	1350
4006-4011	FTA	EMD	1943	1350
4012-4021	FTA	EMD	1944	1350
4022-4032	F3A	EMD	1948	1500
4100-4105	FTB	EMD	1942	1350
4106-4111	FTB	EMD	1943	1350
4112-4121	FTB	EMD	1944	1350
4200-4202	FA1	Alco-GE	1948	1500
4300-4302	FB1	Alco-GE	1948	1500
4500	DR12-3-3000	BLW	1945	3000
4501-4512	DR12-8-3000	BLW	1947	3000
4513	DR12-8-3000	BLW	1948	3000

Motor Cars

Road Number	Builder	Date
2000-2001	GE-Wason	1917
2002-2003	EMC/St.L	1925
2012	Brill	1922
2013-2021	Brill	1927
2022-2023	EMC/St.L	1928
2024-2026	ACF	1935
2027	EMC/St.L	1936
2028	EMC/St.L	1936

Builder Abbreviations:

ACF – American Car & Foundry; Alco – American Locomotive Company; BLW – Baldwin Locomotive Works; BLH – Baldwin-Lima-Hamilton; EMC – Electro-Motive Corporation; EMD – Electro-Motive Division of General Motors; GE – General Electric; St.L – St. Louis Car Company

One of the most famous SAL publicity photos of the *Silver Meteor* is this going-away view complete with orange tree and observation car.

(SAL Photo/W. E. Griffin, Jr. Collection)

By the early 1900s, the State of Florida as well as the entire Southeast began to experience an unprecedented growth in population. With the Civil War and Reconstruction behind them, people from various sections of the country discovered that the South's climate not only provided an excellent place for relaxation and rest but also for permanent or part-time residence. The most remarkable growth was taking place on the east coast of Florida.

At that time, the Seaboard and the Atlantic Coast Line railroads connected the Northeast

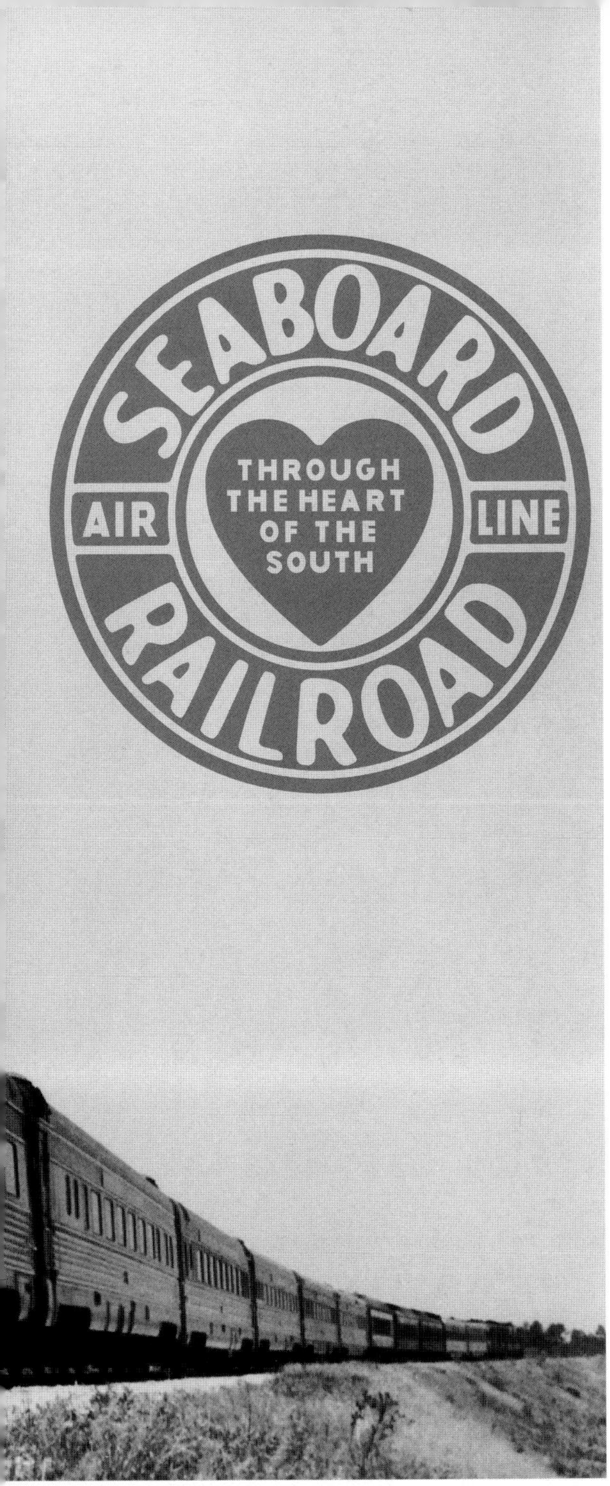

Passenger Service

Chapter 4

with Florida, both roads turning west from Jacksonville and running down the center of the Florida peninsula, angling gradually westward until they reached Tampa. The Florida East Coast Railway had a line running south from Jacksonville, hugging the east coast to the tip of the peninsula. By the time the FEC was completed to Key West in 1912, beautiful winter resorts had been strung down the coast almost to the southern tip of Florida.

Until 1925, the FEC handled the through equipment of both the SAL and ACL passenger trains from Jacksonville down the east coast of Florida. In January of that year, the SAL completed and opened a 204-mile extension of its main line from Coleman to West Palm Beach, with the line reaching Miami in 1927. This new SAL line not only linked both coasts by rail but also opened up for the first time the east coast of Florida to a railroad that ran over its own rails to Richmond and connected there with eastern trunk lines.

Prior to the completion of the Coleman-West Palm Beach line, the Seaboard's all-Florida trains included *The Florida-Cuba Special* (Nos. 1 and 2, later renamed the *Carolina-*

Florida Special) and the all-Pullman winter tourist train, the *Seaboard Florida Limited* (Nos. 191-192), operating between New York and both coasts of Florida. Through car service on these trains was handled between Jacksonville and Miami by the FEC. Both trains operated over SAL tracks from Jacksonville to Tampa, St. Petersburg, Sarasota, and Venice on the west coast. Two other trains, the *Floridian* (Nos. 7 and 8) and the *All Florida Special* (Nos. 103 and 104) also offered service from New York to both coasts, again with the Miami section handled by the FEC. The *Seaboard Fast Mail* (Nos. 3 and 4) operated between New York and Tampa.

The SAL's through service was handled in conjunction with the Richmond, Fredericksburg & Potomac Railroad, which handled the trains between Richmond and Washington, and the Pennsylvania Railroad, which handled them between Washington and New York. Through line expenses and rolling stock for the service were allocated among the three participating railroads based on a proration of the mileage operated by the trains on their respective lines.

When the Coleman-West Palm Beach line was completed in 1925, the Seaboard established new twice-a-day service between St. Petersburg and West Palm Beach operating through Tampa, Plant City, and West Lake Wales independent of its north-south trains then operating between West Lake Wales and West Palm Beach. The railroad also launched an extensive advertising campaign designed to attract traffic to the new service.

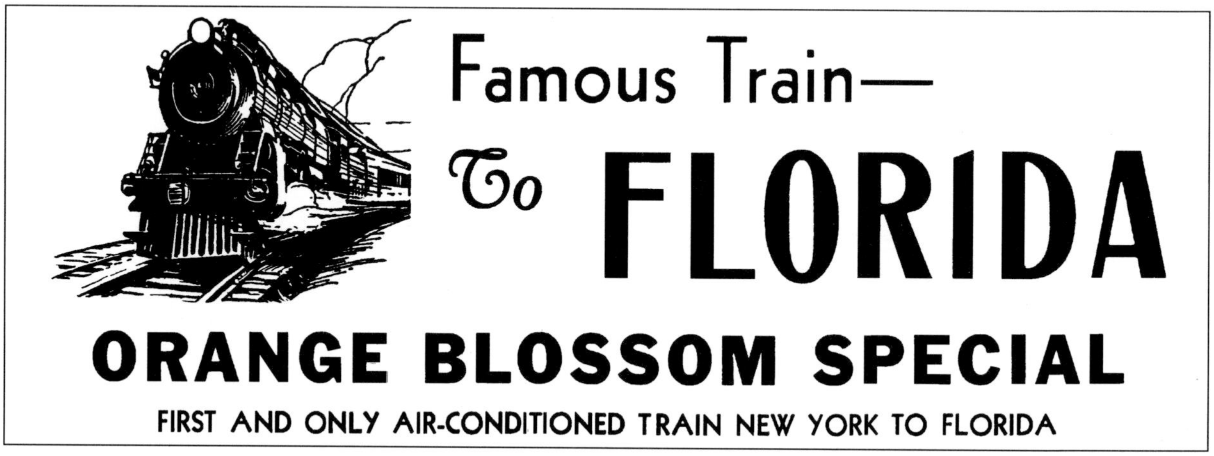

Famous Train—
To FLORIDA
ORANGE BLOSSOM SPECIAL
FIRST AND ONLY AIR-CONDITIONED TRAIN NEW YORK TO FLORIDA

Crowds line the tracks as a smartly decorated *Orange Blossom Special* enters Miami, Fla., for the first time on January 8, 1927. (SAL Photo)

(above) The *Orange Blossom Special* at Hermitage Yard, Richmond, Va., in 1934 with M-2 Class 4-8-2 No. 249.
(Anthony Dementi Photo/W. E. Griffin, Jr. Collection)

The Seaboard's famous *Orange Blossom Special* (Nos. 7 and 8) was placed in service effective with the first trip from New York November 21, 1925, operating via the Gross-Baldwin Cut-off to and from West Palm Beach over the SAL's new line. Every aspect of this all-Pullman winter tourist train accentuated luxury for its passengers. There were showers and valet service, a club car with a barber shop for the men and manicure service for the ladies, and diners that featured the finest cuisine. Connecting with the *Orange Blossom Special* at Baldwin were Trains Nos. 15 and 16 that operated between Jacksonville and St. Petersburg with connections to Sarasota and Venice.

With the completion of the new cross-state line, the SAL no longer required the services of the FEC to handle its trains on the east coast. The last through car service in connection with the FEC was operated on the *Carolina-Florida Special* from New York on December 29, and from Miami on December 31, 1925.

In addition to the *Orange Blossom Special*, the *Seaboard-Florida Limited* operated in two sections to and from the east and west coasts of Florida during the winter season of 1926. In May of that year, a new train, the *Southerner* (Nos. 107 and 108), was established between New York and Sebring, with connections between Jacksonville, Tampa, and St. Petersburg. *The Southerner* operated on a schedule comparable with that of the *Orange Blossom Special* during the winter months.

FIRST TRIP SOUTHBOUND JANUARY 2, 1934
FIRST TRIP NORTHBOUND JANUARY 4, 1934 — **DAILY SCHEDULES**

12.30PM	Lv	**New York** (Penna. Sta.)	PRR	Ar	5 55PM
12.43PM	Lv	**Manhattan Transfer**	"	Ar	5.41PM
12.47PM	Lv	**Newark** (Market St.)	"	Ar	5.37PM
2.06PM	Lv	**North Philadelphia**	"	Ar	4.18PM
2 16PM	Lv	**Philadelphia** (Penna. Sta., 30th St.)	"	Ar	4 08PM
4.05PM	Lv	**Baltimore**	"	Ar	2.10PM
5.20PM	Lv	**Washington**	RF&P	Ar	1 00PM
8.03PM	Lv	**Richmond** (Main St. Sta.)	SAL	Ar	10.12AM
8.38PM	Lv	**Petersburg**	"	Ar	9.37AM
7 30AM	Ar	**West Savannah**	"	Lv	10.26PM
8.58AM	Ar	**Thalmann** (Brunswick-Sea Island)	"	Lv	8.55PM
10.35AM	Ar	**Baldwin**	"	Lv	7.15PM
12.22PM	Lv	**Ocala** (Silver Springs)	"	Lv	5 20PM
12.56PM	Ar	**Wildwood**	"	Lv	4.45PM
2.10PM	Ar	**Auburndale**	"	Lv	3.20PM
2.18PM	Ar	**Winter Haven**	"	Lv	3.10PM
2.29PM	Ar	**West Lake Wales** (Lake Wales-Mtn. Lake)	"	Lv	3 00PM
2.59PM	Ar	**Avon Park**	"	Lv	2.24PM
3.14PM	Ar	**Sebring**	"	Lv	2.12PM
5.18PM	Ar	**West Palm Beach-Palm Beach**	"	Lv	12.15PM
6.15PM	Ar	**Fort Lauderdale**	"	Lv	11.12AM
6.24PM	Ar	**Hollywood**	"	Lv	11.02AM
6.55PM	Ar	**Miami**	"	Lv	10.30AM
2.12PM	Ar	**Dade City**	SAL	Lv	3.23PM
3.00PM	Ar	**Plant City**	"	Lv	2.39PM
3.35PM	Ar	**Tampa**	"	Lv	2.05PM
4.46PM	Ar	**Clearwater**	"	Lv	12.49PM
4.51PM	Ar	**Belleair** (Belleview-Biltmore Hotel)	"	Lv	12.44PM
5.35PM	Ar	**St. Petersburg**	"	Lv	12.05PM
5.50PM	Ar	**Sarasota**	SAL	Lv	11.00AM
6.35PM	Ar	**Venice**	"	Lv	10.10AM

EQUIPMENT (ALL AIR-CONDITIONED)

Club-Library Car (Baggage)..New York-Washington-Tampa-St. Petersburg. (Refreshments-Valet-Bath)
Dining Car....New York-Washington-West Palm Beach-Miami-Tampa-St. Petersburg.
Sleeping Cars:
6 Compt., 3 DR..New York-Washington-Tampa-St. Petersburg.
6 Compt., 3 DR..New York-Washington-West Palm Beach-Palm Beach-Miami.
12 Sec., 1 DR....Washington-West Palm Beach-Palm Beach-Miami.
10 Sec., 2 DR....New York-Washington-Tampa-St. Petersburg.
12 Sec., 1 DR....Washington-Tampa-St. Petersburg.
12 Sec., 1 DR....New York-Washington-Tampa-Sarasota-Venice (southbound Tues., Thurs., Sats.; northbound Thurs., Sats., Mons.).
Lounge Car.........New York-Washington-West Palm Beach-Miami. (10 Sec.)

The line between West Palm Beach and Miami was opened on January 8, 1927, and the first *Orange Blossom Special* operated into Miami, leaving New York on January 7th, arriving Miami on January 8th, and leaving Miami on its initial northward trip on January 9th. During the winter season of 1927, two sections of the *Orange Blossom Special* were operated – one between New York and Miami and another between New York and St. Petersburg – with connection to and from Venice and Fort Myers. Both trains operated via the Gross-Baldwin Cut-off,

ORANGE
BLOSSOM
SPECIAL
COMPLETELY
AIR
CONDITIONED

(facing page) The rear end of the *Orange Blossom Special* with the train's name and advertisement for air conditioned service.
(SAL Photo/CSX Transportation)

(above) The crew of the *Orange Blossom Special* dining cars poses behind the rear end of the train prior to a trip from Miami in an early 1930s-era photo.
(SAL Photo)

(right) In this SAL publicity photo, ladies in Spanish costumes and a city official were on hand to greet the engineer and conductor upon the first arrival of the *Orange Blossom Special* at Tampa, Fla. on December 10, 1937.
(SAL Photo/CSX Transportation)

bypassing Jacksonville. However, shuttle train service was operated between Jacksonville and Gross and Jacksonville and Baldwin, handling passengers for connection with these trains.

The Fort Myers-Naples line on the west coast was opened January 9, 1927, and effective that date, through sleeping car service was established between New York and Naples on the *Seaboard-Florida Limited*, and between New York and Fort Myers on the *West Coast Orange Blossom Special.* At that time, the *Seaboard-Florida Limited* operated in one section between New York and Gross, dividing and converging at that point for and from the east and west coasts of Florida. The east coast section operated through the Gross-Baldwin Cut-off and the west coast section through Jacksonville. The *All-Florida Special* and the *Seaboard Fast Mail* operated as separate trains between Washington and Hamlet, but were consolidated at Hamlet and operated as one train between Hamlet and Florida.

The Florida real estate boom collapsed during the Spring of 1927 and, even with its new routes and services, the SAL's passenger revenues decreased by 20 per cent. The Seaboard's revenues were also affected by the public defection from local rail lines to buses and the increased use of private automobiles. In response, the SAL purchased eleven gas-electric motor cars and twelve trailers in 1927-28 to supplant steam locomotives and reduce operating costs on certain local passenger trains.

During 1928, the *Carolina-Florida Special* was discontinued and operation of the *Seaboard Fast Mail* was discontinued south

(upper left) The *Orange Blossom Special* at Main Street Station in Richmond, Va. On this trip, the observation car had a tail sign in the shape of the Pennsylvania Railroad keystone.
(John W. Barriger, III Photo/St. Louis Mercantile Library)

(above left) In a classic photograph sure to warm the hearts of rail and baseball fans alike, the Boy Scouts of America present an award to Babe Ruth, "King of Baseball," as Ruth, his wife, and daughter board the *Orange Blossom Special* at Philadelphia.
(SAL Photo/CSX Transportation)

(left) Fashion rode the rails on the *Orange Blossom Special.* During an *Orange Blossom Special* Mid-Winter Fashion Show held aboard the train in the 1930s, models from Miami displayed the latest beach creations in the lounge of the train before an audience of interested passengers. In this photo, the girls are modeling acetate, cellophane, and all-silk bathing suits.
(SAL Photo/W. E. Griffin, Jr. Collection)

of Jacksonville. The *Southerner* continued to operate between New York and St. Petersburg. While this train had no connection to and from the east coast of Florida, it did carry a connection for the Fort Myers-Naples line. A new local day train was established between Wildwood and Miami.

During the winter season of 1929, the *Orange Blossom Special* operated in one section through the Gross-Baldwin Cut-off, dividing and converging at Wildwood and serving both coasts of Florida. The *Seaboard-Florida Limited* was operated in one section between New York and Miami, via Jacksonville, with the west coast cars handled south of Jacksonville on the *Carolina-Florida Special*. On April 21th, the *Southern States Special* (Nos. 107 and 108) was established, replacing the *Southerner*.

A new train, the *Carolina Golfer* (Nos. 197 and 198), was added to the service between New York and Pinehurst, N.C., in 1930, relieving the *New York-Florida Limited* of the Pinehurst equipment that it had carried during the winter seasons of previous years. During the summer of 1930, trains Nos. 807 and 808 were added to operate between Wildwood and Miami, connecting at Wildwood with the *Southern States Special*.

The stock market crash of October 1929 had a devastating effect on business generally, including the SAL's passenger traffic. Passenger revenues declined by 20 per cent in 1930 and, on December 23rd of that year, the Seaboard went into receivership.

During 1931, the Seaboard's passenger revenues declined by 25 per cent and the *Seaboard-Florida Limited* was not re-established. Operation of the *Orange Blossom Special* was reduced to a two-night-out schedule between New York and southern Florida, the train continuing to be divided at Wildwood for service to both coasts. No change was made in the operation of the *Southern States Special* or the *New York-Florida Limited* and the *Florida Sunbeam* (Nos. 5 and 6) replaced the *Seaboard Fast Mail* during the winter season with operations extended through to Miami and St. Petersburg. The *Suwanee River Special*, a winter seasonal train that was first established on November 21st with through cars between Cleveland, Detroit/Toledo, and Tampa/St. Petersburg was not re-established during the winter season. Effective June 7th, the Fort Myers-Naples service was reduced to mixed train service between Arcadia and Fort Myers-Naples, connecting with Train Nos. 409 and 410 operating between Plant City and South Boca Grande. This service was operated only three days a week.

By 1932 the country was in the depth of the Depression and SAL's passenger revenues declined 35 per cent from the previous year, amounting to more than a 50 per cent reduction from pre-Depression receipts. However, revenues did not reach their lowest point during the Depression until 1933. In order to attract passengers back to the railroads, the Southeastern roads reduced the basic rail fares and the Pullman surcharge was eliminated. This action did little to increase revenues but did arrest the decline in ridership, resulting in an increase during 1932 of approximately 30 per cent in the number of passengers on Seaboard trains.

Another factor contributing to the increase in ridership was the SAL program, commenced late in 1933, of air conditioning its passenger equipment. SAL was the first railroad in the southern territory to apply this apparatus to its equipment. The Seaboard equipped certain of its dining cars with air-conditioning and obtained air-conditioned sleeping cars from the Pullman Company for operation on the *Orange Blossom Special*. The *Orange Blossom Special* was entirely air conditioned beginning with the start of the train's winter season in January 1934. By the close of 1934, air-conditioned coaches, sleeping, dining, and lounge cars were also placed on the *Southern States Special* (Nos. 107 and 108) and the *New York-Florida Limited* (Nos. 191 and 192).

The result of the reduced fares and the Seaboard's progressive step in air-conditioning its equipment was dramatic. In 1934 the SAL's passenger revenue increased 44 per cent over the previous year and the number of passengers handled increased by 64 per cent.

In addition to its Florida trains, the Seaboard also operated a number of important passenger trains between the Northeast and

Train No. 17, the southbound *Cotton States Special*, with M-2 4-8-2 No. 241 nears Howells Yard, just east of Northside Drive, at Atlanta, Georgia, on March 16, 1947. It is 8:30 in the morning as the train steams by at approximately 60 mph.

(David W. Salter)

COTTON STATES SPECIAL

Diesel Powered Between Richmond and Atlanta

a11:00 PM	Lv. Boston (South Sta.) (ET)...	NYNH&H	Ar.	11:50 PM
c10:10 AM	Lv. New York (Penna. Sta.)....	PRR	Ar.	c 6:15 PM
c12:01 PM	Lv. Philadelphia (30th St. Sta.)	"	Ar.	c 4:25 PM
c 1:37 PM	Lv. Baltimore	"	Ar.	c 2:45 PM
2:50 PM	Lv. Washington	RF&P	Ar.	1:35 PM
5:45 PM	Lv. Richmond (Main St. Sta.)..	SAL	Ar.	10:20 AM
3:30 PM	Lv. Norfolk	FERRY	Ar.	12:05 PM
4:00 PM	Lv. Portsmouth	SAL	Ar.	11:50 AM
8:50 PM	Ar. Raleigh	"	Lv.	6:55 AM
r10:26 PM	Ar. Southern Pines (Pinehurst)	"	Lv.	r 5:16 AM
6:00 AM	Ar. Athens	"	Lv.	10:18 PM
8:00 AM	Ar. Atlanta	"	Lv.	8:30 PM
8:25 AM	Lv. Atlanta	"	Ar.	8:10 PM
12:00 N	Ar. Birmingham (CT)	"	Lv.	3:00 PM
12:25 PM	Lv. Birmingham (CT)	FRISCO	Ar.	2:45 PM
7:05 PM	Ar. Memphis	"	Lv.	8:00 AM
8:55 AM	Lv. Atlanta (ET)	A&WP	Ar.	1:15 PM
12:05 PM	Ar. Montgomery (CT)	"	Lv.	7:40 AM
4:40 PM	Ar. Mobile	L&N	Lv.	2:37 AM
8:25 PM	Ar. New Orleans	"	Lv.	11:00 PM
pp 1:35 PM	Lv. Birmingham (CT)	SOU	Ar.	7:05 AM
9:10 PM	Ar. New Orleans	"	Lv.	9:00 PM

Coaches (Baggage).................			Birmingham-Atlanta to Washington. (Reclining, de luxe seats.) (Air-Conditioned.)
			Washington to New York. (Air-Conditioned.)
			Norlina to Portsmouth-Norfolk. (Reclining, de luxe seats.) (Air-Conditioned.) (Colored coach not Air-Conditioned.)
Dining Car.........................			Birmingham to Greenwood. (Air-Conditioned.)
			Hamlet to Washington. (Air-Conditioned.)
			Norlina to Portsmouth-Norfolk.
			Washington to New York. (Air-Conditioned.)
Sleeping Cars:	Designation	Line No.	
12 Sec., 1 DR........	B-147	6710	Birmingham-Atlanta-Athens to Raleigh-Richmond-Washington to New York. (Air-Conditioned.)
12 Sec., 1 DR........	B- 27	6711	Atlanta-Athens to Raleigh-Richmond-Washington. (Air-Conditioned.)
Observ. Library Car..	......	....	Birmingham-Athens to Greenwood—12 Seats. (Air-Cond.)
Parlor Car...........	"A"	....	Norlina to Portsmouth-Norfolk—12 Seats.
Lounge Car..........	B-111	2747	Hamlet-Raleigh to Richmond-Washington. (10 Sec.) (Air-Conditioned.)

Atlanta/Birmingham via Hamlet. For many years, the most notable train on this route had been Nos. 5 and 6, the *Atlanta-Birmingham Special*. On October 28, 1934, the *Cotton States Special* (Nos. 9 and 10) was established as an independent train between Washington and Birmingham, relieving the *Southern States Special* of its Atlanta-Birmingham equipment.

During the spring of 1935, the Seaboard established a new train, the *Robert E. Lee* (Nos. 5 and 6), between New York and Birmingham, replacing the *Atlanta-Birmingham Special*. This train was completely air-conditioned and its fast schedule reduced the elapsed running time between New York and Birmingham by six hours southward and three hours and thirty-six minutes northward. The establishment of the

E4A No. 3005 with the *Cotton States Special* at Atlanta in 1940.
(Hugh M. Comer Photo/F. E. Ardrey, Jr. Collection)

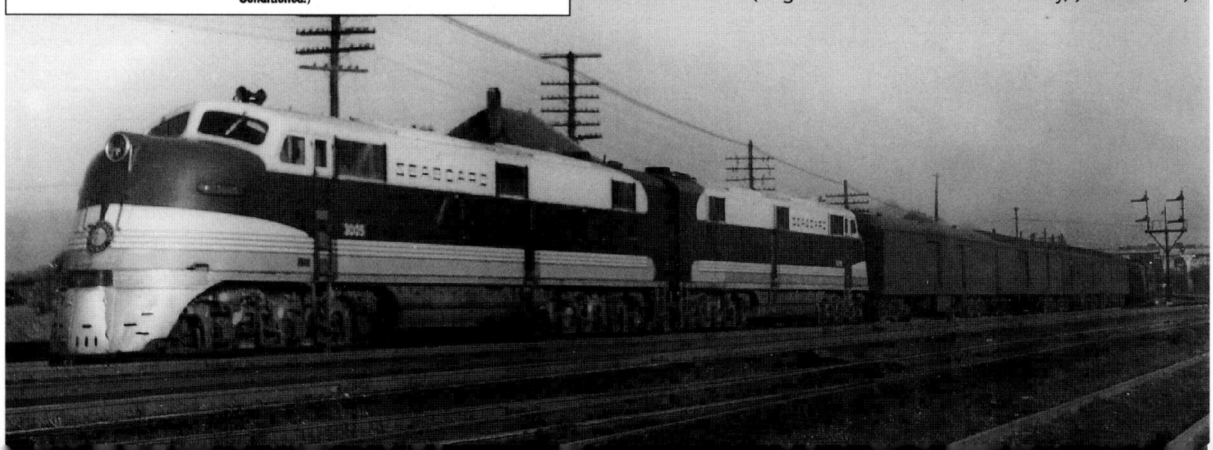

Robert E. Lee permitted the rescheduling of the departure time of the *New York-Florida Limited* and its overall running time was improved by two hours and fifty minutes. When it was found that the traffic did not justify operating an additional train north of Hamlet, the Atlanta-Birmingham business handled by the new *Cotton States Special* was operated north of that point on the *Southern States Special* but continued to operate south of Hamlet as the *Cotton States Special*.

In December 1935 and January 1936, the SAL took delivery of three new AC&F-built air-conditioned rail buses for local service between Richmond and Raleigh, Jacksonville and Tampa, and Jacksonville, Tallahassee and River Junction, Florida. The SAL also received two new EMC-built diesel-electric rail motor cars early in 1935 for service between Wilmington and Rutherfordton, N.C. These EMC rail motor cars were capable of pulling four or five standard coaches.

Passenger service during this period was substantially unchanged with the exception that service to Florida during the winter tourist season was augmented by the inauguration of the *Florida Sunbeam* (Nos. 5 and 6). This train operated between Chicago, Detroit, Cleveland, Cincinnati, and Miami and St. Petersburg, in conjunction with the New York Central and Southern Railways. It operated from January 2, 1936, until April 18, 1936, during its inaugural season, and was continued in seasonal service thereafter.

M Class 4-8-2 No. 200 with Train No. 6, the northbound *Robert E. Lee*, near Mina, Georgia, (just west of Atlanta's Emory University) on the afternoon of February 1, 1947.
(David W. Salter)

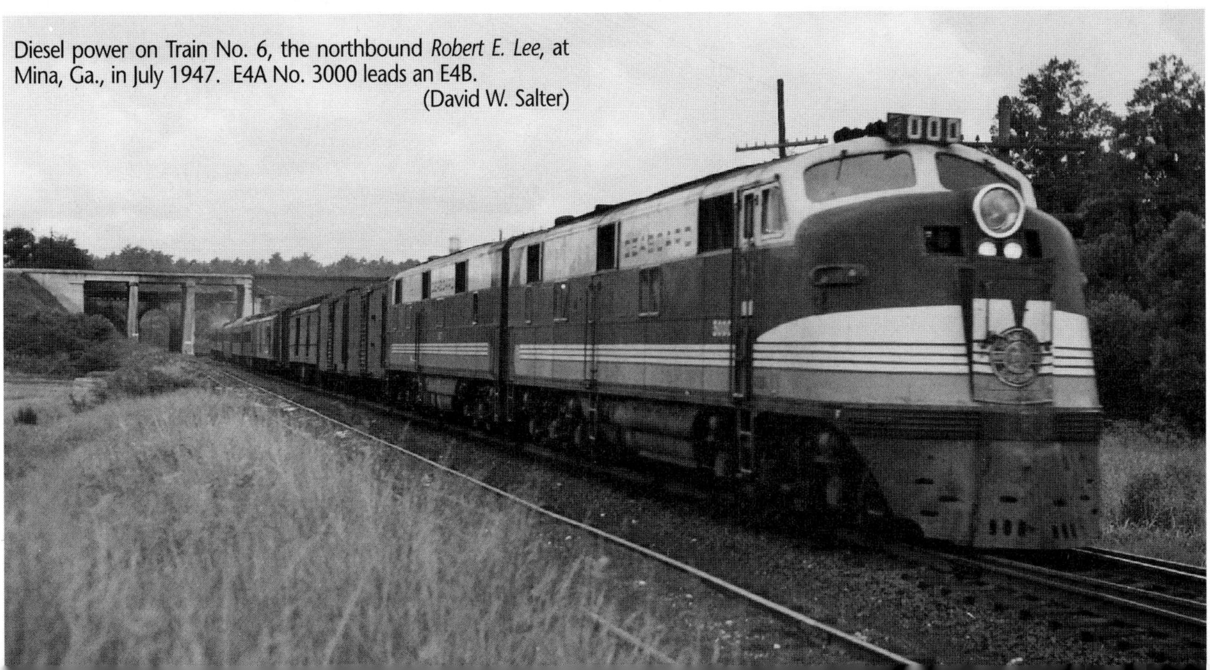

Diesel power on Train No. 6, the northbound *Robert E. Lee*, at Mina, Ga., in July 1947. E4A No. 3000 leads an E4B.
(David W. Salter)

(above) Interior of a deluxe chair coach on *The Robert E. Lee.*
(SAL Photo/W. E. Griffin, Jr. Collection)

(below) M class 4-8-2 No. 213 crosses the L&N Railroad leaving Birmingham, Ala. The First Avenue viaduct is in the background in this 1940 photograph.
(J. E. Jones Photo/F. E. Ardrey, Jr. Collection)

THE ROBERT E. LEE

11 00 AM	Lv	**Boston** (South Sta.) (ET)	NYNH&H	Ar	6 55 PM
4 30 PM	Lv	**New York** (Penna. Sta.)	PRR	Ar	1 50 PM
5 57 PM	Lv	**Philadelphia** (30th St. Sta.)	"	Ar	12 12 PM
7 24 PM	Lv	**Baltimore**	"	Ar	10 41 AM
9 00 PM	Lv	**Washington**	RF&P	Ar	9 45 AM
12 10 AM	Lv	**Richmond** (Main St. Sta.)	SEABOARD	Ar	6 35 AM
4 35 AM	Ar	**Raleigh**	"	Lv	y 2 20 AM
6 40 AM	Ar	**Southern Pines** (Pinehurst)	"	Lv	12 14 AM
2 53 PM	Ar	**Athens**	"	Lv	4 00 PM
4 55 PM	Ar	**Atlanta** (ET)	"	Lv	2 00 PM
8 55 PM	Ar	**Birmingham** (CT)	"	Lv	7 50 AM
10 15 PM	Lv	**Birmingham**	FRISCO	Ar	7 15 AM
6 45 AM	Ar	**Memphis**	"	Lv	J10 30 PM
8 00 PM	Lv	**Atlanta** (ET)	A&WP	Ar	1 10 PM
11 35 PM	Ar	**Montgomery** (CT)	"	Lv	7 20 AM
5 15 AM	Ar	**Mobile**	L&N	Lv	1 55 AM
9 30 AM	Ar	**New Orleans**	"	Lv	9 30 PM
10 00 PM	Lv	**Birmingham** (CT)	SOU.	Ar	7 00 AM
11 38 PM	Ar	**Tuscaloosa**	"	Lv	5 10 AM
2 30 AM	Ar	**Meridian**	"	Lv	2 25 AM
8 55 AM	Ar	**New Orleans**	"	Lv	7 45 PM

Coaches (Baggage).................Birmingham-Atlanta to Washington. (Reclining, de luxe seats.) **(Air-Conditioned.)**
Washington to New York. **(Air-Conditioned.)**
Norlina to Portsmouth-Norfolk. **(Air-Conditioned.)**

Dining Car.........................Birmingham to Hamlet.
Washington to New York. **(Air-Conditioned.)**

Sleeping Cars:	**Designation**	**Line No.**	
12 Sec., 1 DR........	F- 36	2702	Memphis-Birmingham-Atlanta-Athens-Raleigh to Richmond-Washington-New York. **(Air-Conditioned.)**
12 Sec., 1 DR........	B- 94	2760	Raleigh to Richmond-Washington. **(Air-Conditioned.)**
12 Sec., 1 DR........	"S"	2705	Hamlet to Portsmouth-Norfolk. (Handled on trains 2-16.) **(Air-Conditioned.)**
Lounge Car..........	R-109	....	Washington to Raleigh-Hamlet. (10 Sec.) **(Air-Conditioned.)** Birmingham-Atlanta-Athens to Hamlet.

During 1937-38, the SAL operated its all-Pullman steam-powered *East Coast Orange Blossom Special* between New York and Miami on a schedule of 29 hours and northbound on a schedule of 29 hours and 55 minutes. The competing schedule of the ACL-FEC's *Florida Special* was 27 hours 40 minutes southward and 27 hours 45 minutes northward. The ACL also operated a faster service in the handling of its west coast *Florida Special* than the SAL's *West Coast Orange Blossom Special*. To meet this competitive situation, the SAL conducted studies during 1938 which resulted in its purchase of nine 2000-horsepower diesel-electric locomotives.

These nine E4 diesels were purchased from the Electro-Motive Corporation and were delivered in the new "citrus" paint scheme of yellow, dark green, and orange with silver pilots and running gear. To introduce the new diesels, the SAL operated a Diesel Exhibition Tour Train throughout its system. It was met by adoring crowds at every stop.

At the completion of the exhibition tour, the new diesels were assigned to the winter tourist season between Washington, D.C., and Miami on the *East Coast Orange Blossom Special*, departing with their inaugural trip on December 15, 1938. As a result of arrangements with the RF&P, the Seaboard diesel power was operated with its train over the RF&P between Richmond and Washington. The all-Pullman train consisted of 13 cars (including a Boston-Miami sleeper) all equipped with tight-lock couplers, rubber draft gear, and anti-noise devices. This train operated between New York and Miami on a schedule of 26 hours 15 minutes southward and 26 hours 25 minutes northward. The train was so successful that revenues increased 75 per cent over the preceding winter season. During that part of the year in which the *Orange Blossom Special* was not operated, the diesels were used to power the *Southern States Special* between Richmond and Miami and Trains Nos. 9 and 6 between Hamlet and Atlanta.

Local school bands played at many towns visited by the Diesel Exhibition Tour Train. This was the scene during the stop at Plant City, Florida, in November 1938.
(SAL Photo/CSX Transportation)

(above) The Diesel Exhibition Tour Train – with an *Orange Blossom Special* sign on the rear car – stops at Sarasota, Florida, in November 1938.

(SAL Photo/CSX Transportation)

(below) The Diesel Exhibition Tour Train comprised E4 A-B-A set Nos. 3000,3100, and 3001; two lightweight coaches; dining car No. 1009 *Silver Springs*; and three Pullmans. The train was a great public relations success, as seen at Dade City, Florida, in November 1938.

(SAL Photo/CSX Transportation)

On February 2, 1939, the SAL introduced its new diesel-powered, streamlined, all-coach train, the *Silver Meteor* (Nos. 57 and 58). The train consisted of one EMC E4 "A" diesel and seven air-conditioned Budd-built lightweight stainless steel passenger coaches. The new train operated alternately every third day between New York and Miami and New York and St. Petersburg until June 5th. The train was so successful that the SAL purchased two additional trains of like equipment. Effective June 6th the operation was changed, with the train dividing at Wildwood on each trip and serving both Miami and St. Petersburg. The operation continued in this manner until December 1, 1939. By the summer of 1940, the popular *Silver Meteor* was being operated on a daily basis and the Wildwood to St. Petersburg leg of the run was powered by streamlined 4-6-2 steam locomotives. The *Silver Meteor* rounded out one million miles of service on November 10, 1940, and it was expanded to a 14-car daily train powered by two diesel units in December of that year.

(below) An admiring crowd welcomes the first *Silver Meteor* to Miami on February 3, 1939.
(SAL Photo/W. E. Griffin, Jr. Collection)

The combination of the SAL's new diesels, air-conditioned cars, and streamlined equipment had an immediate positive effect on the revenues from passenger service. Receipts for 1939 increased 27 per cent over those for 1938, and revenues for 1940 and 1941 increased by 19 per cent and 46 per cent respectively. However, the SAL's greatest challenge was yet to come.

On December 7, 1941, the Japanese attacked Pearl Harbor. This was promptly followed by a declaration of war by the United States against Japan and the other Axis nations. As the country mobilized for war, the Seaboard – as well as the other American railroads – began participation in the greatest movement of manpower in the nation's history. Most of the important military camps of World War I were rebuilt and many new centers for specialized military training were established. The SAL played a major role in the transportation of military personnel to and from the many Southern training locations. Camp Blanding, near Starke, Florida, was originally activated in December 1940 and became one of the principal military posts along the Seaboard. Twenty new military posts served by the Seaboard were opened in 1942, including Camp Butner near Wilkin, N.C.; Cecil

FASTEST SCHEDULES

Ever Operated between Eastern Cities and Florida

25 Hours New York - Miami

23 Hours FIFTY MINUTES New York - St. Petersburg

Field (Naval Air Base) near Otis, Fla.; Drew Field (Army Airpost) near Tampa; Army Basic Flying School at Lynn, Ga.; Army Air Fields at St. Petersburg and Venice, Fla.; and the Army Air school at Miami Beach.

During 1942, the Army and Navy took over many of the principal hotels in Miami Beach, a substantial number in Miami proper, and most of the principal hotels in the Clearwater-St. Petersburg area. At year's end it was estimated that the military forces in the Miami area alone numbered approximately 70,000. SAL's passenger revenues for 1942 increased 146 per cent.

During the war, the *Orange Blossom Special* and the *Florida Sunbeam* were not operated, but an extra section of the *Silver Meteor* was established effective December 6, 1942, carrying coaches and sleeping cars with service to both coasts of Florida during the winter season. Because of heavy mail and express traffic, Trains Nos. 3 and 4 were operated in two sections and Trains Nos. 45 and 46 were established between Washington and Hamlet to take care of the strictly local service. All trains during the war were heavily patronized. Test checks by the railroad indicated that about 60 per cent of the passengers were traveling on government orders. However, civilian traffic was also heavy due to restrictions upon the use of gasoline and tires. Schedules were substantially lengthened to allow for additional time at stations to handle the large increase in passenger, mail, and express traffic. Each year new records were set for passenger traffic handled by the railroad.

With the end of the Second World War, twenty-two military camps and posts along the Seaboard's lines were closed and the activities of eight remaining camps were substantially curtailed. Military travel was significantly reduced and, coupled with the removal of wartime restrictions on the use of private automobiles, the SAL experienced a sizable decrease in passenger earnings.

To attract the traveling public back to its trains, the SAL developed a strategic plan that incorporated aggressive marketing, more attractive schedules, modern equipment, and a high standard of service. The SAL also restored its winter tourist trains. The *Orange Blossom Special* resumed operations during the winter season between New York and both coasts of Florida effective December 12, 1946. The *Florida Sunbeam* was re-established during the winter season with service between Chicago-Detroit-Cleveland and Florida effective December 6, 1946.

SILVER METEOR

New York, Jacksonville, Miami, Tampa, Sarasota, Venice and St. Petersburg

All accommodations must be reserved in advance

Diesel-Powered *Seaboard Dining Service*

57-157		DAILY TRAINS			158-58
10 00AM	Lv	Boston (So. Station) (EST)	NYNH&H	Ar	5 45PM
2 50PM	Lv	New York (Penna. Station)	PRR	Ar	10 25AM
3 05PM	Lv	Newark	"	Ar	10 10AM
4 24PM	Lv	North Philadelphia	"	Ar	8 55AM
4 34PM	Lv	Philadelphia (30th Street Station)	"	Ar	8 45AM
5 03PM	Lv	Wilmington	"	Ar	8 15AM
6 05PM	Lv	Baltimore	"	Ar	7 13AM
7 05PM	Lv	Washington	RF&P	Ar	6 10AM
a 9 38PM	Lv	Richmond (Main Street Station)	SAL	Ar	a 3 27AM
a10 05PM	Lv	Petersburg	"	Ar	a 2 58AM
12 20AM	Ar	Raleigh	"	Lv	12 40AM
2 10AM	Ar	Hamlet	"	Lv	10 52PM
4 15AM	Ar	Columbia	"	Lv	8 45PM
6 43AM	Ar	Savannah	"	Lv	6 23PM
a 7 50AM	Ar	Thalmann (Brunswick-Sea Island)	"	Lv	a 5 10PM
9 10AM	Ar	Jacksonville	"	Lv	4 00PM
9 25AM	Lv	Jacksonville	"	Ar	3 45PM
a10 19AM	Ar	Waldo (Gainesville)	"	Lv	a 2 44PM
a10 59AM	Ar	Ocala (Silver Springs)	"	Lv	a 2 04PM
11 30AM	Ar	Wildwood (Homosassa Springs)	"	Lv	1 40PM
a12 36PM	Ar	Winter Haven (Cypress Gardens)	"	Lv	a12 25PM
a12 46PM	Ar	W. Lake Wales-Lake Wales (Bok Tower)	"	Lv	a12 18PM
a 1 06PM	Ar	Avon Park	"	Lv	a11 54AM
a 1 17PM	Ar	Sebring (Highlands Hammock State Park)	"	Lv	a11 44AM
2 50PM	Ar	West Palm Beach-Palm Beach	"	Lv	10 18AM
a 2 57PM	Ar	Lake Worth	"	Lv	a10 09AM
a 3 07PM	Ar	Delray Beach	"	Lv	a 9 58AM
a 3 17PM	Ar	Deerfield Beach (Boca Raton Club)	"	Lv	a 9 48AM
3 35PM	Ar	Fort Lauderdale	"	Lv	9 34AM
a 3 46PM	Ar	Hollywood	"	Lv	a 9 25AM
4 25PM	Ar	Miami	"	Lv	9 00AM
6 00PM	Lv	Miami	FLORIDA GREYHOUND LINES	Ar	4 25AM
9 30PM	Ar	Key West	" " "	Lv	12 30AM
11 45AM	Lv	Wildwood (Homosassa Springs)	SAL	Ar	1 20PM
a12 24PM	Ar	Dade City	"	Lv	a12 24PM
a12 51PM	Ar	Plant City	"	Lv	a11 59AM
1 30PM	Ar	Tampa	"	Lv	11 30AM
2 35PM	Ar	Clearwater (Belleview-Biltmore Hotel)	"	Lv	10 20AM
a 2 48PM	Ar	Bay Pines (Madeira Bch.-Reddington Bch.)	"	Lv	a10 04AM
3 20PM	Ar	St. Petersburg	"	Lv	9 45AM
1 45PM	Lv	Tampa	SAL	Ar	11 10AM
3 15PM	Ar	Palmetto-Ellenton	"	Lv	9 26AM
3 25PM	Ar	Bradenton	"	Lv	9 20AM
3 45PM	Ar	Sarasota	"	Lv	9 00AM
4 40PM	Ar	Venice	"	Lv	8 15AM

a–Conditional stop; Consult Ticket Agent.

(Coach Seats Reserved Without Extra Cost)

	Designation S.B.	Designation N.B.	Line No.	
BAGGAGE DORMITORY				New York-Miami.
COACH (56 Recl. Seats)	11-E	11-E	....	New York-Miami.
10 SEC., 1 DR 2 Cpt.	SA-45	B-51	6774	New York-Miami.
8 SEC., 5 DBR	SA-46	B-53	6765	New York-Miami.
6 SEC., 6 DBR	SA-47	B-52	6765	New York-Miami.
RECLINING SEAT P&B CAR				Wildwood-St. Petersburg.
10 SEC., 1 DR 2 CPT.	SA-49	B-48	2741	New York-Sarasota-Venice.
8 SEC., 1 DR 3 DBR	SA-50	B-59	6772	New York-St. Petersburg.
8 SEC. 1 DR 3 DBR	SA-51	B-58	2751	New York-St. Petersburg.
SAL DINING CAR				New York-St. Petersburg.
COACH (56 Recl. Seats)	18-W	18-W	....	New York-St. Petersburg.
COACH (52 Recl. Seats)	19-W	19-W	....	New York-St. Petersburg.
SAL DINING CAR				New York-Miami.
COACH (56 Recl. Seats)	12-E	12-E	....	New York-Miami.
COACH (56 Recl. Seats)	13-E	13-E	....	New York-Miami.
COACH (52 Recl. Seats)	14-E	14-E	....	New York-Miami.
COACH (52 Recl. Seats)	15-E	15-E	....	New York-Miami.
TAVERN OBSERVATION CAR				New York-Miami.

Presenting
A New STREAMLINED TRAIN
The ADVANCE SILVER METEOR
To
FAMOUS RESORTS ON BOTH COASTS of FLORIDA
Leaves December 12th from New York at 10:05 a.m., operating through West Savannah and the Gross-Baldwin Cut-off and northbound through Jacksonville and Savannah, arriving West Palm Beach 10:00 a.m., Miami 11:40 a.m., Tampa 8:50 a.m., St. Petersburg 10:35 a.m., with connections at Tampa to Boca Grande. Northbound will leave St. Petersburg 9:15 a.m., (Sarasota 8:45 a.m.), Tampa 11:10 a.m., Miami 8:25 a.m., West Palm Beach 9:50 a.m., Jacksonville 3:45 p.m., Savannah 6:10 p.m., arriving Washington 6:15 a.m., New York 10:40 a.m.
Coaches will afford comfortable adjustable seats, which must be reserved in advance at no extra charge; commodious rest rooms; wide windows and individual car attendants. Pullman, observation-lounge, tavern and dining cars will complete the train. A passenger service agent and registered nurse will be available on the train to all passengers. New stainless steel, streamlined coaches are now being built and will be added to the train on delivery.

On November 10, 1940, the *Silver Meteor* reached and passed its millionth mile. This publicity photograph to celebrate the event was taken at milepost 1023 north of Wildwood, Florida.
(SAL Photo/W. E. Griffin, Jr. Collection)

SEABOARD

SEABOARD RAILROAD
SILVER
METEOR
20

Aboard the SILVER FLEET

(facing page, top) Train No. 57, the southbound *Silver Meteor* East Coast Section, behind E7A No. 3024 at Winter Haven, Florida, in April 1960.

(David W. Salter)

(facing page, bottom) The passenger service agent and conductor of the *Silver Meteor* are among those enjoying the 20th Anniversary cake served on board the train upon arrival at Miami on February 4, 1959.

(SAL Photo/CSX Transportation)

(right) The *Silver Meteor's* baggagemaster at work aboard the train.

(SAL Photo)

(below) One of the duties of the Stewardess-Registered Nurse was to assist the train's conductor and passenger agent, as seen here aboard the *Silver Meteor.*

(SAL Photo)

BEACH

(facing page) SAL Stewardess-Registered Nurse Mary Noble assists a child from the *Silver Meteor* upon the train's arrival in West Palm Beach, Florida. All SAL streamliners carried Registered Nurses as regular members of the train crew.

(SAL Photo)

(above) Chair-Buffet-Observation Car No. 6500 was on the rear of the *Silver Meteor* for this station stop in Jacksonville, Florida.

(SAL Photo/CSX Transportation)

(below) Interior view of a *Silver Meteor* coach, decorated with scenes of the Florida beaches.

(SAL Photo)

The Seaboard implemented its plan to modernize the company's passenger equipment by placing an order in 1946 for new lightweight streamlined passenger equipment for use in the *Silver Meteors* between New York and Florida and in two new trains – the *Silver Comet* (Nos. 33 and 34) and the *Silver Star* (Nos. 21 and 22).

The *Silver Comet* was inaugurated between New York-Atlanta and Birmingham on May 18, 1947. Carrying both sleeping cars and lightweight, streamlined coaches and feature cars, this train enjoyed excellent patronage. The *Silver Star* was also introduced in 1947 as a new winter seasonal train. Inaugurated on December 12th, it operated between New York and both coasts of Florida with a consist that included sleeping cars and lightweight, streamlined coaches and feature cars (diners, lounges, and tavern observations). In response to the demand for additional streamliner service, the *Silver Star* commenced operation on August 1, 1948, as a year-round train between New York and Miami. On December 17, 1948, its operation was expanded to also provide winter service to and from St. Petersburg.

The lightweight, streamlined sleeping cars that had been ordered in 1946 for the *Silver Fleet* (*Meteor, Comet,* and *Star*) were delayed by the manufacturers (Budd, Pullman-Standard, and AC&F) and did not arrive on the property until 1949. These sleeping cars featured all-room type accommodations, each consisting of six double bedrooms and ten roomettes. They were the first sleeping cars of their type to be operated in the South. They were equipped with trucks of the latest design to eliminate road shocks and vibrations. To assure smooth starting and stopping, the cars also were equipped with roller bearings, tight-lock couplers and rubber draft gears. Of the 31 cars put into service, 25 were named for principal cities along the Seaboard route.

At the same time the Seaboard was emphasizing the passenger service of its *Silver Fleet*, it began to cut back or discontinue service on certain of its less important passenger trains. The SAL did continue to operate the *Sunland* (Nos. 7 and 8) and the *Palmland* between Washington and both coasts of Florida and the *Orange Blossom Special* was retained as an all-Pullman winter season

The *Silver Meteor* in the later years rolls through Florida behind two E8A diesels.
(SAL Photo/W. E. Griffin, Jr. Collection)

train. The *Florida Sunbeam* was not re-established after the 1948-1949 winter season and thereafter midwestern passenger traffic was routed via the Washington-Richmond-Jacksonville gateways.

The Seaboard added another streamlined train with the inauguration of the *Gulf Wind* (Nos. 38 and 39) on July 31, 1949. This train offered Pullman and coach service and replaced the *New Orleans-Florida Express*, one of two daily local trains (the other was the *New Orleans-Florida Limited*) that operated over the Gulf route between Jacksonville and New Orleans in conjunction with the L&N Railroad. The *Gulf Wind* offered an improved daily schedule and direct connections to and from Florida and the Pacific

Coast, via the Southern Pacific's famed *Sunset Limited.*

However, even as the Seaboard was modernizing its equipment and offering improved schedules and service, its passenger business declined in the face of strong competition from the airlines and private automobiles. Seaboard's New York to Miami business was seriously affected in 1951 when the airlines offered air coach fares between those two cities for daytime schedules which compared favorably with rail coach fares.

Hence, as early as the 1950s, the Seaboard was required to consolidate certain of its local passenger trains and to discontinue the operation of others. Some of the discontinuances were as follows: Passenger trains Nos. 13 and 14 between Portsmouth and Norlina were curtailed on October 1, 1950. Trains Nos. 19 and 20 between Hamlet and Rutherfordton were discontinued on December 10, 1950. Trains Nos. 17 and 18 between Cuthbert, Ga. and Tallahassee, Fla., and Trains Nos. 1 and 2 between Tampa and St. Petersburg were retired on February 1, 1951. Trains Nos. 11 and 12 between Savannah and Montgomery were also withdrawn in 1951. Trains Nos. 25 and 26 between Hamlet and Charleston were discontinued on December 31, 1956. Trains Nos. 11 and 12 between Wildwood and Tampa ended operations on November 13, 1965. The operation of Trains Nos. 36 and 37 between Jacksonville and Chattahoochee was suspended effective October 18, 1966.

(above) Train No. 33, the southbound *Silver Comet*, with E7A No. 3030 leading an A-A-A consist configuration, enters Atlanta, Georgia, on Southern Railway tracks at Jefferson Street on May 1, 1947.

(David W. Salter)

(below) Movie actress Jean Parker christens the new *Silver Comet* in ceremonies at Pennsylvania Station, New York City, on May 18, 1947.

(SAL Photo)

SILVER COMET

New York, Washington, Richmond, Norfolk, Raleigh, Athens, Atlanta, Birmingham, the Southwest

Diesel-Powered *All accommodations reserved*

33	DAILY TRAINS			34
7 30AM	Lv **Boston** (So. Station) (EST)	NYNH&H	Ar	5 45PM
12 35PM	Lv **New York** (Penna Station)	PRR	Ar	12 45PM
12 50PM	Lv **Newark**	"	Ar	12 28PM
1 59PM	Lv **North Philadelphia**	"	Ar	11 21AM
2 09PM	Lv **Philadelphia** (30th Street Station)	"	Ar	11 12AM
2 37PM	Lv **Wilmington**	"	Ar	10 43AM
3 40PM	Lv **Baltimore**	"	Ar	9 41AM
5 00PM	Lv **Washington**	RF&P	Ar	8 20AM
7 35PM	Lv **Richmond** (Main Street Station)	SAL	Ar	5 42AM
a 8 02PM	Lv **Petersburg**	"	Ar	a 5 14AM
a 9 31PM	Ar **Henderson**	"	Lv	a 3 41AM
10 15PM	Ar **Raleigh**	"	Lv	3 00AM
12 05AM	Ar **Hamlet**	"	Lv	1 15AM

17-7	*Connections at Hamlet*			8	22-18
4 20PM	Lv **Norfolk**	PORTSMOUTH FERRY	Ar	......	8 40AM
4 40PM	Lv **Portsmouth**	SAL	Ar	......	8 25AM
8 44PM	Lv **Henderson**	"	Ar	8 21AM	......
9 40PM	Lv **Raleigh**	"	Ar	7 25AM	3 45AM
10 28PM	Lv **Sanford**	"	Lv	6 37AM	......
10 58PM	Lv **Southern Pines** (Pinehurst)	"	Lv	6 07AM	......
11 35PM	Ar **Hamlet**	"	Lv	5 35AM	2 05AM

33	SILVER COMET			34
12 25AM	Lv **Hamlet**	SAL	Ar	1 00AM
1 30AM	Ar **Monroe**	"	Lv	11 55PM
a 3 52AM	Ar **Greenwood**	"	Lv	a 9 37PM
5 37AM	Ar **Athens**	"	Lv	7 54PM
a 6 45AM	Ar **Emory University**	"	Lv	a 6 43PM
7 10AM	Ar **Atlanta**	"	Lv	6 20PM
7 25AM	Lv **Atlanta**	"	Ar	6 00PM
a 8 38AM	Ar **Rockmart**	"	Lv	a 4 50PM
a 8 55AM	Ar **Cedartown**...(EST)	"	Lv	a 4 34PM
10 25AM	Ar **Birmingham**..(CST)	"	Lv	1 15PM
	Connections at Atlanta and Birmingham			
12 05PM	Lv **Birmingham**..(CST)	FRISCO	Ar	7 00AM
6 45PM	Ar **Memphis**	"	Lv	10 00PM
8 35AM	Lv **Atlanta**......(EST)	A&WP	Ar	1 15PM
11 30AM	Ar **Montgomery**.(CST)	"	Lv	7 40AM
4 30PM	Ar **Pensacola**	L&N	Lv	12 25AM
3 10PM	Ar **Mobile**	"	Lv	2 35AM
6 55PM	Ar **New Orleans**	"	Lv	11 00PM
10 30AM	Lv **Atlanta**......(EST)	C OF GA	Ar	5 55PM
1 15PM	Ar **Columbus**	"	Lv	3 10PM
9 30AM	Lv **Atlanta**......(EST)	C OF GA	Ar	6 00PM
12 20PM	Ar **Macon**	"	Lv	3 20PM
3 25PM	Ar **Albany**	"	Lv	12 40PM

a—Conditional stop; Consult Ticket Agent.

(Coach Seats Reserved)

	Designation S.B.	Designation N.B.	Line No.	
P&B Dormitory (18 Recl. Seats)	21-B	21-B	....	Washington-Birmingham.
Coach (36 Recl. Seats)	22-B	22-B	....	New York-Birmingham.
Coach (52 Recl. Seats)	28-B	28-B	....	(SEE NOTE) Portsmouth-Atlanta.
10 Sec., 1 Dr., 2 Cpt.	B-3	B-4	6777	(SEE NOTE) Portsmouth-Atlanta.
10 Rmtte., 6 Dbr.	R-365	B-70	6906	Washington-Atlanta.
10 Sec., 1 Dr., 2 Cpt.	R-366	B-71	2737	Washington-Birmingham.
10 Rmtte., 6 Dbr.	S-119	B-72	6903	New York-Birmingham.
10 Sec., Lounge	S-120	B-74	6773	New York-Birmingham.
SAL Diner				New York-Birmingham.
Coach (52 Recl. Seats)	23-B	23-B	...	New York-Birmingham.
Coach (52 Recl. Seats)	24-B	24-B	...	New York-Birmingham.
Tavern Observation				New York-Birmingham.

NOTE—Handled on Trains 7 and 8 between Norlina and Hamlet.

The *Silver Comet* in the later years is being pulled into Birmingham Union Station, Birmingham, Alabama, with SDP35 No. 1108 on the head end. Train No. 34 has a mixed consist of passenger equipment on this March 1965 afternoon.

(David W. Salter)

Observation car No. 6401 on the *Silver Star* as the train operates over the Pennsylvania Railroad between Washington, D.C., and New York City.

(M. D. McCarter Collection)

6401
SILVER STAR

SILVER STAR

New York, Washington, Richmond, Jacksonville and Miami

All accommodations must be reserved in advance

Diesel-Powered — *Seaboard Dining Service*

21		DAILY TRAINS			22
10 00PM	Lv	Boston (So. Station) (EST)	NYNH&H	Ar	7 30PM
9 30AM	Lv	New York (Penna. Station)	PRR	Ar	2 10PM
9 45AM	Lv	Newark	"	Ar	1 54PM
10 57AM	Lv	North Philadelphia	"	Ar	12 35PM
11 07AM	Lv	Philadelphia (30th Street Station)	"	Ar	12 25PM
11 34AM	Lv	Wilmington	"	Ar	11 56AM
12 35PM	Lv	Baltimore	"	Ar	10 41AM
1 50PM	Lv	Washington	RF&P	Ar	9 20AM
4 23PM	Lv	Richmond (Main Street Station)	SAL	Ar	6 37AM
a 4 50PM	Lv	Petersburg	"	Ar	a 6 04AM
......	Lv	Portsmouth	"	Ar	8 25AM
6 58PM	Ar	Raleigh	"	Lv	3 50AM
8 45PM	Ar	Hamlet	"	Lv	2 05AM
10 53PM	Ar	Columbia	"	Lv	12 01AM
a 1 13AM	Ar	West Savannah	"	Lv	......
......	Ar	Savannah (Union Station)	"	Lv	9 40PM
a 2 14AM	Ar	Thalmann (Brunswick-Sea Island)	"	Lv	a 8 29PM
3 30AM	Ar	Jacksonville	"	Lv	7 20PM
a 4 38AM	Ar	Waldo	"	Lv	a 6 00PM
a 5 18AM	Ar	Ocala (Silver Springs)	"	Lv	a 5 21PM
5 50AM	Ar	Wildwood (Homosassa Springs)	"	Lv	4 55PM
a 6 56AM	Ar	Winter Haven (Cypress Gardens)	"	Lv	a 3 37PM
a 7 06AM	Ar	W. Lake Wales-Lake Wales (Bok Tower)	"	Lv	a 3 28PM
a 7 26AM	Ar	Avon Park	"	Lv	a 3 04PM
a 7 36AM	Ar	Sebring (Highlands Hammock State Park)	"	Lv	a 2 53PM
9 10AM	Ar	West Palm Beach-Palm Beach	"	Lv	1 26PM
a 9 17AM	Ar	Lake Worth	"	Lv	a 1 16PM
a 9 27AM	Ar	Delray Beach	"	Lv	a 1 04PM
a 9 37AM	Ar	Deerfield Beach (Boca Raton Club)	"	Lv	a12 53PM
10 03AM	Ar	Fort Lauderdale	"	Lv	12 41PM
a10 13AM	Ar	Hollywood	"	Lv	a12 29PM
a10 30AM	Ar	Hialeah	"	Lv	a12 12PM
10 45AM	Ar	Miami	"	Lv	12 05PM
12 01PM	Lv	Miami	FLORIDA GREYHOUND LINES	Ar	10 30AM
4 10PM	Ar	Key West	" " "	Lv	7 00AM
		Connection at Wildwood with No. 8			
......	Lv	Wildwood	SAL	Ar	4 35PM
......	Ar	Dade City	"	Lv	3 42PM
......	Ar	Zephyrhills	"	Lv	a 3 27PM
......	Ar	Plant City	"	Lv	3 00PM
......	Ar	Tampa	"	Lv	2 30PM
......	Lv	Tampa	TAMIAMI TRAIL TOURS BUS	Ar	b12 20PM
......	Ar	Bradenton	"	Lv	b11 05AM
......	Ar	Sarasota	"	Lv	b10 40AM
......	Ar	Venice	"	Lv	b10 00AM

a–Conditional stop; Consult Ticket Agent.
b–Via Bus, SAL tickets honored.

(Coach Seats Reserved)

	Designation S.B.	Designation N.B.	Line No.	
Baggage Dormitory				New York-Miami.
10 Rmtte., 6 Dbr.	S-109	B-45	6905	New York-Miami.
8 Sec., 5 Dbr.	S-110	B-46	2700	New York-Miami.
6 Cpt. Buff. Lounge	S-111	B-47	6779	New York-Miami.
6 Cpt., 3 Dr.	S-112	B-55	2761	New York-Port Boca Grande.
10 Rmtte., 6 Dbr.	S-113	B-56	6908	New York-St. Petersburg.
8 Sec., 5 Dbr.	S-114	B-57	2767	New York-St. Petersburg.
SAL Diner				New York-St. Petersburg.
Coach (52 Recl. Seats)	7-W	7-W	....	New York-St. Petersburg.
Coach (52 Recl. Seats)	8-W	8-W	....	New York-St. Petersburg.
SAL Diner				New York-Miami.
Tav. Coach (24 Recl. Seats)	2-E	2-E	....	New York-Miami.
Coach (52 Recl. Seats)	3-E	3-E	....	New York-Miami.
Coach (52 Recl. Seats)	4-E	4-E	....	New York-Miami.
Coach (52 Recl. Seats)	5-E	5-E	....	New York-Miami.
Obv. Coach (40 Recl. Seats)	6-E	6-E	....	New York-Miami.

(facing page, top) Led by E7A No. 3018, Train No. 21, the southbound *Silver Star*, departs Main Street Station in Richmond, Virginia, on October 17, 1952.

(facing page, middle) All Aboard the *Silver Star* at Raleigh, N.C., on June 20, 1951.

(Both, W. E. Griffin, Jr. Collection)

(facing page, bottom) Interior view of lounge car on the *Silver Star.*

(SAL Photo/W. E. Griffin, Jr. Collection)

(right) The SAL inaugurated the *Silver Star* on December 12, 1947. During ceremonies at Pennsylvania Station in New York City, Diana Lynn, a young motion picture star, was inducted into the Seminole Indian tribe by Chief Billie Osceola. The new stainless-steel, Budd-built train departed on its first trip after the ceremonies.

(SAL Photo/CSX Transportation)

(below) The northbound *Silver Star,* with two E7s and 18 cars, rolls past GP7 No. 1763 at Henderson, N.C., in December 1964.

(Curt Tillotson, Jr.)

THE CAMELLIA

tt†6:00AM	Lv Boston (South Sta.) (ET)	NYNH&H	Ar	9:10PM
c11:05AM	Lv New York (Penna. Sta.) (ET)	PRR	Ar	c 3:45PM
c12:41PM	Lv North Philadelphia	"	Ar	c 2:22PM
c12:58PM	Lv Philadelphia (30th St. Sta.)	"	Ar	c 2:13PM
c 1:35PM	Lv Wilmington	"	Ar	c 1:44PM
c 2:50PM	Lv Baltimore	"	Ar	c12:42PM
4:00PM	Lv Washington	RF&P	Ar	11:30AM
6:55PM	Lv Richmond (Main St. Sta.)	SAL	Ar	8:32AM
7:27PM	Lv Petersburg	"	Ar	8:05AM
4:50PM	Lv Norfolk	Ferry	Ar	10:35AM
5:10PM	Lv Portsmouth	SAL	Ar	10:20AM
10:05PM	Lv Raleigh	SAL	Ar	5:20AM
o11:30PM	Lv Southern Pines (Pinehurst)	"	Ar	o 4:00AM
A 1:54AM	Lv Camden	"	Ar	A 1:36AM
2:40AM	Ar Columbia	"	Lv	1:00AM
5:40AM	Ar Savannah (Union Station)	"	Lv	10:06PM
L 6:56AM	Ar Thalmann (Bruns.-Sea Isl.)	"	Lv	L 8:43PM
8:25AM	Ar Jacksonville	"	Lv	7:25PM
10:49AM	Ar Ocala (Silver Springs)	"	Lv	5:10PM
11:25AM	Ar Wildwood (Homosassa Springs)	"	Lv	4:40PM
1:03PM	Ar Winter Haven (Cypress Gardens)	"	Lv	2:48PM
1:15PM	Ar W. Lake Wales-Lake Wales (Bok Tower)	"	Lv	2:40PM
1:37PM	Ar Avon Park	"	Lv	2:16PM
1:50PM	Ar Sebring (Highlands Hammock State Park)	"	Lv	2:03PM
3:27PM	Ar West Palm Beach-Palm Beach	"	Lv	12:20PM
4:34PM	Ar Fort Lauderdale	"	Lv	11:15AM
5:30PM	Ar Miami	"	Lv	10:30AM
1:50PM	Ar Tampa	SAL	Lv	2:00PM
3:55PM	Ar St. Petersburg	"	Lv	12:01PM
2:15PM	Lv Tampa	SAL	Ar	w 1:26PM
3:54PM	Ar Bradenton	"	Lv	w12:10PM
4:25PM	Ar Sarasota	"	Lv	w11:50AM
5:10PM	Ar Venice	"	Lv	w11:15AM
2:30PM	Lv Tampa	TTT Bus	Ar	1:26PM
6:20PM	Ar Fort Myers	"	Lv	10:00AM

DIESEL POWERED (Raleigh–Miami, both directions)

	Designation S.B.	Designation N.B.	Line No.	
BAGGAGE CAR				New York-Miami.
COACH				New York-Miami.
COACH				New York-Miami.
COACH				New York-Miami
COACH				Portsmouth-Norlina.
PASSENGER & BAGGAGE CAR				Jacksonville-St. Petersburg.
COACH				New York-St. Petersburg.
COACH				Tampa-Sarasota-Venice.
DINING CAR				New York-Washington.
SAL DINING CAR				Washington-Sebring.
BUFFET LOUNGE COACH (Light refreshments only)				Wildwood-St. Petersburg.
10 SECTION LOUNGE	R-101	B-114	2779	Washington-Jacksonville.
10 SEC., 1 DR 2 CPT.	SA- 5	B-110	2772	New York-Miami.
10 SEC., 1 DR 2 CPT.	SA- 7	B-112	2723	New York-St. Petersburg.
12 SEC., 1 DR.	B-17	B-18	6702	Portsmouth-Jacksonville.
COACH (52 Recl. Seats)	28-B	28-B		Portsmouth-Atlanta. (SEE NOTE).
10 SEC., 1 DR 2 CPT.	B- 5	B- 6	6777	Portsmouth-Atlanta. (SEE NOTE)

NOTE—Handled on Trains 33 and 34 between Hamlet and Atlanta.

Train No. 8, the northbound *Sun Queen*, arrives at Main Street Station in Richmond, Virginia. The *Sun Queen* was renamed the *Camellia* in 1947. The train was again renamed in December 1948, becoming the *Sunland*.

(SAL Photo/W. E. Griffin, Jr. Collection)

(above) Train No. 8, the northbound *Camellia,* rolls by at approximately 75 mph on September 15, 1947. The train is at Oleta, Florida, north of Hialeah, with No. 3004 leading another E4A.
(David W. Salter)

(below) Three E7As, led by No. 3018, pause at the Henderson, N.C., station with Train No. 8, the northbound *Sunland*, in March 1964. With an 8:21 a.m. departure, the 17-car train will arrive in Richmond, Virginia, before noon for interchange to the RF&P.
(Curt Tillotson, Jr.)

SUNLAND

Washington, Richmond, Norfolk and Florida with connections to and from New York and Boston

Diesel-Powered

7		DAILY TRAINS			8
10 00PM	Lv	Boston (So. Station) (EST)	NYNH&H	Ar	10 25PM
11 30AM	Lv	New York (Penna. Station)	PRR	Ar	5 45PM
11 45AM	Lv	Newark	"	Ar	5 29PM
1 10PM	Lv	Philadelphia (30th Street Station)	"	Ar	4 13PM
1 39PM	Lv	Wilmington	"	Ar	3 42PM
2 45PM	Lv	Baltimore	"	Ar	2 41PM
3 25PM	Ar	Washington	"	Lv	2 00PM
3 40PM	Lv	Washington	RF&P	Ar	1 45PM
6 35PM	Lv	Richmond (Main Street Station)	SAL	Ar	10 40AM
7 05PM	Lv	Petersburg	"	Ar	10 10AM
4 20PM	Lv	Norfolk	PORTSMOUTH FERRY	Ar	
4 40PM	Lv	Portsmouth	SAL	Ar	
5 08PM	Lv	Suffolk	"	Ar	
5 33PM	Lv	Franklin	"	Ar	
6 07PM	Lv	Boykins	"	Ar	
6 46PM	Lv	Weldon	"	Ar	See
8 00PM	Ar	Norlina	"	Lv	Page 6
8 25PM	Lv	Norlina	SAL	Ar	8 55AM
8 44PM	Ar	Henderson	"	Lv	8 21AM
9 30PM	Ar	Raleigh	"	Lv	7 35AM
10 28PM	Ar	Sanford	"	Lv	6 37AM
10 58PM	Ar	Southern Pines (Pinehurst)	"	Lv	6 07AM
11 35PM	Ar	Hamlet	"	Lv	5 35AM
1 14AM	Ar	Camden	"	Lv	3 28AM
2 00AM	Ar	Columbia	"	Lv	2 50AM
5 15AM	Ar	Savannah (Union Station)	"	Lv	11 45PM
6 35AM	Ar	Thalmann (Brunswick-Sea Island)	"	Lv	10 14PM
8 10AM	Ar	Jacksonville	"	Lv	9 00PM
8 45AM	Lv	Jacksonville	"	Ar	7 30PM
9 32AM	Ar	Starke	"	Lv	6 35PM
9 47AM	Ar	Waldo	"	Lv	6 17PM
10 40AM	Ar	Ocala (Silver Springs)	"	Lv	5 33PM
11 15AM	Ar	Wildwood	SAL	Lv	5 00PM
11 25AM	Lv	Wildwood	SAL	Ar	4 35PM
12 04PM	Ar	Dade City	"	Lv	3 42PM
12 15PM	Ar	Zephyrhills	"	Ar	a 3 27PM
12 33PM	Ar	Plant City	"	Lv	3 00PM
1 25PM	Ar	Tampa	"	Lv	2 30PM
1 45PM	Lv	Tampa	SAL	Ar	b12 20PM
3 15PM	Ar	Palmetto-Ellenton	"	Lv	b11 15AM
3 25PM	Ar	Bradenton	"	Lv	b11 05AM
3 45PM	Ar	Sarasota	"	Lv	b10 40AM
4 40PM	Ar	Venice	"	Lv	b10 00AM

a-Conditional stop; consult ticket agent.
b-Via Bus, SAL tickets honored.

	Designation S.B.	Designation N.B.	Line No.		
Baggage Car					Washington-Miami.
Coaches					Washington-Miami.
Passenger and Baggage Car					Jacksonville-Tampa.
Coach					Washington-Tampa.
Coach					Tampa-Sarasota-Venice.
Dining Car					Washington-Hamlet.
Dining Car					Portsmouth-Norlina.
Parlor-Diner					Jacksonville-Miami.
10 Sec., 1 Dr., 2 Cpt.	R-360	B-110	2722		Washington-Miami.
10 Sec., 1 Dr., 2 Cpt.	B-17	B-18	6702		Portsmouth-Tampa.
Coach (52 Recl. Seats)	28-B	28-B	....	(SEE NOTE)	Portsmouth-Atlanta.
10 Sec., 1 Dr., 2 Cpt.	B-3	B-4	6777	(SEE NOTE)	Portsmouth-Atlanta.

NOTE—Handled on Trains 33 and 34 between Hamlet and Atlanta.

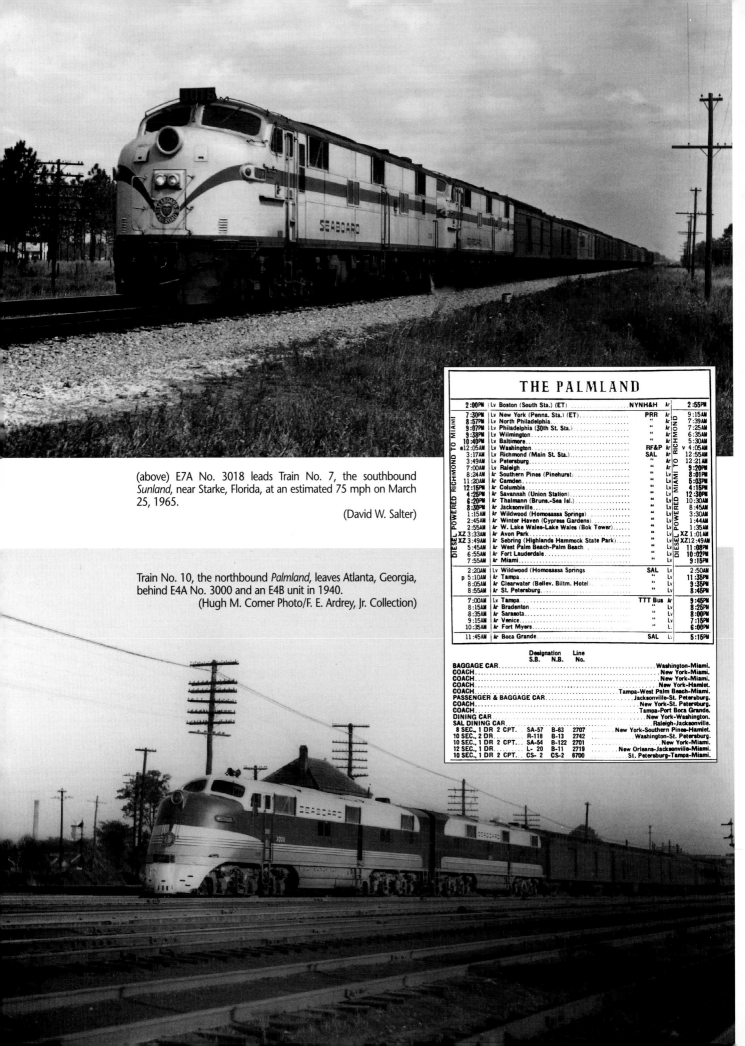

(above) E7A No. 3018 leads Train No. 7, the southbound *Sunland*, near Starke, Florida, at an estimated 75 mph on March 25, 1965.

(David W. Salter)

THE PALMLAND

DIESEL POWERED RICHMOND TO MIAMI / DIESEL POWERED MIAMI TO RICHMOND

2:00PM	Lv	Boston (South Sta.) (ET)	NYNH&H	Ar	2:55PM
7:30PM	Lv	New York (Penna. Sta.) (ET)	PRR	Ar	9:15AM
8:57PM	Lv	North Philadelphia	"	Ar	7:39AM
9:07PM	Lv	Philadelphia (30th St. Sta.)	"	Ar	7:25AM
9:38PM	Lv	Wilmington	"	Ar	6:35AM
10:40PM	Lv	Baltimore	"	Ar	5:30AM
e12:05AM	Lv	Washington	RF&P	Ar	v 4:05AM
3:17AM	Lv	Richmond (Main St. Sta.)	SAL	Ar	12:55AM
3:49AM	Lv	Petersburg	"	Ar	12:21AM
7:00AM	Lv	Raleigh	"	Ar	9:20PM
8:24AM	Ar	Southern Pines (Pinehurst)	"	Lv	8:01PM
11:20AM	Ar	Camden	"	Lv	5:03PM
12:15PM	Ar	Columbia	"	Lv	4:15PM
4:25PM	Ar	Savannah (Union Station)	"	Lv	12:30PM
6:20PM	Ar	Thalmann (Bruns.-Sea Isl.)	"	Lv	10:30AM
8:30PM	Ar	Jacksonville	"	Lv	8:45AM
1:15AM	Ar	Wildwood (Homosassa Springs)	"	Lv	3:30AM
2:45AM	Ar	Winter Haven (Cypress Gardens)	"	Lv	1:44AM
2:55AM	Ar	W. Lake Wales-Lake Wales (Bok Tower)	"	Lv	1:35AM
XZ 3:33AM	Ar	Avon Park	"	Lv	XZ 1:01AM
XZ 3:49AM	Ar	Sebring (Highlands Hammock State Park)	"	Lv	XZ12:49AM
5:45AM	Ar	West Palm Beach-Palm Beach	"	Lv	11:08PM
6:55AM	Ar	Fort Lauderdale	"	Lv	10:02PM
7:55AM	Ar	Miami	"	Lv	9:15PM
2:20AM	Lv	Wildwood (Homosassa Springs	SAL	Lv	2:50AM
p 5:10AM	Ar	Tampa	"	Lv	11:35PM
8:05AM	Ar	Clearwater (Bellev. Biltm. Hotel	"	Lv	9:35PM
8:55AM	Ar	St. Petersburg	"	Lv	8:45PM
7:00AM	Lv	Tampa	TTT Bus	Ar	9:45PM
8:15AM	Ar	Bradenton	"	Lv	8:25PM
8:35AM	Ar	Sarasota	"	Lv	8:00PM
9:15AM	Ar	Venice	"	Lv	7:15PM
10:35AM	Ar	Fort Myers	"	L.	6:00PM
11:45AM	Ar	Boca Grande	SAL	Lv	5:15PM

	Designation S.B.	Designation N.B.	Line No.	
BAGGAGE CAR				Washington-Miami.
COACH				New York-Miami.
COACH				New York-Miami.
COACH				New York-Hamlet.
COACH				Tampa-West Palm Beach-Miami.
PASSENGER & BAGGAGE CAR				Jacksonville-St. Petersburg.
COACH				New York-St. Petersburg.
COACH				Tampa-Port Boca Grande.
DINING CAR				New York-Washington.
SAL DINING CAR				Raleigh-Jacksonville.
8 SEC., 1 DR 2 CPT.	SA-57	B-63	2707	New York-Southern Pines-Hamlet.
10 SEC., 2 DR	R-118	B-13	2742	Washington-St. Petersburg.
10 SEC., 1 DR 2 CPT.	SA-54	B-122	2701	New York-Miami.
12 SEC., 1 DR	L- 20	B-11	2719	New Orleans-Jacksonville-Miami.
10 SEC., 1 DR 2 CPT.	CS- 2	CS-2	6700	St. Petersburg-Tampa-Miami.

Train No. 10, the northbound *Palmland*, leaves Atlanta, Georgia, behind E4A No. 3000 and an E4B unit in 1940.

(Hugh M. Comer Photo/F. E. Ardrey, Jr. Collection)

(above) E7A No. 3017 with the northbound *Cotton Blossom* departing Emory University, Atlanta, Georgia, in August 1948.
(David W. Salter)

(right) M-2 No. 260 with the southbound *Cotton Blossom* at Winder, Georgia, on January 11, 1948.
(R. D. Sharpless Photo/F. E. Ardrey, Jr. Collection)

(below right) Train No. 6, the northbound *Cotton Blossom,* rolls through Weems, Alabama, behind E7A No. 3040 on September 5, 1948.
(F. E. Ardrey, Jr.)

THE COTTON BLOSSOM

11:00 AM	Lv. Boston (South Sta.) (ET)	NYNH&H	Ar.	b 7:55 PM
4:30 PM	Lv. New York (Penna. Sta.)	PRR	Ar.	1:55 PM
6:11 PM	Lv. Philadelphia (30th St. Sta.)	"	Ar.	12:16 PM
7:42 PM	Lv. Baltimore	"	Ar.	10:42 AM
9:00 PM	Lv. Washington	RF&P	Ar.	9:15 AM
12:25 AM	Lv. Richmond (Main St. Sta.)	SAL	Ar.	5:40 AM
4:35 AM	Ar. Raleigh	"	Lv.	1:45 AM
6:55 AM	Ar. Southern Pines (Pinehurst)	"	Lv.	11:35 PM
10:10 AM	Ar. Monroe	"	Lv.	9:05 PM
3:35 PM	Ar. Athens	"	Lv.	3:35 PM
5:40 PM	Ar. Atlanta	"	Lv.	1:35 PM
6:00 PM	Lv. Atlanta	"	Ar.	1:10 PM
9:30 PM	Ar. Birmingham (CT)	"	Lv.	7:30 AM
10:30 PM	Lv. Birmingham (CT)	FRISCO	Ar.	7:00 AM
6:55 AM	Ar. Memphis	"	Lv.	10:40 PM
7:25 PM	Lv. Atlanta (ET)	A&WP	Ar.	1:15 PM
11:00 PM	Ar. Montgomery (CT)	"	Lv.	7:40 AM
3:50 AM	Ar. Mobile	L&N	Lv.	2:37 AM
7:30 AM	Ar. New Orleans	"	Lv.	11:00 PM
....	Lv. Birmingham (CT)	SOU	Ar.	7:05 AM
	Ar. New Orleans	"	Lv.	9:00 PM

	Designation S.B.	Designation N.B.	Line No.	
PARLOR CAR				New York-Washington.
DINING CAR				New York-Washington.
COACHES				New York-Washington.
PASSENGER & BAGGAGE CAR				Washington-Birmingham.
COACH				Washington-Birmingham.
SAL DINING CAR				Hamlet-Athens.
12 SEC., 1 DR	R-110	B-148	2702	Washington-Atlanta.

GULF WIND

Jacksonville, Tallahassee, Pensacola, Mobile and New Orleans

No. 39		Daily Trains				No. 38	
		Connections at Jacksonville					
1st Day	9 00AM	Lv	Miami	SAL	Ar	4 25PM	1st Day
"	b 9 25AM	Lv	Hollywood	"	Ar	b 3 46PM	"
"	9 34AM	Lv	Ft. Lauderdale	"	Ar	3 35PM	"
"	b 9 48AM	Lv	Deerfield Bch. (Boca Raton Club)	"	Ar	b 3 17PM	"
"	b 9 58AM	Lv	Delray Beach	"	Ar	b 3 07PM	"
"	b10 09AM	Lv	Lake Worth	"	Ar	b 2 57PM	"
"	10 18AM	Lv	West Palm Beach-Palm Beach	"	Ar	2 50PM	"
"	b11 44AM	Lv	Sebring (Highlands Hammock State Park)	"	Ar	b 1 17PM	"
"	b11 54AM	Lv	Avon Park	"	Ar	b 1 06PM	"
"	b12 18PM	Lv	West Lake Wales-Lake Wales (Bok Tower)	"	Ar	b12 46PM	"
"	b12 25PM	Lv	Winter Haven (Cypress Gardens)	"	Ar	b12 36PM	"
"	9 45AM	Lv	St. Petersburg	"	Ar	3 20PM	"
"	10 20AM	Lv	Clearwater	"	Ar	2 35PM	"
"	8 15AM	Lv	Venice	"	Ar	4 40PM	"
"	9 00AM	Lv	Sarasota	"	Ar	3 45PM	"
"	11 30AM	Lv	Tampa	"	Ar	1 30PM	"
"	3 45PM	Ar	Jacksonville	"	Lv	9 25AM	"
		GULF WIND					
1st Day	5 00PM	Lv	Jacksonville	SAL	Ar	8 45AM	2nd Day
"	6 06PM	Lv	Lake City	"	Lv	7 26AM	"
"	6 29PM	Lv	Live Oak	"	Lv	7 03AM	"
"	b 7 03PM	Lv	Madison	"	Lv	b 6 30AM	"
"	8 21PM	Lv	Tallahassee	"	Lv	5 30AM	"
"	8 57PM	Lv	Quincy	"	Ar	4 53AM	"
"	9 25PM	Ar	Chattahoochee	"	Lv	4 30AM	"
"	9 35PM	Lv	Chattahoochee	L&N	Ar	4 25AM	"
2nd Day	12 15AM	Ar	Pensacola (CT)	"	Lv	11 36PM	1st Day
"	12 25AM	Lv	Pensacola	"	Ar	11 26PM	"
"	1 30AM	Ar	Flomaton	"	Lv	10 30PM	"
"	3 20AM	Ar	Mobile	"	Lv	8 45PM	"
"	7 20AM	Ar	New Orleans	"	Lv	5 00PM	"
		Connections at New Orleans					
1st Day	10 30AM	Lv	New Orleans (CT)	SO. PAC.	Ar	a4 00PM	3rd Day
"	8 00PM	Ar	Houston	"	Lv	a8 30AM	"
2nd Day	2 10AM	Ar	San Antonio	"	Lv	a4 00AM	"
"	6 30PM	Ar	El Paso	"	Lv	a2 30PM	2nd Day
3rd Day	2 40AM	Ar	Tucson	"	Lv	a7 55AM	"
"	....	Ar	Phoenix (MT)	"	Lv	a5 20AM	"
"	3 15PM	Ar	Los Angeles (PT)	"	Lv	a8 00PM	1st Day
4th Day	8 00AM	Ar	San Francisco	"	Lv	7 15AM	"
1st Day	7 30AM	Lv	New Orleans (CT)	T&P	Ar	6 15AM	2nd Day
"	8 30PM	Ar	Dallas	"	Lv	5 30PM	1st Day
"	10 00PM	Ar	Fort Worth	"	Lv	4 25PM	"
2nd Day	12 50PM	Ar	El Paso (MT)	"	Lv	12 50AM	"

a–Sunset Limited, extra fare train. Advance reservations required.
b–Conditional stop; consult ticket agent.

EQUIPMENT

LOUNGE CAR
Between Jacksonville and New Orleans—5 Dbl. Bedrooms, Buffet.

SLEEPING CARS
Between Jacksonville and New Orleans—Sections, Roomettes., Dbl. Bedrooms.

COACHES
Between Jacksonville and New Orleans.

DINING CARS
Between Jacksonville and Tallahassee.
New Orleans to Mobile.

BAGGAGE SERVICE
Between All Points.

(top) *The New Orleans-Florida Limited*, Train Nos. 36 and 37 provided air conditioned coach, dining car and sleeping car service in conjunction with the L&N Railroad between Jacksonville, Florida, and New Oleans, Louisiana. M-1 Class 4-8-2 No. 216 is westbound with Train No. 37 at Olustee, Florida, on February 19, 1949.

(William J. Husa, Jr.)

(above) Train No. 37 is departing Live Oak, Florida, with ten cars for New Orleans on July 31, 1932. The locomotive is P class 4-6-2 No. 856.

(Otto Perry Photo/Denver Public Library – Western History Department Collection)

(facing page) On July 31, 1949, the SAL inaugurated the operation of the *Gulf Wind*, Train Nos. 38 and 39, with lightweight air-conditioned reclining seat coaches, dining car, and sleeping car service between Jacksonville and New Orleans. The train also featured a 10-section buffet-lounge car. The *Gulf Wind's* observation car posed at Jacksonville on March 19, 1964.

(Railroad Avenue Enterprises)

The
Gulf Wind

(above) M-2 4-8-2 No. 268 gets ready to depart Suffolk, Virginia, with Train No. 17 on January 1, 1949. Portsmouth Sub-Division passenger trains were unnamed during the steam era.

(H. Reid)

Train No. 17 leaves Portsmouth, Virginia, for Norlina, N.C., where it will connect with the *Southern States Special.* M-2 4-8-2 No. 262 has charge of this Portsmouth Sub-Division train in the winter of 1949.

(L. D. Moore, Jr.)

TIDEWATER

Norfolk-Portsmouth, Atlanta, Birmingham, Columbia, Savannah and Florida

Diesel-Powered *Seaboard Dining Service*

17-7	DAILY TRAINS			22-18
4 20PM	Lv Norfolk	PORTSMOUTH FERRY	Ar	8 30AM
4 40PM	Lv Portsmouth	SAL	Ar	8 25AM
5 08PM	Lv Suffolk	"	Ar	7 49AM
5 33PM	Lv Franklin	"	Ar	7 18AM
6 07PM	Lv Boykins	"	Ar	6 56AM
6 40PM	Lv Weldon	"	Ar	6 18AM
8 00PM	Ar Norlina	"	Lv	5 20AM
8 25PM	Lv Norlina	"	Ar	a 4 52AM
8 44PM	Lv Henderson	"	Ar	......
9 40PM	Lv Raleigh	"	Ar	3 45AM
10 58PM	Lv Southern Pines	"	Ar	......
11 35PM	Ar Hamlet		Lv	2 05AM
33				**34**
12 25AM	Lv Hamlet	SAL	Ar	1 00AM
1 30AM	Ar Monroe	"	Lv	11 55PM
a 3 52AM	Ar Greenwood	"	Lv	a 9 37PM
5 37AM	Ar Athens	"	Lv	7 54PM
a 6 45AM	Ar Emory University	"	Lv	a 6 43PM
7 10AM	Ar Atlanta	"	Lv	6 20PM
7 25AM	Lv Atlanta	"	Ar	6 00PM
10 25AM	Ar Birmingham...(CT)	"	Lv	1 15PM
7				**22**
11 59PM	Lv Hamlet	SAL	Ar	1 55AM
2 00AM	Ar Columbia	"	Lv	12 01AM
5 15AM	Ar Savannah (Union Station)	"	Lv	9 40PM
8 10AM	Ar Jacksonville	"	Lv	7 20PM
57	*Connections at Jacksonville*			**22**
9 25AM	Lv Jacksonville	SAL	Ar	7 05PM
a10 59AM	Ar Ocala	"	Lv	a 5 21PM
11 30AM	Ar Wildwood (Homosassa Springs)	"	Lv	4 55PM
a12 36PM	Ar Winter Haven	"	Lv	a 3 37PM
a12 46PM	Ar West Lake Wales	"	Lv	a 3 28PM
a 1 17PM	Ar Sebring	"	Lv	a 2 53PM
2 50PM	Ar West Palm Beach	"	Lv	1 26PM
3 35PM	Ar Fort Lauderdale	"	Lv	12 41PM
4 25PM	Ar Miami	"	Lv	12 05PM
157				**8**
11 45AM	Lv Wildwood	SAL	Ar	4 35PM
1 30PM	Ar Tampa	"	Lv	2 30PM
2 35PM	Ar Clearwater	"	Lv	......
3 20PM	Ar St. Petersburg	"	Lv	......
1 45PM	Lv Tampa	SAL	Ar	b12 20PM
3 25PM	Ar Bradenton	"	Lv	b11 05AM
3 45PM	Ar Sarasota	"	Lv	b10 40AM
4 40PM	Ar Venice	"	Lv	b10 00AM

a–Conditional stop; Consult Ticket Agent. b–Via Bus, SAL tickets honored.

EQUIPMENT

LOUNGE CAR
Between Hamlet and Atlanta—10 Sections.
Between Hamlet and Birmingham—Tavern Coach.

SLEEPING CARS
Between Portsmouth and Atlanta—Sections, Dbl. Bedrooms.
Between Hamlet and Birmingham—Roomettes, Dbl. Bedrooms.
Between Portsmouth and Jacksonville—Sections, Dbl. Bedrooms.

COACHES
Between Portsmouth and Atlanta.
Between Hamlet and Birmingham (Seats reserved).
Between Portsmouth and Jacksonville.

DINING CARS
Between Portsmouth and Norlina.
Between Hamlet and Birmingham.
Jacksonville to Norlina.

BAGGAGE SERVICE
Between All Points.

(above) Train No. 17, the *Tidewater*, nears Suffolk, Virginia, enroute to Norlina, N.C., behind E8A No. 3049 in September 1954.
(Mallory Hope Ferrell)

(below) Photographer L. D. Moore, Jr. posed his wife and son with Train No. 17, the *Tidewater*, as it departed Portsmouth, Virginia, in 1950.
(L. D. Moore, Jr.)

Even the famed *Orange Blossom Special* departed – and without the fanfare that had accompanied its inaugural run. In its annual report to the stockholders the Seaboard simply said: "During 1954, your Company provided substantially the same passenger service as in the preceding year, with the exception that the *Orange Blossom Special*, a seasonal winter train between New York and Florida, was not operated."

As ridership and revenues continued to decline, the Seaboard persisted in its efforts to provide the finest in passenger service. In 1955 it placed orders with Pullman-Standard and Budd for 25 lightweight streamlined sleeping cars and coaches to be assigned to the *Silver Meteor* and *Silver Star*. These cars were delivered in 1956 and included center-lounge coaches and the unusual "Sun Lounge" cars with five bedrooms and a bar-lounge.

When Seaboard merged with ACL in 1967, it was still operating a fleet of passenger trains whose service and equipment were the equal of any railroad in the country. Those trains were the *Silver Meteor*, the *Silver Comet*, the *Silver Star*, the *Sunland*, the *Palmland*, the *Tidewater*, the *Gulf Wind*, and Passenger, Mail and Express Trains Nos. 3 and 4, and Nos. 5 and 6-8.

PASSENGER, MAIL AND EXPRESS

Nos. 3-11 and 12-4

Passenger and Baggage Car	Washington-Hamlet.
Passenger and Baggage Car	Hamlet-Atlanta.
Coach	Washington-Hamlet.
Coach	Hamlet-Atlanta.

PASSENGER, MAIL AND EXPRESS—Nos. 36-37

Baggage Car	Jacksonville-Flomaton.
Coaches	Jacksonville-Flomaton.

Nos. 15 and 16

Passenger and Baggage Car	Atlanta-Birmingham.
Coach	Atlanta-Birmingham.

No. 2

Passenger and Baggage Car	Jacksonville to Hamlet
Coach	Jacksonville to Hamlet

Southbound Passenger, Mail and Express Train No. 3 rolls through Norlina, N.C. E7As 3036 and 3030 have charge of the 14-car train on this December afternoon in 1966.

(Curt Tillotson, Jr.)

(above) M-2 4-8-2 No. 243 crosses the diamond at Raleigh Tower, Raleigh, N.C., in the winter of 1943 with northbound Passenger, Mail and Express Train No. 4.

(Wiley M. Bryan)

(below) Two generations of motive power move an 18-car Train No. 3 near Norlina, N.C., on a December afternoon in 1966. E7A No. 3025 and SDP35 No. 1109 are moving the long Passenger, Mail and Express train at a good clip.

(Curt Tillotson, Jr.)

(left) Portsmouth Sub-Division Local No. 11 crosses Godwin Street as it departs Portsmouth, Virginia, enroute to Norlina, N.C., and its connection with Local No. 3. P-class Pacific No. 861 has charge of the train in the 1949 photo.

(L. D. Moore, Jr.)

(below left) Local No. 13, operating between Wilmington and Charlotte, N.C., is at Wadesboro, N.C., behind P-2 class 4-6-2 No. 845 in May 1951.

(Robert G. Lewis)

M-2 class 4-8-2 No. 255 takes water during its station stop with Passenger, Mail and Express Train No. 2 at Savannah, Georgia, on August 1, 1939.

(Otto Perry Photo/Denver Public Library – Western History Department Collection)

Local Train No. 11, which operated on the line between Savannah, Georgia, and Montgomery, Alabama, is just east of Pitts, Georgia, on the afternoon of January 2, 1948. Motive power is provided by P-4 4-6-2 No. 876, a former Western Maryland locomotive.

(David W. Salter)

P-2 class 4-6-2 No. 823 and M-1 class 4-8-2 No. 221 double-head Passenger, Mail and Express Train No. 15 near Powder Springs, Georgia, in July 1948. No. 15 handled local passenger service between Birmingham and Atlanta.

(David W. Salter)

RAILWAY EXPRESS AGENCY.
RESS AGENCY.

BOARD
MOTOR COACH

(facing page, top) The public views one of the new AC&F rail cars on display at Main Street Station in Richmond, Virginia.
(SAL Photo/W. E. Griffin, Jr. Collection)

(facing page, bottom) Boarding an AC&F motor rail car. These cars were used on the lines between Richmond/Raleigh, Jacksonville/River Junction, and Jacksonville/Tampa.
(SAL Photo/W. E. Griffin, Jr. Collection)

(right) Brill rail motor car No. 2017 in service at Raleigh, N.C., in a circa 1920s view.
(Bruce Lewis Photo/Robert K. Durham Collection)

(above) The SAL acquired two rail cars from St. Louis/EMC in April 1936. No. 2027, in its original paint scheme, is at Hamlet, N.C., in November 1937.

(H. K. Vollrath Collection)

(below) St. Louis/EMC rail car No. 2027, with a version of the citrus paint scheme, is at Cordele, Georgia, in June 1948.

(H. K. Vollrath Collection)

(facing page, top) Repainted in the citrus colors, rail car No. 2028 stops at Cordele, Georgia, in August 1948.

(H. K. Vollrath Collection)

(facing page, bottom) Rail car No. 2028 southbound in the streets of Sarasota, Florida, with two streamline cars – a coach and a Pennsylvania Railroad sleeper – on November 25, 1966.

(William J. Husa, Jr.)

SEABOARD
2028
2028
UNITED STATES MAIL
RAILWAY POST OFFICE

SEABOARD
2028
2028

Chapter 5 Passenger Equipment

(above) SAL coach No. 261 was originally built for service on the Raleigh and Gaston in 1862. The 44-foot long coach had a baggage section in the middle, plus 32 coach seats and a coal stove at each end to heat the car in winter.
(SAL Photo/CSX Transportation)

(facing page) A SAL tavern-observation car on the rear of the *Silver Comet* is photographed at Washington Terminal.
(SAL Photo)

SILVER
COMET

(above) SAL coach No. 7 was 50 feet in length, weighed 44,350 lbs. and carried 58 passengers. It was built in 1890.

(left) This interior view of an SAL coach is typical of the company's accommodations for travelers in the early 1900s.

(below) SAL coach No. 405 is another "old timer" that was built prior to the formation of the company. It was sublettered "CC" for the Carolina Central Railroad.

(facing page, top) This gem is SAL combine car No. 101.
(Four SAL Photos/CSX Transportation)

(facing page, middle) Ventilated box-express car No. 748 was built by Pullman in 1945. These cars were painted Pullman green and were frequently found on the head end of Train Nos. 3 and 4.
(Bob's Photo Collection)

(facing page, bottom) Diagram of the SAL ventilated box-express car.
(W. E. Griffin, Jr. Collection)

SEABOARD AIR LINE
101

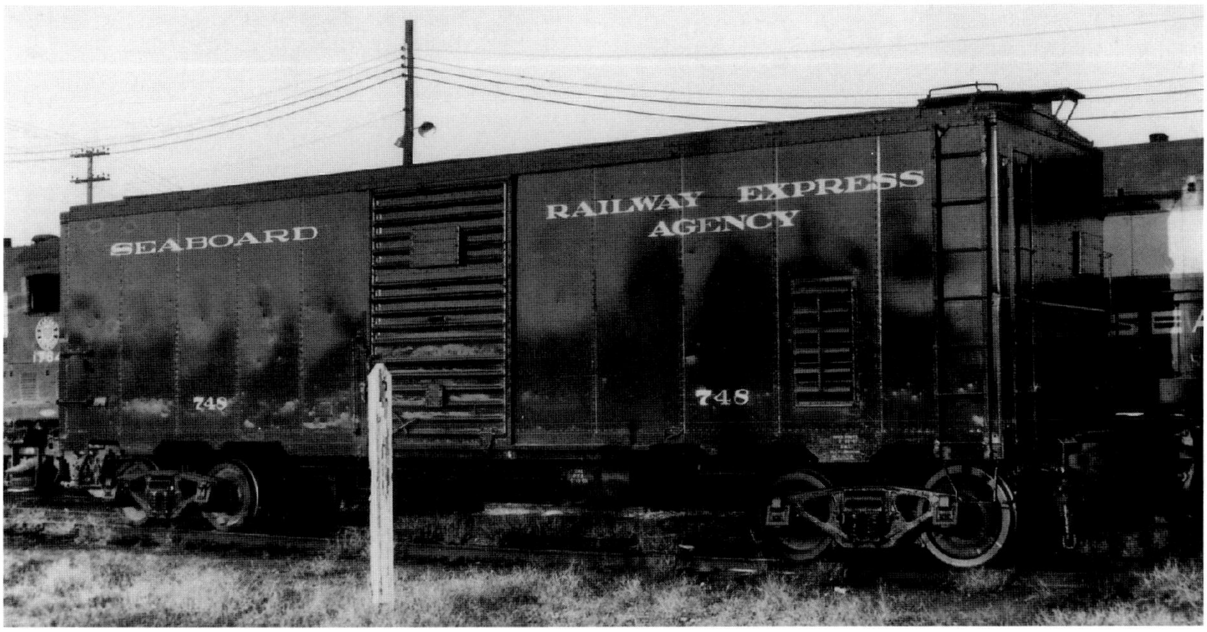
SEABOARD
RAILWAY EXPRESS
AGENCY
748
748

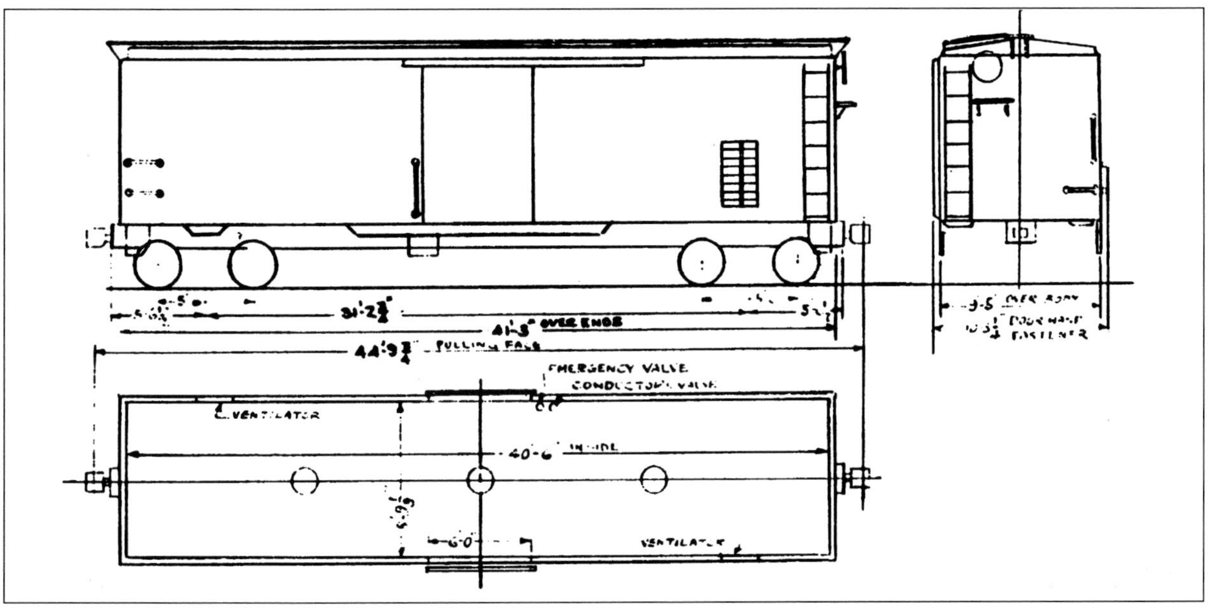
EMERGENCY VALVE
VENTILATOR
40'-6" INSIDE
6'-0"
VENTILATOR

SEABOARD
UNITED STATES MAIL
RAILWAY POST OFFICE
171
171

SEABOARD
UNITED STATES MAIL
RAILWAY POST OFFICE
157

SEABOARD

(facing page, top) Passenger and Mail Car No. 171 was built by Pullman in 1911.

(Smithsonian Institution)

(facing page, middle) Mail car No. 157 was built for the SAL by Pullman-Standard in 1913. It is shown at Richmond, Virginia

(SAL Photo)

(facing page, bottom) The Postal Clerk snares a mail bag "on the fly" from SAL Mail Car No. 153 as Train No. 3 rolls through Bracey, Virginia.

(Wiley M. Bryan)

(above) The interior of SAL mail car No. 157.

(SAL Photo)

(middle right) Express car No. 366 is seen at Washington Terminal in 1940. It was built in 1926 by Pullman.

(T. W. Dixon Jr. Collection)

(right) Combination Passenger and Baggage car No. 280 was built by AC&F in 1926. The 280 was equipped with deluxe seats.

(Bob's Photo Collection)

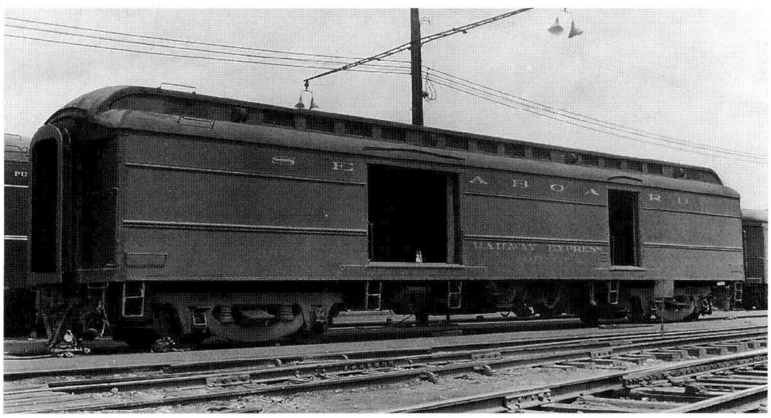

(above) SAL heavyweight Passenger Coach No. 821 was built by AC&F in 1926 and was later equipped with deluxe seats.
(Smithsonian Institution)

(below) PC10 class "American Flyer" Passenger Coach No. 830 was built by Pullman in 1936 and is here seen at Richmond, Virginia , in the late 1960s.
(Railroad Avenue Enterprises)

(bottom) PC10 class "American Flyer" Passenger Coach No. 832 in its unique semi-streamlined condition as delivered by Pullman makes up part of the consist of the *Orange Blossom Special* at Raleigh, N.C.
(Henry L. Kitchen)

(above) An "American Flyer" combination baggage/coach car and passenger coach are the first two cars on the SAL's Diesel Exhibition Tour Train behind E4 diesel set Nos. 3000-3100-3001 as the train heads north over the tracks of the Pennsylvania Railroad in Washington, D.C., en route to New York City's Pennsylvania Station in December 1938.

(W. E. Griffin, Jr. Collection)

(below) The public was invited to tour the new "American Flyer" lightweight passenger coaches that were carried on the head end of the Diesel Exhibition Tour Train.

(SAL Photo/CSX Transportation)

(above) DC8 class dining car No. 225, the *Lake Istokpoga*, was one of 19 *Lake* series diners delivered by Pullman in 1925-26.

(Smithsonian Institution)

Welcome

to delicious meals in the "Old South" manner

Seaboard dining cars are delightful settings for your choice of tempting menu selections. The service is friendly, and three meals cost as little as $4.40 . . . and if you really want to pamper yourself, try our charcoal-broiled steak dinner at only $4.75.

(below) Heavyweight Dining Car No. 1004 was built by Pullman in 1922.

(Smithsonian Institution)

(bottom) SAL kitchen crew members take a few minutes from their duties to pose outside heavyweight dining car No. 1004.

(SAL Photo)

(above) In 1947, SAL rebuilt and renovated a number of its dining cars at the company's Portsmouth passenger car shops for the winter travel season. In this interior view of one of the rebuilt diners, Steward W. A. Roberts is at right. From left to right are Waiters Chester Jones, Luther Cheatham, H. L. Thomas, L. H. Miller, Julius Frazier, and C. F. Hammond.

(SAL Photo/W. E. Griffin, Jr. Collection)

(below) Heavyweight Sleeper Car No. 1231, the *Bartlett Tower*, had 8 sections, 1 drawing room, and 3 double bedrooms. It is at Atlanta in April 1966.

(C. L. Goolsby Collection)

Seaboard's SILVER FLEET

(above) Lightweight baggage-dormitory car No. 6050 was built new for the SAL by Budd in 1947.

(W. E. Griffin, Jr. Collection)

(below) Lightweight baggage-dormitory car No. 6058, shown here on the *Silver Meteor*, was built by Budd in 1947 for the Florida East Coast Railroad as the *St. Johns River*. It was purchased by SAL from the FEC in 1965.

(C. L. Goolsby Collection)

(facing page, top) Lightweight passenger coach No. 6218 was purchased from Budd in 1947 and seated 52 passengers.

(SAL Photo)

(facing page, bottom) Interior view of lightweight coach No. 6218.

(SAL Photo)

SEABOARD
6218

SEABOARD
6238

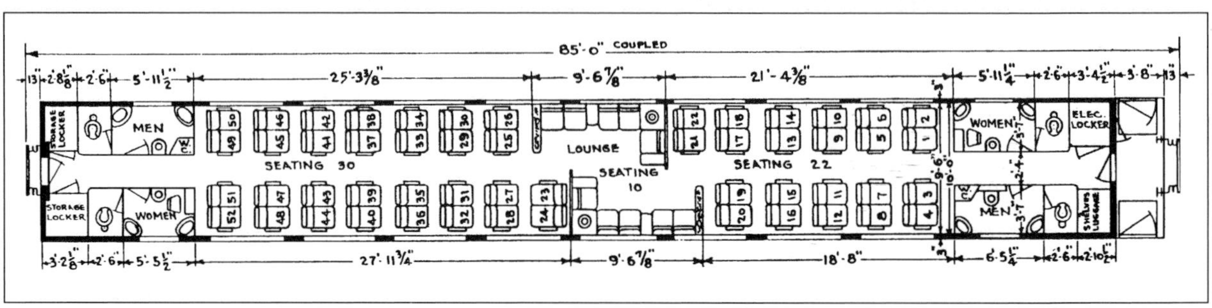
85'-0" COUPLED
13"
2'-8 1/8"
2'-6"
5'-11 1/2"
25'-3 3/8"
9'-6 7/8"
21'-4 3/8"
5'-11 1/4"
2'-6"
3'-4 1/2"
3'-8"
13"
STORAGE LOCKER
MEN
C.E.
WOMEN
STORAGE LOCKER
SEATING 30
LOUNGE
SEATING 10
SEATING 22
WOMEN
ELEC. LOCKER
MEN
C.E.
SHELVES LUGGAGE
9'-6"
10'-0"
3'-7"
2'-4"
3'-7"
3"
3"
3'-2 1/8"
2'-6"
5'-5 1/2"
27'-11 3/4"
9'-6 7/8"
18'-8"
6'-5 1/4"
2'-6"
2'-10 1/2"

(facing page, top) Lightweight coach-lounge car No. 6238 was built by Pullman-Standard in 1955. The car's interior length was 78'6" and it had a seating capacity of 62 passengers.
(Smithsonian Institution)

(facing page, middle and bottom) Interior view and floor plan diagram of coach-lounge car No. 6238.
(Smithsonian Institution/Diagram, W. E. Griffin, Jr. Collection)

(above) Lightweight 56-seat coach No. 6263 was purchased from Budd in 1946. The car's interior length was 78'2".
(Railroad Avenue Enterprises)

(below) Built by Budd in 1947 as the *Fort Matanzas*, the SAL acquired diner No. 6117 from FEC in 1965.
(C. L. Goolsby Collection)

An interior view of one of SAL's lightweight dining cars.
(SAL Photo/W. E. Griffin, Jr. Collection)

(above) Lightweight dining car No. 6120 was built by Pullman-Standard in 1950. It was photographed at Atlanta.
(C. L. Goolsby Collection)

(below) The porter prepares his sleeper car for departure from the station. Note the fluted roof on this car – a rarity for Pullman-Standard construction – specified by SAL to match its Budd-built equipment.
(SAL Photo)

PULLMANS *to the Sun*

(above) SAL sleeping car *Camden* had 4 roomettes, 1 compartment, 5 double bedrooms, and 4 sectons.

(SAL Photo)

(right) The interior of the SAL's luxurious six-double bedroom/ten-roomette sleeping cars embodied all the latest innovations in modern passenger train equipment and appointments.

(SAL Photo)

(below) SAL sleeping Car No. 42, the *West Palm Beach*, was built by Budd in 1949. This car had six double bedrooms and ten roomettes.

(W. E. Griffin, Jr. Collection)

SEABOARD
PALM BEACH

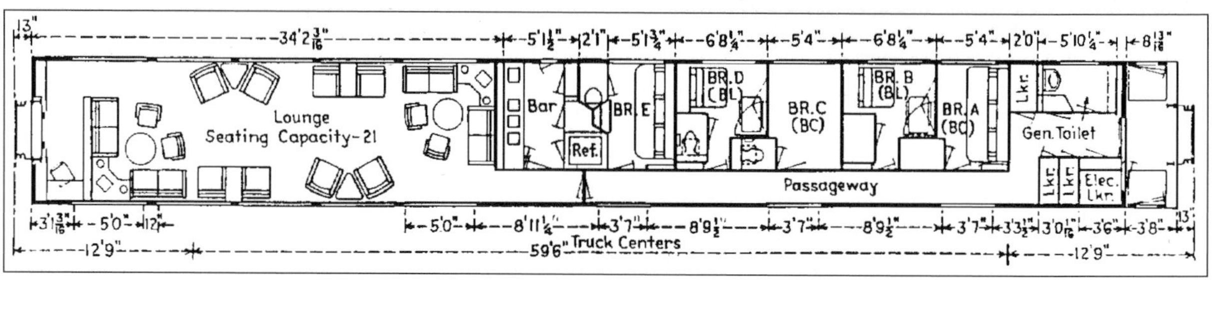
Lounge
Seating Capacity-21
Bar
Ref.
BR. E
BR. D (BL)
BR. C (BC)
BR. B (BL)
BR. A (BC)
Lkr.
Gen. Toilet
Passageway
Lkr.
Lkr.
Elec. Lkr.
Truck Centers
59'6"
12'9"
12'9"

(above) In 1956 Pullman-Standard built three distinctive sleeper-lounge cars with curved, tinted non-glare glass windows in the roofs of the lounge sections. Known as the *Sun Lounge* cars, they were named the *Miami Beach, Hollywood Beach,* and *Palm Beach* and their interiors were designed with the thought of capturing a true Florida resort atmosphere. This is a builder's view of the *Palm Beach.*

(W. E. Griffin, Jr. Collection)

(facing page) Interior view of lounge section of a *Sun Lounge* car looking toward the rear of the car.

(W. E. Griffin, Jr. Collection)

(above) Coach-observation car No. 6400 was built for the SAL by Budd in 1939 and was rebuilt in 1943. It seated 48 passengers in the coach section and 20 in the observation section.

(W. E. Griffin, Jr. Collection)

(facing page, top) Interior view of a Budd-built *Silver Meteor* observation car.

(SAL Photo)

(facing page, bottom) An interior view of the tavern section of one of the SAL tavern-observation cars.

(SAL Photo)

(above) Tavern-observation car No. 6604 was built by Budd in 1947. It seated 24 passengers in the observation section and 34 in the tavern. This view of the car was taken at Miami, Florida.

(Railroad Avenue Enterprises)

(right) In the 1960s, the SAL added diaphragms to three Budd-built tavern-observation cars to permit mid-train operation. Here one of these cars brings up the rear of the *Silver Star* as it operates over the RF&P in March 1962.

(W. E. Griffin, Jr.)

(below) Diagram of an SAL tavern-observation car.

(W. E. Griffin, Jr. Collection)

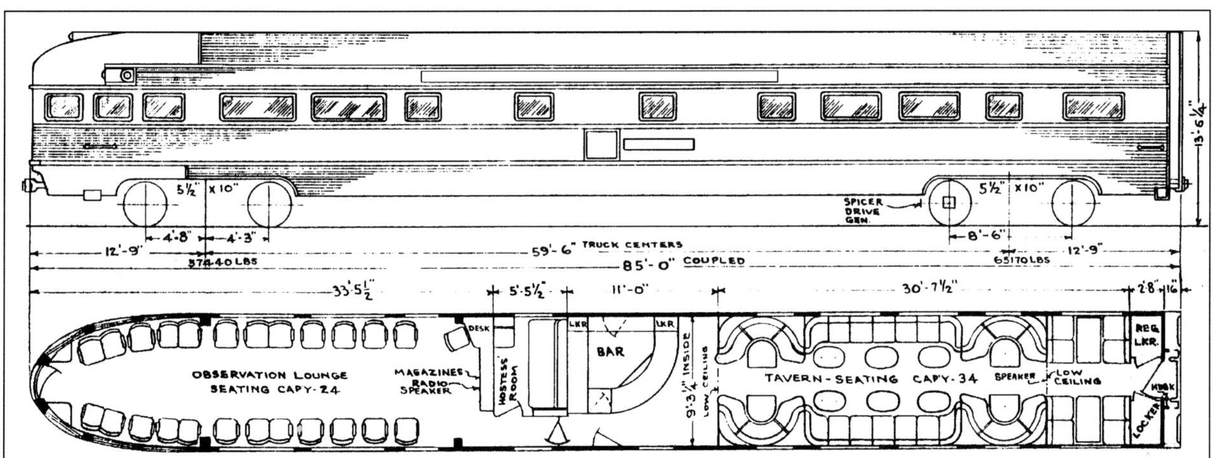

SEABOARD AIR LINE RAILROAD CO.

Cars marked "Seaboard" unless otherwise indicated in column headed "Markings and Kind of Cars."

Send reports of passenger train cars interchanged and address correspondence regarding passenger train car mileage or per diem statements to C. H. Crumpler, General Superintendent Transportation, Richmond, Va.

The passenger train cars of this Company are numbered and classified as follows:

A. A. R. Mech. Desig.	Markings and Kind of Cars	Car Numbers or Names	Seating Cap'y	Length of Comp't Bag. or Exp. ft.	Length of Comp't Mail ft.	Length of Car Inside ft.	Length of Car Inside in.	Length of Car Over Buffer ft.	Length of Car Over Buffer in.	Rate Mileage	Rate Per Diem	No. of Cars
	Note X											
PV..e	Business, Steel, Note AC②	Jacksonville	...	...	...	74	1	84	1	......	......	1
PV..o	Business, Steel, Note AC②	Norfolk	...	...	...	74	2	84	..	......	......	1
PV..e	Business, Steel Under-frame..Note AC③	Raleigh	...	...	...	72	..	81	2	......	......	1
PV..e	Business, Steel, Note AC②	Richmond	...	...	...	71	8	82	..	......	......	1
PV..e	Business, Steel, Note AC③	Savannah	...	...	...	68	1	79	3	......	......	1
PV..e	Business, Steel, Note AC③	Southland	...	...	...	75	1	83	5	......	......	1
PV..e	Business, Steel Under-frame..Note AC③	Tampa	...	...	...	61	2	71	5	......	......	1
PV..e	Business, Steel, Note AC③	Virginia	...	...	...	73	4	83	5	......	......	1
PV..e	Business, Steel, Note AC②	Birmingham	...	...	...	72	10	82	7	......	......	1
BLF..	Special Flat, Twin Van Body, FLEXI-VAN Service.......Note H	1, 2	...	...	...	...	...	86	9	......	......	2
MB..e	Bagg. & Mail, Steel (See Exceptions)	80 to 90	...	39	30	69	4	73	3	.162	$25.65	7
BE...e	Baggage & Express, Steel Exception	84	...	...	...	69	4	73	3	.086	16.15	1
MB..e	Bagg. & Mail, Steel	96, 97	...	40	30	70	..	74	2	.162	25.65	2
MB..e	" " "	98, 99	...	55	15	70	..	74	2	.162	25.65	2
MB..e	" " "	100 to 111	...	40	30	70	..	74	2	.162	25.65	12
MB..e	" " "	112, 113	...	55	15	70	..	74	2	.162	25.65	2
MA..e	Postal, Steel.......	150 to 156	...	...	...	60	..	64	..	.133	21.85	6
MA..e	" "	157	...	...	...	60	..	73	3	.162	25.65	1
MB..e	Mail & Bagg., Steel	171	...	35	30	65	6	69	5	.133	21.85	1
MB..e	" " "	172, 173	...	35	30	65	6	69	5	.133	21.85	2
CSB..e	Baggage-Dormitory, All Steel...Note AC①	180	...	30	...	76	7	83	8	.191	35.15	1
CSB..e	Baggage-Dormitory, All Steel...Note AC②	183	...	30	...	76	7	83	8	.175	29.95	1
CSB..e	Baggage-Dormitory, All Steel...Note AC①	184	...	30	...	76	7	83	8	.191	35.15	1
CSB..e	Baggage-Dormitory, All Steel. Note AC①	185, 186	...	32	...	77	7	84	8	.191	35.15	2
CSB..e	Baggage-Dormitory, All Steel...Note AC①	187	...	31	...	77	7	84	8	.191	35.15	1
DA..e	Dining, Steel. Notes A, AC①	225 to 243	A	...	...	75	8	82	1	.191	35.15	8
CA..e	Comb. Bagg. & Pass., Steel Note AC①	265	32	29	...	78	1	79	10	.191	35.15	1
CA...e	Comb. Baggage & Pass., Steel..Notes A, AC①	271 to 282	A	30	...	73	2	79	8	.191	35.15	12
CA...e	Comb. Bagg. & Pass., Steel	283	34	30	...	69	3	76	4	.162	25.65	1
CA...e	Comb. Baggage & Pass., Steel...Note AC①	285 to 288	48	27	...	77	5	84	7	.191	35.15	4
BEM.e	Baggage Express, Steel..	300 to 335	...	...	...	69	4	74	..	.086	16.15	34
BEM.e	" " " ..	336 to 341	...	...	...	70	..	74	..	.086	16.15	6
BEM.e	" " " ..	342 to 347	...	...	...	71	9	78	1	.086	16.15	6
BEM.e	" " " ..	349	...	...	...	72	10	82	5	.086	16.15	1
BEM.e	" " " ..	350	...	...	...	78	8	82	1	.086	16.15	1
BEM.e	" " " ..	352	...	...	...	69	8	80	4	.086	16.15	1
BEM.e	" " " ..	353	...	...	...	73	2	79	10	.086	16.15	1
BEM.e	" " " ..	354, 355	...	...	...	69	4	73	3	.086	16.15	2
BEM.e	Bagg. & Express, Steel....	360 to 391	...	...	...	60	..	63	4	.067	13.30	31
BEM.e	" " "	392	...	...	...	72	10	82	5	.086	16.15	1
BEM.e	" " "	393 to 395	...	...	...	69	11	74	2	.086	16.15	3
BEM.e	" " "	432, 433	...	...	...	62	3	66	4	.067	13.30	2
PB...e	Coach, Steel. Note AC①	575	66	...	...	69	4	78	2	.191	35.15	1
PB...e	" " Notes A, AC①	583 to 589	A	...	...	71	8	81	..	.191	35.15	3
PB..e	" Steel. Note AC①	594	68	...	...	71	8	81	..	.191	35.15	1
PB...e	" " Note AC①	598	68	...	...	71	8	81	..	.191	35.15	1
BX....	Box, Express, Steel.	700 to 754	...	...	...	40	6	44	..	.048	9.50	54
PB...e	Coach, Steel...... Notes A, AC①	807 to 826	A	...	...	71	8	81	1	.191	35.15	20
PB...e	" Steel. Note AC①	830 to 835	76	...	...	74	3	84	7	.191	35.15	6
PB...e	" " Note AC①	840, 841	54	...	...	70	..	79	3	.191	35.15	2
PB...e	" " Note AC①	842 to 845	58	...	...	70	..	79	3	.191	35.15	4
PB...e	" " Note AC①	846 to 848	45	...	...	70	..	79	3	.191	35.15	3
......e	Coach-Grill, Steel Note AC①	849	18	...	...	70	..	79	3	.191	35.15	1
PB...e	Coach, Steel..Note AC①	850	64	...	...	70	..	79	3	.191	35.15	1
PB...e	" " Note AC①	851 to 857	58	...	...	70	..	79	3	.191	35.15	7
......e	Coach-Grill, Steel Note AC①	858	18	...	...	70	..	79	3	.191	35.15	1
PB...e	Coach, Steel..Note AC①	859	45	...	...	70	..	79	3	.191	35.15	1
	Note X											
DA..e	Dining, Steel. Note AC①	1008, 1009	36	...	...	75	8	81	5	.191	$35.15	2
PS...e	Sleeper, Steel. Notes T, AC①	1201	...	...	...	75	7	82	6	.191	35.15	1
PS...e	Sleeper, Steel, Notes T, AC①	1202	...	...	...	77	7	84	6	.191	35.15	1
PS...e	Sleeper, Steel, Notes U. AC①	1233	...	...	...	73	10	83	6	.191	35.15	1
PS...e	Sleeper, Steel. Notes S, AC①	1253 to 1260	...	...	...	72	10	82	5	.191	35.15	7
PS...e	Sleepers, Steel..Notes B, AC①	1270 to 1273	...	...	...	74	8	82	7	.191	35.15	4
BH..e	Horse, Express, Steel	1300 to 1313	...	...	...	74	..	77	8	.086	16.15	12
ED..e	Oil-Electric Motor, Steel..	2028	...	33	15	...	...	75	1	......	......	1
CSP..e	Comb. Baggage & Pass., Steel...Note AC①	6004, 6005	18	22	...	78+		85	..	.191	35.15	2
CSB..e	Baggage-Dormitory, Stl. Note AC①	6050 to 6056	...	27	...	78	..	85	..	.191	35.15	7
DA..e	Dining, Steel, Note AC①	6100 to 6105	48	...	...	82	..	84	8	.191	35.15	6
DA..e	" " Note AC①	6106 to 6114	48	...	...	81	..	85	..	.191	35.15	9
PB...e	Coach, Steel, Note AC①	6200 to 6207	60	...	...	78	..	84	8	.191	35.15	8
PB...e	" Steel. Note AC①	6208 to 6214	56	...	...	78	..	85	..	.191	35.15	7
PB...e	" Steel. Note AC①	6215 to 6226	52	...	...	78	..	85	..	.191	35.15	12
PB...e	" Steel, Note AC①	6227 to 6231	50	...	...	78	4	85	..	.191	35.15	5
PB...e	Coach-Lounge, Steel. Note AC①	6232 to 6234	44	...	...	78	4	85	..	.191	35.15	3
PB...e	Coach-Lounge, Steel. Note AC①	6235 to 6241	62	...	...	78	6	85	..	.191	35.15	7
PB...e	Coach, Steel, Note AC①	6242 to 6251	52	...	...	78	6	85	..	.191	35.15	10
......e	Coach-Tavern, Steel. Note AC①	6300	60	...	...	78	..	84	8	.191	35.15	1
......e	Coach-Tavern, Steel. Note AC①	6301, 6302	60	...	...	78	..	85	..	.191	35.15	2
PBO.e	Coach, Observation, Steel Note AC①	6400	68	...	...	83	..	84	10	.191	35.15	1
PBO.e	Coach, Observation, Steel Note AC①	6401, 6402	72	...	...	83	..	85	..	.191	35.15	2
PO...e	Coach, Observation, Steel Note AC①	6500 to 6502	54	...	...	82	..	85	..	.191	35.15	3
......e	Tavern-Observation, Steel...Note AC①	6600 to 6605	58	...	...	82	..	85	..	.191	35.15	6
PS...e	Sleepers, Steel..Notes C, D, Z, AC①	Note D	D	...	...	78	5	85	..	......	......	3
PS...e	Sleepers, Steel..Notes C, E, Z, AC①	Note E	E	...	...	78	6	85	..	......	......	13
PS...e	Sleepers, Steel..Notes C, F, Z, AC①	Note F	F	...	...	78	3	85	..	......	......	6
PS...e	Sleepers, Steel..Notes G, Z, AC①	Clover Harvest	G	...	...	75	7	82	6	......	......	1
PS...e	Sleepers, Steel..Notes J, Z, AC①	Note J	J	...	...	75	7	82	6	......	......	4
PS...e	Sleepers, Steel..Notes K, Z, AC①	Note K	K	...	...	76	7	83	6	......	......	3
PS...e	Sleepers, Steel..Notes L, Z, AC①	Note L	L	...	...	73	10	83	6	......	......	5
PS...e	Sleepers, Steel..Notes M, Z, AC①	Note M	M	...	...	72	10	82	5	......	......	4
PS...e	Sleepers, Steel..Notes C, N, Z, AC①	Note N	N	...	...	78	6	85	..	......	......	6
PS...e	Sleepers, Steel..Notes C, P, Z, AC①	Note P	P	...	...	78	6	85	..	......	......	6
PS...e	Sleepers, Steel..Notes C, Q, Z, AC①	Note Q	Q	...	...	78	6	85	..	......	......	3
PS...e	Sleepers, Steel..Notes C, R, Z, AC①	Note R	R	...	...	78	6	85	..	......	......	3
	Total......											451

Note A—The seating capacities of cars in series 225 to 243, 271 to 282, 583 to 589 and 807 to 826 are as follows:

Car Numbers	Seating Capacity	Car Numbers	Seating Capacity	Car Numbers	Seating Capacity
225 to 227	36	589	68	817	68
229	36	807	68	818	74
237	48	808	48	819	48
240, 241	36	809	68	820	70
243	36	810	48	821	74
271 to 276	36	811	68	822	60
277, 278	38	812 to 814	48	823 to 825	74
279 to 282	36	815	68	826	64
583, 586	64	816	48		

Note B—Sleepers in series 1270 to 1273 have 10 Sections and Observation Lounge each.

Types of Air Conditioning indicated by following notes: AC① Electro-Mechanical; AC② Ice System; AC③ Waukesha; AC④ Steam Ejector.

Seaboard Air Line Railroad Co.—Continued.

Note C—The following cars in these series are streamlined:

Atlanta	Henderson	Ocala	Sarasota
Avon Park	Hialeah	Orlando	Savannah
Bay Pines	Hollywood Beach	Palm Beach	Sebring
Birmingham		Petersburg	Southern Pines
Boca Grande	Jacksonville	Pinehurst	Stone Mountain
Camden	Kennesaw Mountain	Portsmouth	Tallahassee
Cedartown		Raleigh	Tampa
Charlotte	Lake Wales	Red Mountain	Venice
Clearwater	Miami	Richmond	West Palm Beach
Columbia	Miami Beach	St. Petersburg	Winter Haven
Fort Lauderdale	Norfolk		

Note D—Individual names of Sleepers having 6 Double Bed Rooms, Lounge and Buffet:
Kennesaw Mountain   Red Mountain   Stone Mountain

Note E—Individual names of Sleepers having 6 Double Bed Rooms and 10 Single Bed Rooms; inside length 78 ft. 6 in.:

Atlanta	Jacksonville	Petersburg	Richmond
Birmingham	Norfolk	Portsmouth	Savannah
Charlotte	Orlando	Raleigh	Tampa
Columbia			

Note F—Individual names of Sleepers having 6 Double Bed Rooms and 10 Single Bed Rooms; inside length 78 ft. 3⅝ in.:

Lake Wales	St. Petersburg	West Palm Beach
Miami	Sarasota	Winter Haven

Note G—Named Sleeper "Clover Harvest" has 8 Sections and 5 Double Bed Rooms.

Note H—Cars numbered 1 and 2 are passenger equipped and have roller bearings. These cars are for handling storage mail on passenger trains.

Note J—Individual names of Sleepers having 6 Sections and 6 Double Bed Rooms; inside length 75 ft. 7½ in.:
Poplar Brook   Poplar Castle   Poplar City   Poplar Creek

Note K—Individual names of Sleepers having 6 Sections and 6 Double Bed Rooms; inside length 76 ft. 7½ in.:
Poplar Road   Poplar Run   Poplar Springs

Note L—Individual names of Sleepers having 8 Sections, 1 Drawing Room, 3 Double Bed Rooms:

Bartlett Tower	Pinnacle Tower	Weepers Tower
Chimes Tower	Siebers Tower	

Note M—Individual names of Sleepers having 10 Sections, 1 Drawing Room, 2 Compartments:

Lake Alexander	Lake Chicot	New Portage
Lake Borgne		

Note N—Individual names of Sleepers having 4 Roomettes, 1 Compartment, 5 Double Bedrooms and 4 Sections:

Bay Pines	Cedartown	Pinehurst
Camden	Henderson	Southern Pines

Note P—Individual names of Sleepers having 11 Double Bedrooms:

Avon Park	Ocala	Tallahassee
Hialeah	Sebring	Venice

Note Q—Individual names of Sleepers having 5 Double Bedrooms and 1 Lounge:
Hollywood Beach   Miami Beach   Palm Beach

Note R—Individual names of Sleepers having 5 Double Bedrooms, 2 Compartments and 2 Drawing Rooms:
Boca Grande   Clearwater   Fort Lauderdale

Note S—Cars in series 1253 to 1260 have 10 Sections, 1 Drawing Room, 2 Compartments.

Note T—Sleeping cars numbered 1201 and 1202 have 8 Sections and 5 Double Bedrooms.

Note U—Sleeping car numbered 1233 has 8 Sections, 1 Drawing Room, 3 Double Bedrooms.

Note X—The head end passenger train cars of this Company, except Box-Express cars in series 700 to 754 are equipped with small door each end to permit passage from one car to another.

Passenger carrying cars are equipped with vestibules. Generator equipment, toilet and washing facilities are as follows:

Electric generator, 1 flush toilet, 1 wash basin—
171 172 173 283

Electric generator, 2 flush toilets, 2 wash basins—

265	271	285	807	811	818	823	850	6400
	to	to		815	820	824		6401
	282	288	809	817	821	825	859	6402

Electric generator, 2 flush toilets, 3 wash basins—
575 589

Electric generator, 3 flush toilets, 4 wash basins—
583 586

Electric generator, 4 flush toilets, 4 wash basins—
594 808 812 814 819 826 6004 6005
598 810 813 816 822

Electric generator, 2 flush toilets, 4 wash basins—
830 to 835 6200 to 6202

Electric generator, 2 flush toilets, 2 wash basins, 2 dental lavatories—
840 to 848 851 to 857

Electric generator, 3 flush toilets, 3 wash basins—
849 858 6300 6301 6302 6500 6501 6502

Electric generator, 2 flush toilets, 5 wash basins—
6203 to 6207

Electric generator, 4 flush toilets, 6 wash basins—
6208 to 6214

Electric generator, 4 flush toilets, 6 wash basins, 4 dental bowls—
6215 to 6226

Electric generator, 2 flush toilets, 1 urinal, 4 wash basins, 2 dental bowls—
6227 to 6234

Electric generator, 4 flush toilets, 8 wash basins, 4 dental bowls—
6235 to 6241

Electric generator, 3 flush toilets, 4 wash basins, 2 dental bowls—
6242 to 6251

Note Z—Named cars in these series are leased to the Pullman Co. All mileage reports and charges incurred incident to repairs and operation should be made to the Pullman Co., Chicago, Ill.

(*Mar., 1963*)

SAL Train No. 34, the northbound *Silver Comet*, passes over tracks shared by the Southern and Central of Georgia railroads at Weems, Alabama, on April 4, 1948. One of the Seaboard's classic Budd-built observations cars carries the drumhead.
(F. E. Ardrey, Jr.)

Chapter 6

Freight Service

As late as May of 1948, watermelons were still being shipped in ventilated boxcars. Here the melons are being loaded onto SAL ventilated boxcar No. 79972 at Summerfield, Florida.
(SAL Photo)

The Seaboard's tracks extended from Richmond and Norfolk-Portsmouth on the north, through Virginia, North and South Carolina, Georgia, Alabama, and Florida. It served the capital city of each of those six states, their principal cities and resorts, connecting them with the balance of the nation and the world. The Seaboard Air Line also served all important ports of the South Atlantic states, including Norfolk, Wilmington, Charleston, and Savannah.

However, the Seaboard's 4,150-mile system was closely paralleled by other rail carriers, principally the Southern Railway and the Atlantic Coast Line Railroad. Like its two

rivals, the Seaboard was essentially a north-south carrier and was forced to compete each day for its share of the commerce moving between the Northeast and Florida along the Atlantic Seaboard.

Burdened since the 1920s with a heavy debt structure and operating a single-track railroad system that was inferior to the double-track physical plant of its principal competitors, the Seaboard found itself forever cast in the role of the underdog. To survive it had to be more innovative and offer better service. In its freight operations, SAL was the first railroad in the Southeast to adopt diesel power, install Centralized Traffic Control, and employ a full time industrial forester. The Seaboard was also one of the first railroads to offer through trailer-on-flatcar (TOFC) service to the Northeast.

On its southbound trains, the Seaboard brought the diverse products of the Northeast's manufacturing centers to the Southeastern states. Aboard its northbound trains moved the mining and agricultural products and manufactured goods of the developing South.

During the steam era, manufacturing and miscellaneous traffic made up approximately 34 per cent of the traffic mix, with forest

(above) The SAL's perishable traffic originated in Central Florida and, in the early years, fruits and vegetables were shipped in ventilated boxcars such as No. 27699 that was built for the SAL in 1914.

(C. L. Goolsby Collection)

(left) Watermelons being loaded onto SAL ventilated boxcar No. 83409 at Sumter County, Georgia, in 1929.

(W. E. Griffin, Jr. Collection)

(facing page) By 1920, the Fruit Growers Express Company was organized to supply railroads with refrigerator and ventilated type cars. The refrigerator cars were equipped with ice bunkers to cool the fruit and vegetables during the trip to market. These cars had to be re-iced a various points en route. Here, refrigerator cars are being iced on the SAL at Baldwin, Florida, in December 1947.

(SAL Photo)

products comprising 20 per cent, products of mines 14 per cent, and agricultural products roughly 10 per cent. This traffic mix changed over the years and by the diesel era, transportation of mineral products had easily become the Seaboard's chief commodity.

The transportation of fresh fruits and vegetables to Northern markets provided the Seaboard with one of its earliest sources of through traffic. Strawberries, melons, and vegetables from the coasts of the Carolinas and fresh vegetables and citrus fruits from the winter gardens of Florida produced a valuable source of revenue during the winter and early spring. Assembled at points such as Winter Garden, Zellwood, Orlando, Clearwater, Lake Wales, and Plant City, the Florida perishables were loaded onto special ventilated and insulated box cars for shipment on fast unit trains. Until the advent of mechanically refrigerated box cars in the 1950s, it was essential that these older ventilated cars be re-iced at various points along the route to maintain each load's required temperature.

While the perishable traffic was an important source of revenue for the Seaboard, it was a seasonal business at best and always subject to favorable yield and market conditions. Often the carloads of perishables were simply waybilled to the RF&P's Potomac Yard at Alexandria, Virginia, where they were held for diversion or reconsignment. Beginning in the early 1930s, the Seaboard's citrus fruit traffic from Florida was greatly diminished by competition from water and highway carriers. Much of this traffic was lost to the Seaboard until the outbreak of World War II, when the menace of enemy submarines along the Atlantic coast caused the diversion to rail of a large volume of import and export traffic that normally would have been handled via coastal shipping to the North Atlantic ports.

Much of the perishable traffic was again lost by the railroad to the highway motor carriers and the refrigerated steamship lines with the end of the war.

As the South transformed itself from an agrarian to an industrial economy, the Seaboard established an industrial relations department that was successful in locating important traffic-producing industries along its line. A separate agricultural department helped the Seaboard to overcome the losses in the shipment of staples such as cotton and tobacco by promoting forestry and establishing pulp and paper companies as well as other wood-using industries along its lines.

By the 1920s the six Southeastern states served by the Seaboard possessed the greatest untapped reservoir of pine and hardwoods in the nation. The forest areas of Georgia and Florida alone possessed over 36 million acres and the growth rate of the Southern pine – a yard a year in height – was unmatched anywhere. The Seaboard employed professional foresters and industrial agents to promote reforestation and the relocation of the pulp industry to the South. In less than two decades, the number of pulp-board and paper mills in the South doubled. The Seaboard was rewarded for its efforts when plants located on its line at points such as Franklin, Virginia, Charleston and Georgetown, South Carolina, Savannah, Georgia, and Fernandina, Florida.

Of particular importance to the Seaboard was the revenue derived from the conveyance of mining products. Clay, stone, sand and gravel moved from various points on the line and coal was routed to the Southeast from the Chesapeake & Ohio mine fields via the Seaboard's connection with the Clinchfield at Bostic Yard near Rutherfordton, North Carolina. Iron ore, sheet, and structural iron originated at Birmingham, Alabama, and were shipped by way of the Atlanta Division.

(facing page) Forest products, especially shipments of pulpwood, were hauled in great quantities by SAL. Pulpwood was loaded from truck to railcar at many small towns located along the Seaboard Air Line.

(W. E. Griffin, Jr. Collection)

(above) Dry phosphate is loaded into SAL covered hoppers at the Coronet Phosphate Company, Coronet, Florida, in January 1947.

(SAL Photo by William Rittase/W. E. Griffin, Jr. Collection)

The Seaboard also enjoyed significant revenues from the steady growth in the transportation of phosphate minerals from the mines of South Florida. Used in the production of fertilizer, ammunition, and diverse products, dry phosphate (hard rock) was mined at Dunnellon and Arcadia, Fla., while wet phosphate (pebbles of mineral slurried to remove impurities) was mined in the so-called Bone Valley in the vicinity of Mulberry and Bartow, Florida. The Seaboard primarily moved both wet and dry phosphate in short hauls from the mines to Florida processing plants or to the Seddon Island docks at Tampa or via the former Charlotte Harbor & Northern line to Port Boca Grande. The Seaboard also shared in its division of the line haul revenues secured from the shipments of fertilizer to other points in the nation and Canada.

As was the case with the majority of American railroads, the volume of freight traffic handled by the Seaboard reached its peak during the Second World War. The discontinuance in early 1942 of coastal and intercoastal steamship service diverted large volumes of traffic, including sugar, petroleum and perishables, to all-rail routes. The early years of the war also saw the establishment of

(above) The phosphate industry was of great important to the SAL, with the majority of this traffic originating in the Bone Valley area east of Tampa, Florida. These 100-ton phosphate hoppers are at Yeoman Yard in Tampa on May 21, 1966.
(SAL Photo/W. E. Griffin, Jr. Collection)

(below) The SAL also transported gravel and rock from various quarries located along the system. Most SAL ballast was mined at the Greystone, N.C., quarry. In this view, a Q-3 Mike awaits the loading of ballast into gondolas at Greystone.
(H. Alan Paul Collection)

many new and the expansion of some existing military installations in the territory served by the Seaboard, resulting in the movement of large quantities of construction materials and supplies. Throughout the war years, the Seaboard also handled large increases in steel and other materials for shipbuilding, critical war materials, and Lend-Lease traffic.

By 1943 the Seaboard was operating a daily average of 261 freight trains (as well as a record number of passenger and troop trains) and although the increased revenues of these busy years expedited the company's return to profitability, it also stretched the capacity of its single-track railroad to the limits. The wear sustained by the Seaboard's aging roster of steam locomotives during the war hastened the conversion to diesel power, and a series of train accidents in 1942 led to the installation of block signals and centralized traffic control (CTC).

The Seaboard emerged from the war a much improved railroad. Between 1946 and 1950, the entire main line was equipped with CTC and automatic signals. The motive power fleet was completely dieselized by the early 1950s. The installation of these and other safety features allowed the Seaboard to increase the speed of its trains, eventually enabling it to offer the fastest freight schedules in the country.

Except for traffic originating or terminating at Portsmouth, Va., the Seaboard's north-south through traffic was classified and blocked at the RF&P's Potomac Yard in Alexandria, Va. Through SAL freight trains operated between Richmond, Va. and Washington, D.C., over the RF&P gave the SAL a gateway for its traffic into the Northeast in competition with other Southern railroads.

This through traffic was interchanged between the SAL and RF&P at Richmond, VA., with all transfer work performed by SAL yard crews assigned to SAL's Hermitage Yard. The SAL yard crews delivered northbound trains from Hermitage Yard to any available empty track at RF&P's Acca Yard, which adjoined Hermitage Yard to the north. Southbound trains destined for delivery to the SAL were yarded on designated interchange tracks in Acca Yard by RF&P road crews and were subsequently pulled to Hermitage Yard by SAL yard crews. When whole trains were moved intact, the yard crews often double-headed F-7 Class 0-6-0s and during the busy years of the Second World War, F-9 0-8-0s were utilized in transfer service. During the diesel era, 1200-horsepower Baldwin RS12s were assigned to Hermitage for transfer work and other heavy switching duties.

Some of the SAL's premier freight trains moved via Hemitage Yard to the Potomac Yard gateway. In the steam era these included No. 86, *The Red Fox*, the fast Florida perishable train; No. 87, *The Migrator*; No. 89, *The Capitol*; No. 88, *The Ironmaster*, between Hermitage and Hamlet, NC; and, No. 80, *The Marketer* between Hermitage and Hialeah. In the diesel era, the principal trains were No. 27, spelled during this period as both *The Capital* and *The Capitol*; No. 75, *The Merchandiser*; No. 82, *The Courier*; No. 88, *The Ironmaster*; Through Freight 280 and the TOFC Special TT-23, sometimes referred to as *The Razorback*.

Hermitage Yard was the northern terminal of the Seaboard and continuous yard service was maintained at that facility. In addition to the transfer work, Hermitage yard crews also assembled and broke up SAL road trains and performed industrial switching for traffic brought to the yard by the numerous SAL road switcher assignments that operated out of Hermitage to Bellwood, Hopewell, and Alberta (which until the 1959 merger of the Virginian and Norfolk & Western was the SAL's interchange point for traffic with the Virginian Railway). Interchange with the C&O was accomplished at the SAL's Brown Street Yard, located just north of Main Street Station in Richmond, and with the N&W and ACL at Petersburg, Virginia.

About ninety-eight miles south of Hermitage, the SAL's line from Richmond reached Norlina, N.C., the important junction point with the SAL's line to Portsmouth, Virginia. The line from Norlina extended in a north-easterly direction for approximately 115 miles through Weldon, N.C., and Boykins and Suffolk, Va., to the Portsmouth yard (known as Shops). A portion of the right-of-

(above) Due to their power and equal distribution of weight, the SAL favored Decapods, such as D-class No. 519, for service on lines with light track and bridge loadings.
(Railroad Avenue Enterprises)

(below) D-class 2-10-0 No. 507 assaults the grade with a freight train near Macon, Ga., on the Macon, Dublin and Savannah line on May 22, 1946.
(Jay Williams Collection)

(facing page, top) Doubleheading Class D Decapods Nos. 516 and 507 make about 20 m.p.h. up the grade into Pitts, Georgia, with eastbound through freight No. 82 on September 6, 1947.

(facing page, bottom) Both locomotives darken the sky with smoke as eastbound through freight No. 82 rolls by just east of Penia, Ga. Class D3 No. 533 and Class D No. 502 Decapods have charge of the train on the morning of September 30, 1947.
(Both, David W. Salter)

516

533

way on this line was built by the Portsmouth and Roanoke Railroad, the oldest predecessor company of the Seaboard Air Line. During various periods of the SAL's history, important locomotive and car shops, as well as a division of the corporate offices, were located at Portsmouth. Until 1958 the SAL's corporate headquarters building was located in Norfolk at the corner of Plume and Granby streets. The SAL also maintained a fleet of seven barges and a tug boat in Norfolk harbor which moved freight shipments to and from the railroad's three large terminal warehouse piers located on the Portsmouth side of the Elizabeth River, not far from the downtown Portsmouth train station.

During the steam era, the "Red Ball" trains on the Portsmouth Subdivision were No. 85, *The Merchandiser* and No. 82, *The Courier*, both of which operated between Portsmouth and Birmingham via Hamlet, N.C. Two through freights operated between Portsmouth and North Carolina were No. 79, *The Governor* and No. 72, *The Textiler*. No. 85, no longer known as *The Merchandiser*, and No. 82, *The Courier*, remained as the principal trains on this line during the diesel era.

The 150 miles of railroad south of Norlina to Hamlet, N.C., provided the heaviest concentration of traffic on the whole system. With no alternate route available, all SAL trains to or from Richmond and Portsmouth operated over the same line to Hamlet via Raleigh. It was a busy segment of track on a predominantly single-track section of railroad. The only section of double-track on this line was the SAL/Southern Railway joint trackage arrangement between Raleigh and Cary (Fetner). A significant branch line to Durham and Oxford, N.C., diverged from the main line about 40 miles north of Raleigh at Henderson, N.C. The light rail and bridge loading restrictions on the Durham Branch dictated that the 2-10-0 Decapods and RSC six-axle Alco road switchers be used on that line.

About 100 miles south of Raleigh, the central hub of the entire Seaboard system was located at the little town of Hamlet, N.C. During the steam era the Hamlet freight yard had a capacity of nearly 3,000 cars, exclusive of running and service tracks. North of the main yard and contiguous to the northbound freight main line were located the largest ice manufacturing plant on the railroad, icing platforms, and tracks for the icing of perishable traffic. Hamlet was also a principal transfer point for less-than-carload traffic. A freight transfer station was located to the west of the main line opposite the main yard.

(below) Rolling an eastbound freight train of 41 cars at White House, Florida, on October 12, 1929 is P-1 class 4-6-2 No. 826. (Otto Perry Photo/Denver Public Library – Western History Department Collection)

(right) Decapod No. 515 moves its train through Durham, N.C., on April 4, 1949.

(R. B. Carneal)

(below) Just getting underway from Wadesboro, N.C., on the line between Hamlet and Charlotte, N.C., SAL freight train Extra 418 East is doubleheading with Q-3 2-8-2 No. 418 and M-2 4-8-2 No. 249 on August 12, 1947.

(H. Reid)

The convergence and divergence of SAL routes to and from Hamlet made it a major point for the consolidation and distribution of traffic to and from the various lines. In 1953, the SAL began construction of a new retarder-equipped classification yard at Hamlet. The new yard, dedicated on January 31, 1955, was built at a cost of 8-1/2 million dollars and at the time was the most modern freight car classification yard in the South. The new yard also contained facilities for the repair and servicing of diesel locomotives.

At Hamlet, freight traffic converged and diverged from five main lines and three operating divisions. From the north came the traffic from Raleigh, Portsmouth-Norfolk, and Richmond via the Virginia Division. Tracks of the Virginia Division's Wilmington Subdivision came from the east and included a 79-mile section of tangent track that is said to be the nation's longest. Through freights Nos. 77 and 78 plied this line between Hamlet and the port of Wilmington, N.C.

From the west came the traffic of the 500-mile line from Birmingham via Monroe, N.C., and Atlanta. An important branch extended 160 miles to the northwest from Monroe to Charlotte and Rutherfordton, N.C. During the steam era, No. 85 *The Merchandiser*, No. 89 *The Capitol*, No. 82

The Courier and No. 88 *The Ironmaster* operated between Hamlet and Birmingham. Through freights Nos. 91 and 92 operated between Charlotte and Bostic Yard, just east of Rutherfordton, where interchange was made with the Clinchfield Railroad. During the diesel era, the principal trains on this line included No. 27 *The Capital* from Birmingham to Hamlet, No. 28 *The Courier* from Atlanta to Hamlet, No. 88 *The Ironmaster* from Birmingham to Atlanta, No. 89 *The Tar Heel* from Hamlet to Bostic, and numerous through freights.

South of Hamlet were two main line routes to Savannah. Running east out of Hamlet and then south through Charleston to Savannah was the 260-mile stretch of low-grade trunk line known as the "East Coast Line." This was the principal SAL freight route over which perishable trains from Florida and other high-speed and tonnage freights were operated. The western route, known as the "Columbia Line," was a 248-mile line that headed southwest from Hamlet straight to Columbia, S.C., and then turned south to Savannah. This was the line used by the SAL's through passenger trains between New York and Florida.

SAL Virginia Division freight train Extra 430 South is in the pass track at Grandy, Virginia, in the summer of 1943 giving Fireman Wiley M. Bryan an opportunity to photograph his train. Motive power is Q-3 Mikado No. 430, equipped with an Elvin "paddle type" stoker.

(Wiley M. Bryan)

At Savannah, the SAL's old Alabama Division diverged from the main line and extended west for a distance of 337 miles to Montgomery, Alabama, with important branch lines to Columbus and Macon, Georgia. This was an important freight line and during both the steam and diesel eras the principal trains were No. 81 *The Clipper* and No. 82 *The Alaga* between Montgomery and Savannah.

South of Savannah, all Seaboard trains shared a single main line route to Gross, Florida, where the lines split again. The original SAL main line from Savannah to Jacksonville passed through Everett, Georgia, and Yulee, Florida. In 1925 the SAL constructed a cut-off line running approximately 13 miles from Gross, just north of Yulee, in a southwesterly direction to Callahan, Florida, connecting with the original Florida Railroad line between Fernandina and Cedar Key. The Gross Cut-off established a direct route for freight trains to the Seaboard's important yard at Baldwin, Florida.

Baldwin Yard, located approximately 18 miles west of Jacksonville, was the junction point for the SAL's north-south lines from Richmond to Miami and Tampa and its east-west lines from Jacksonville to Chattahoochee, Florida, and Bainbridge, Georgia. Traffic moving west and south and to Jacksonville, was brought into Baldwin by trains from Savannah. Traffic moving north and south and to Jacksonville was brought to Baldwin by trains from Tallahassee. Traffic moving north and west and to Jacksonville was brought to Baldwin by trains from Wildwood.

(above) Looking north at Hermitage Yard in Richmond in 1947. Hermitage was the most northern point on the SAL.
(W. E. Griffin, Jr. Collection)

(below) Q-3 Mikado No. 352 with a short southbound local freight from Savannah rumbles across the SAL's crossing at grade with the Southern Railway at Everett, Georgia, in 1940.
(Hugh M. Comer)

(facing page, top) Q-3 2-8-2 No. 443 is at milepost 9, approaching Chester, Virginia, with Extra 443 South on April 27, 1947.
(August A. Thieme)

(facing page, bottom) Rolling by with a clean stack at an estimated 60 m.p.h. is Q-3 Mike No. 445 with a northbound freight approaching Baldwin, Florida, on March 26, 1949.
(David W. Salter)

445
445

AIR CONDITIONED ICE REFRIGERATORS
COAL AND OIL
2502

(facing page, top) In a classic view, R-1 2-6-6-4 No. 2502 rounds the curve at Raleigh, N.C., with a *Red Ball* freight in 1942.
(Homer R. Hill)

(facing page, bottom) Eastbound through freight No. 82 is at Harryat, Georgia, behind Class B-1 2-10-2 No. 2493 on March 17, 1948.
(David W. Salter)

(above) The SAL had many freight houses for handling LCL freight, like this one at Richmond, Va. This 1948 view looks north from Main Street Station's platform. The truck is turning onto Franklin Street.
(W. E. Griffin, Jr. Collection)

(below) Many automobiles were shipped over the SAL in special boxcars, as in this 1937 view.
(SAL Photo/CSX Transportation)

H-1 Class 2-8-0 No. 920 rolls a westbound local freight through a stand of Georgia pines just west of Pitts, Georgia, on June 14, 1947. The former GF&A Consolidation joined the SAL roster in 1929.

(David W. Salter)

Stepping out in fine fashion is L-2S Class 4-6-0 No. 654 with a westbound local freight near Seville, Georgia, on a clear April morning in 1947. The train passed at an estimated speed of 35 mph.

(David W. Salter)

(bottom) Mixed Train No. 102 is at Alachua, Florida, behind Class L-4-S 4-6-0 on its return run from Bell to Starke, Fla., on April 6, 1946. The Starke to Bell Mixed Train was photographer Husa's favorite and he photographed it with 4-6-0s, 4-6-2s and finally 2-10-0s in the final days of steam.

(William J. Husa, Jr.)

South of Baldwin, the tracks of the Seaboard extended throughout Florida. In fact, approximately 1,452 miles (or about 24 per cent) of the SAL's total system mileage was operated in the state. The SAL divided the state into two operating divisions with the North Florida Division offices located at Jacksonville and the South Florida Division offices at Tampa.

West of Jacksonville, one line extended approximately 200 miles across the Florida Panhandle through Baldwin and Tallahassee to Chattahoochee (River Junction), Florida. An important branch diverged from that route at Tallahassee and extended south to St. Marks on the Gulf and north to Columbus, Ga., through Bainbridge, Ga., connecting with the SAL's Savannah to Montgomery line at Richland, Georgia. During the steam era this line via Tallahassee, Bainbridge, and Columbus or Montgomery was an important route for perishable traffic moving from Florida to the Midwest. During this period, the principal trains were No. 83, West Jacksonville to Chattahoochee; No. 85, unnamed, and No. 84 *The Pioneer*, from Montgomery to West Jacksonville via Tallahassee; and No. 86 *The Victor* from Montgomery to Bainbridge where it was consolidated with No. 74 *The Cavalcade*, operating from Columbus to West Jacksonville. By the diesel era, this line was used for only local freight service, with the majority of through east-west traffic routed via Baldwin, Savannah, and Montgomery.

South of Jacksonville, all SAL freight trains operated over the same main line from Baldwin to Waldo. The Wannee Branch extended westward on this line from Starke to Bell. South of Waldo, the Seaboard essentially had two main lines running down the Florida peninsula, one down the east coast through Palm Beach and Miami to Homestead, and another down the west coast through Tampa and Fort Myers.

The Brooksville line extended west of Waldo via Gainesville, Dunnellon, and Brooksville to Tampa. The principal main line extended south of Waldo through Ocala and Wildwood (where a line branched off eastward to Lake Charm and Ocoee) to Coleman. At that point, one main line turned west through Plant City

D-2 2-10-0 No. 527 at Alachua, Fla. with Mixed Train No. 102 on the line from Starke to Bell, Florida, on November 5, 1949.
(William J. Husa, Jr.)

to Tampa, St. Petersburg, and Fort Myers and the other turned eastward via Auburndale, Sebring, across the Everglades to Okeechobee, and down the east coast of Florida via West Palm Beach, Fort Lauderdale, Miami, and Homestead.

Tampa was a prominent business city. It was the port of entry for Cuban products and the outlet for Florida lumber and phosphate. The Seaboard built lines from Tampa and extended them down the length of the Pinellas Peninsula to St. Petersburg and around Tampa Bay south to Bradenton and southeast to Arcadia. During the steam era, some of the principal north/south trains operating in Florida included No. 74 *The Cavalcade*, between Baldwin and Hialeah; No. 87 *The Migrator*, between Hermitage and Hialeah; No. 84 *The Pioneer*, between Montgomery and Tampa via Baldwin; No. 86 *The Red Fox*, between Hermitage and Florida and, No. 80 *The Marketer*, between Hialeah and Hermitage with sections from Fort Myers and Tampa consolidated into No. 80 at Baldwin.

In the diesel era, the principal trains included No. 75 *The Merchandiser*; No. 80 *The Marketer*; TT-23 and TT-25 *The TOFC Specials*; No. 75 *The Cavalcade* from Jacksonville to Hialeah; No. 81, also called *The Cavalcade*, from Jacksonville to Tampa; No. 87 *The Migrator*, and numerous through freights.

SEABOARD AIR LINE RAILROAD
4502
4502
SEABOARD

SEABOARD
3032
323

(facing page, top) The Baldwin Centipedes were photographer Husa's favorite SAL diesels. He recorded this view of No. 4502 with a southbound freight train at Wildwood, Florida, on May 6, 1950.

(facing page, bottom) E7A Nos. 3031 and 3032 depart Waldo, Florida, with a southbound passenger train meeting a northbound perishable train behind Centipede No. 4501 on November 12, 1949.

(above) In an extremely rare photo, FTA No. 4018, an FTB, and a 2-8-2 roll a northbound perishable train at Campville, Florida, in 1948. A classic view of steam and first-generation diesel on the SAL

(right) FT No. 4021 with an FTB unit heads up a northbound freight at Hawthorne, Florida, on November 25, 1949.

(Four Photos, William J. Husa, Jr.)

(below) Train No. 85, the southbound daily Portsmouth Subdivision through freight, is just west of Macon, N.C., with a 135-car consist in April 1969 behind GP9 No. 1916 and two GP7s.

(Curt Tillotson, Jr.)

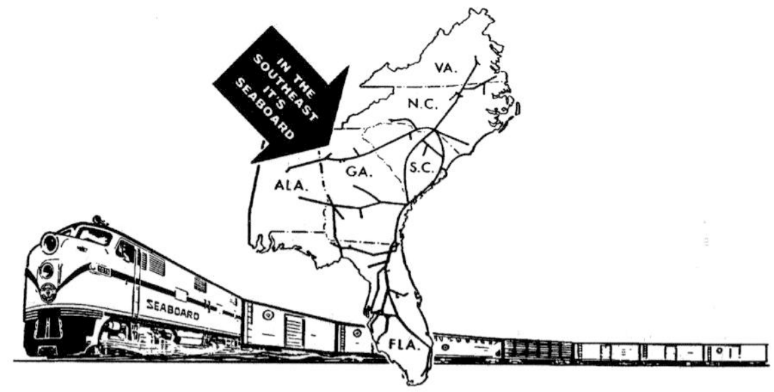

(left) SAL Train No. 27, *The Capital*, operating between Richmond and Atlanta/Birmingham passes Neuse, N.C., behind FTA No. 4002 and a single FTB unit.
(SAL Photo/W. E. Griffin, Jr. Collection)

(below) Train No. 27, the southbound *Capital*, has ample motive power for its 126-car train. It is shown passing Train No. 88, the *Ironmaster*, at Henderson, N.C., in October 1962. Lead unit FTA No. 4004 is assisted by an FTB and three E7As.
(Curt Tillotson, Jr.)

(facing page) The Conductor on SAL northbound Train No. 80, *The Marketer*, positions himself to inspect the passage of southbound Train No. 85, *The Merchandiser*, which is being led by FA1 No. 4202. This meet is taking place just north of Hamlet, N.C.
(SAL Photo/W. E. Griffin, Jr. Collection)

4202
SEABOARD
5301
SEABOARD
AIR LINE RAILROAD COMPANY
Schedule
— OF —
"THE MARKETER"
AND CONNECTING TRAINS
A Fast Dependable
Freight Service
— FOR —
FRUITS and VEGETABLES
— FROM —
FLORIDA
— TO —
Eastern Northern and Western
Points
SEASON 1952–53

SEABOARD

SEABOARD
WILKINSON

(facing page, top) Train No. 82, *The Courier*, is on No. 2 track for a meet with southbound Train No. 27 at Ridgeway, N.C. Three GP7s and their 85-car train bask in the sun in this splendid shot.

(facing page, bottom) After setting off and picking up from the Henderson, N.C. yard, Train No. 82, *The Courier*, is departing town on its journey to Portsmouth in January 1966. GP30 No. 526 and two GP9s have charge of the 93-car train.

(Two Photos, Curt Tillotson, Jr.)

(above) The SAL participated in this solid train movement of livestock from Florida to Kansas in April 1952. Here, the train is on the SAL at Bainbridge, Georgia, behind RSC2 No. 1508.

(SAL Photo)

(below) Two RSC3s hustle into the clear to meet southbound Train No. 75. With a headend load of pulpwood, the local is approaching Norlina, N.C., in October 1965.

(Curt Tillotson, Jr.)

(above) That's U.S. Route 158 on the left, the pass track and house track on the right. The train is No. 85, southbound at Macon, N.C., and nearing Norlina on its run to Raleigh. GP30 No. 520 is assisted by two GP7s as it moves the 122-car train over the Portsmouth Subdivision in September 1966.

(Curt Tillotson, Jr.)

(above) Three Alco C420s (Nos. 129, 128, and 130) head up a five-diesel consist to roll this southbound freight through Starke, Florida, on April 16, 1967.

(William J. Husa, Jr.)

(below) Extra 1119 North is in the pass track at Paschall, N.C., awaiting southbound Train No. 27. SDP35 No. 1119, a GP30 and an F3A are handling the 58-car phosphate extra on January 1965.

(Curt Tillotson, Jr.)

(facing page, bottom) SDP35 No. 1111 and two GP30s head up the first unit coal train operated over the Virginia Division to the Chesterfield County plant of Virginia Electric Power Company at Wheelwright, Va., on January 6, 1965.

(W. E. Griffin, Jr. Collection)

129
129
SEABOARD
129
128

SEABOARD
520

July 1, 1965

Seaboard Railroad Condensed Freight Schedules

READ DOWN — EASTERN STANDARD TIME — READ UP

VIRGINIA CITIES-BOSTIC-CHARLESTON-SAVANNAH-FLORIDA

TT-23	No. 89	No. 27	No. 75		No. 86	No. 280		No. 88	
¶7 45 AM Tu		8 00 AM Tu	1 30 AM Tu	Lv. Potomac Yard (R. F. & P.) Ar.	♯10 45 AM We	10 30 PM We			
¶10 30 AM Tu	5 30 PM Tu	11 45 AM Tu	9 15 AM Tu	Lv. Richmond Ar.	♯5 25 AM We	4 30 PM We		11 00 PM We	
	8 15 PM Tu		11 00 AM Tu	Lv. Petersburg Ar.	♯4 15 AM We			9 00 PM We	
	12 20 AM We			Lv. Henderson Ar.				4 30 PM We	
	1 45 AM We			Ar. Raleigh Lv.				3 30 PM We	
	4 00 AM We			Lv. Raleigh Ar.				3 00 PM We	
	6 45 AM We			Ar. Aberdeen Lv.					
¶4 00 PM Tu	7 30 AM We	6 00 PM Tu	5 00 PM Tu	Ar. Hamlet Lv.	¶9 30 PM Tu	8 00 AM We		12 01 PM We	
			No. 85-75			280-82			
			5 00 AM Tu	Lv. Portsmouth Ar.		8 00 PM We			
			5 00 PM Tu	Ar. Hamlet Lv.		8 00 AM We			
		No. 92	No. 46			No. 45		No. 89	
		9 00 PM Mo	12 30 PM Tu	Lv. Bostic Ar.		2 30 PM We		8 00 PM We	
		2 30 AM Tu	3 00 PM Tu	Lv. Charlotte Ar.		11 00 AM We		3 30 PM We	
		7 00 AM Tu	6 00 PM Tu	Ar. Hamlet Lv.		8 00 AM We		11 30 AM We	
	No. 71	No. 175	No. 75			No. 70	No. 280		
¶4 45 PM Tu	3 00 PM We	8 45 PM Tu	8 15 PM Tu	Lv. Hamlet Ar.	¶9 00 PM Tu	4 00 AM We	5 00 AM We		
	7 00 PM We			Ar. Poston Lv.		1 00 AM We			
				Ar. Georgetown Lv.		6 00 PM Tu			
	11 00 PM We	12 01 AM We		Ar. Charleston Lv.		9 30 PM Tu			
				Lv. Charleston Ar.			12 45 AM We		
¶10 15 PM Tu		3 10 AM We	2 40 AM We	Ar. Savannah Lv.	¶2 15 PM Tu		9 30 PM Tu		
	No. 93					No. 80		No. 72	
¶10 30 PM Tu	4 30 PM We	5 00 AM We	3 15 AM We	Lv. Savannah Ar.	¶1 30 PM Tu	3 00 PM Tu	8 00 PM Tu	6 30 PM Tu	
	10 15 AM Th			Ar. Fernandina Beach Lv.				11 00 AM Tu	
♯1 00 AM We	12 30 AM Th		6 00 AM We	Ar. Jacksonville Lv.			4 30 PM Tu	12 30 PM Tu	
		8 30 AM We		Ar. Baldwin Lv.	¶10 10 AM Tu	11 30 AM Tu			
	TT-25	No. 67						No. 76	TT-24
♯1 30 AM We	†7 30 PM Mo	12 01 PM We	10 30 AM We	Lv. Jacksonville Ar.				3 00 AM We	10 00 AM Tu
		1 30 PM We	11 30 AM We	Lv. Baldwin Ar.	¶10 00 AM Tu	11 00 AM Tu		12 01 AM We	
		4 00 PM We		Ar. Ocala Lv.				7 00 PM Tu	
		5 00 PM We		Ar. Wildwood Lv.	¶7 00 AM Tu	8 00 AM Tu		6 00 PM Tu	6 00 AM Tu
♯7 00 AM We		7 00 AM Th		Ar. Orlando Lv.		12 01 AM Tu			
	†11 30 PM Mo	8 00 PM We		Ar. West Lake Wales Lv.		3 30 AM Tu		7 30 AM Tu	
		11 45 PM We		Ar. West Palm Beach Lv.		11 30 PM Mo		2 00 AM Tu	
♯11 30 AM We	¶4 30 AM Tu	3 00 AM Th	10 00 PM We	Ar. Miami (S.A.L.) Lv.		9 00 PM Mo		11 30 PM Mo	7 30 PM Mo
			9 30 PM We	Ar. Miami (F.E.C.) Lv.					
TT-23	TT-25		No. 81			No. 68	No. 94		
♯1 30 AM We	†7 30 PM Mo		11 30 AM We	Lv. Jacksonville Ar.		12 30 PM Tu			
			1 00 PM We	Lv. Baldwin Ar.		9 30 AM Tu	5 00 AM Tu		
♯7 00 AM We	¶4 30 AM Tu		9 00 PM We	Ar. Tampa Lv.		1 30 AM Tu			
			7 30 AM Th	Ar. St. Petersburg Lv.		6 00 PM Mo			
			5 00 AM Th	Ar. Palmetto Lv.		9 00 PM Mo			
			1 30 PM Th	Ar. Sarasota Lv.		7 15 PM Mo			
				Mulberry Lv.			10 00 PM Mo		

VIRGINIA CITIES-BOSTIC-CHARLOTTE-ATLANTA-BIRMINGHAM

	No. 89	No. 75	No. 27		No. 86	No. 280	No. 88		
		1 30 AM Tu	8 00 AM Tu	Lv. Potomac Yard (R. F. & P.) Ar.	♯10 45 AM We	10 30 PM We			
	5 30 PM Mo	9 15 AM Tu	11 45 AM Tu	Lv. Richmond Ar.	♯5 25 AM We	4 30 PM We	11 00 PM We		
	8 15 PM Mo	11 00 AM Tu		Lv. Petersburg Ar.	♯4 15 AM We		9 00 PM We		
	4 00 AM Tu			Lv. Raleigh Ar.			3 00 PM We		
	7 30 AM Tu	5 00 PM Tu	6 00 PM Tu	Ar. Hamlet Lv.	¶9 30 PM Tu	8 00 AM We	12 01 PM We		
		No. 85-75				No. 280-82			
		5 00 AM Tu		Lv. Portsmouth Ar.		8 00 PM We			
		5 00 PM Tu		Ar. Hamlet Lv.		8 00 AM We			
No. 85		No. 45			No. 98	No. 28	No. 92	No. 30	No. 46
6 30 AM We	11 30 AM Tu	8 00 AM We	7 30 PM Tu	Lv. Hamlet Ar.	6 30 PM Tu	3 00 AM We	7 00 AM We	12 30 PM We	6 00 PM Tu
8 30 AM We			8 50 PM Tu	Ar. Monroe Lv.	4 30 PM Tu	12 01 AM We		9 00 AM We	
No. 71			No. 95			No. 96		No. 72	
†9 00 AM We			2 30 AM We	Lv. Monroe Ar.		7 30 PM Tu		†7 00 AM We	
†11 45 AM We	3 30 PM Tu	11 00 AM We	4 00 AM We	Ar. Charlotte Lv.		6 00 PM Tu	2 30 AM We	†6 00 AM We	3 00 PM Tu
	8 00 PM Tu	2 30 PM We		Ar. Bostic Lv.			9 00 PM Tu		12 30 PM Tu
No. 85			No. 27			No. 28		No. 30	
9 00 AM We			9 00 PM Tu	Lv. Monroe Ar.	4 00 PM Tu	11 15 PM Tu		7 30 AM We	
11 00 AM We				Lv. Clinton Ar.	2 00 PM Tu			5 00 AM We	
11 45 AM We			11 45 PM Tu	Ar. Greenwood Lv.	1 00 PM Tu	9 00 PM Tu		3 45 AM We	
2 30 PM We				Ar. Athens Lv.		5 00 PM Tu		12 01 AM We	
7 00 PM We			3 30 AM We	Ar. Atlanta Lv.	8 30 AM Tu	2 30 PM Tu		9 30 PM Tu	
	No. 83						No. 86		
	11 00 AM We		3 45 AM We	Lv. Atlanta Ar.	6 30 AM Tu	12 30 PM Tu	¶2 00 AM Tu		
	2 40 PM We			Ar. Cedartown Lv.			†11 00 PM Mo		
	3 45 PM We			Ar. Wellington Lv.			†8 30 PM Mo		
	9 30 PM We		8 00 AM We	Ar. Birmingham Lv.	1 00 AM Tu	7 00 AM Tu	†5 00 PM Mo		

HAMLET-COLUMBIA-SAVANNAH

No. 93		No. 94	
‡10 00 PM Tu	Lv. Hamlet Ar.	¶7 00 AM We	
†4 00 AM We	Ar. McBee Lv.	†4 00 AM We	
†6 00 AM We	Ar. Columbia Lv.	†8 00 PM Tu	
†7 30 AM We	Lv. Columbia Ar.	†6 00 PM Tu	
†7 30 PM We	Ar. Savannah Lv.	†8 00 AM Tu	

HAMLET-WILMINGTON

No. 78		No. 79	
‡1 00 PM Mo	Lv. Hamlet Ar.	‡2 00 AM Tu	
‡7 00 PM Mo	Ar. Wilmington Lv.	‡8 00 PM Mo	

READ DOWN — EASTERN STANDARD TIME — READ UP

MONTGOMERY-FLORIDA

		No. 82-96	No. 84		No. 85	No. 91-81		
		‡10 00 AM Tu	3 30 PM Tu	Lv. Montgomery Ar.	7 30 AM We	8 30 PM Tu		
		‡4 00 PM Tu	10 00 PM Tu	Ar. Tallahassee Lv.	10 00 PM Tu			
		‡10 00 PM Tu	3 30 AM We	Ar. Baldwin Lv.	5 00 PM Tu	6 00 AM Tu		
		‡11 59 PM Tu	4 30 AM We	Ar. Jacksonville Lv.	4 00 PM Tu	5 00 AM Tu		
		No. 677	No. 677		No. 680			
		7 00 AM We	7 00 AM Th	Ar. Orlando Lv.	12 01 AM Tu			
		TT-123	No. 81		No. 68			
		♯7 00 AM We	9 00 PM We	Ar. Tampa Lv.	1 30 AM Tu			
		TT-23	No. 75		No. 80			
		♯11 30 AM We	10 00 PM We	Ar. Miami (S.A.L.) Lv.	9 00 PM Mo			
			9 30 PM We	Ar. Miami (F.E.C.) Lv.				

BIRMINGHAM-COLUMBUS-FLORIDA (VIA CofGA-COLUMBUS-SAL)

	CGa-46	CGa-34	CGa-38		CGa-29			
	2 00 AM Tu	6 30 AM Tu	2 30 PM Tu	Lv. Birmingham Ar.	5 00 PM We			
	9 00 AM Tu	1 00 PM Tu	7 30 PM Tu	Ar. Columbus Lv.	11 00 AM We			
	No. 96	No. 74			No. 85-99	No. 91		
	‡11 15 AM Tu	9 30 PM Tu		Lv. Columbus Ar.	7 30 AM We	6 30 PM Mo		
	‡4 00 PM Tu	3 00 AM We		Ar. Tallahassee Lv.	10 00 PM Tu			
	‡10 00 PM Tu	6 30 AM We		Ar. Baldwin Lv.	5 00 PM Tu	6 00 AM Mo		
	‡11 59 PM Tu	7 30 AM We		Ar. Jacksonville Lv.	4 00 PM Tu	5 00 AM Mo		
	No. 677	No. 677			No. 680			
	7 00 AM We	7 00 AM Th		Ar. Orlando Lv.	12 01 AM Tu			
	TT-123	No. 81			No. 68			
	♯7 00 AM We	9 00 PM We		Ar. Tampa Lv.	1 30 AM Tu			
	TT-23	No. 75			No. 80			
	♯11 30 AM We	10 00 PM We		Ar. Miami (S.A.L.) Lv.	9 00 PM Mo			
		9 30 PM We		Ar. Miami (F.E.C.) Lv.				

BIRMINGHAM-ATLANTA-FLORIDA (VIA SAL-ATLANTA-CofGA-MACON-SAL)

	No. 86	No. 98	No. 28			No. 27		
	5 00 PM Mo	1 00 AM Tu	7 00 AM Tu	Lv. Birmingham Ar.		8 00 AM Th		
	2 00 AM Tu	6 30 AM Tu	12 30 PM Tu	Ar. Atlanta Lv.		3 45 AM Th		
	CGa-34		CGa-88			CGa-29		
	10 30 AM Tu		6 00 PM Tu	Lv. Atlanta Ar.		8 30 AM We		
	2 30 PM Tu		9 00 PM Tu	Ar. Macon Lv.		5 30 AM We		
	No. 88					No. 89		
	10 00 PM Tu			Lv. Macon Ar.		3 30 AM We		
	2 45 AM We			Ar. Savannah Lv.		9 30 PM Tu		
No. 93	No. 175		No. 75		No. 80	No. 280	No. 72	
4 30 PM We	5 00 AM We		3 15 AM We	Lv. Savannah Ar.	3 00 PM Tu	8 00 PM Tu	6 30 PM Tu	
10 15 AM Th				Ar. Fernandina Beach Lv.			11 00 AM Tu	
12 30 AM Th			6 00 AM We	Ar. Jacksonville Lv.		4 30 PM Tu	12 30 PM Tu	
	8 30 AM We			Ar. Baldwin Lv.	11 30 AM Tu			
	No. 677				No. 680	No. 680		
	7 00 AM Th			Ar. Orlando Lv.	12 01 AM Tu	12 01 AM Tu		
	No. 81				No. 68			
	9 00 PM We			Ar. Tampa Lv.	1 30 AM Tu			
	No. 75				No. 80			
	10 00 PM We			Ar. Miami (S.A.L.) Lv.	9 00 PM Mo			
	9 30 PM We			Ar. Miami (F.E.C.) Lv.				

BIRMINGHAM-ATLANTA-FLORIDA (VIA ACL-CORDELE-SAL)

	See Note 1						See Note 1	
		2 00 AM Tu	3 30 PM Tu	Lv. Birmingham Ar.	10 30 AM We			
	8 30 PM Mo	6 00 AM Tu	6 30 PM Tu	Lv. Atlanta Ar.	6 30 AM We		11 00 PM Tu	
				Lv. Cordele Lv.				
	5 30 AM Tu	11 00 PM Tu	7 30 AM We	Ar. Jacksonville Lv.	4 30 PM Tu		1 00 PM Tu	
	7 00 AM We	♯7 00 AM We	7 00 AM Th	Ar. Orlando Lv.	12 01 AM Tu		12 01 AM Tu	
	9 00 PM Tu	♯7 00 AM We	9 00 PM We	Ar. Tampa Lv.	1 30 AM Tu		1 30 AM Tu	
				Ar. Auburndale Lv.			10 30 PM Mo	
	10 00 PM Tu	♯11 30 AM We	10 00 PM We	Ar. Miami Lv.	9 00 PM Mo		7 30 PM Mo	

MONTGOMERY-SAVANNAH

No. 82		No. 81
10 00 AM Tu	Lv. Montgomery Ar.	8 30 PM Tu
8 00 AM We	Lv. Americus Lv.	11 30 AM Tu
9 00 AM We	Ar. Cordele Lv.	4 00 AM Tu
12 01 PM We	Lv. Vidalia Lv.	2 30 AM Tu
4 00 PM We	Ar. Savannah Lv.	11 00 PM Mo

HARTSVILLE-SUMTER-FLORENCE

Nos. 111-115	No. 125		No. 126	Nos. 112-116
†6 30 AM Mo		Lv. McBee		†7 00 PM Tu
†7 30 AM Mo		Ar. Hartsville Lv.		†5 00 PM Tu
:10 30 AM Mo	4 00 PM Mo	Lv. Hartsville Ar.	2 30 PM Mo	•3 30 PM Tu
:1 30 PM Mo		Ar. Sumter Lv.		•12 01 PM Tu
	7 00 PM Mo	Lv. Florence Ar.	11 30 AM Mo	
	10 00 PM Mo	Ar. Poston Lv.	8 00 AM Mo	

* Daily. † Daily, except Sunday. ‡ Daily, except Saturday. ¶ Daily, except Monday.
♯ Daily, except Tuesday. : Monday, Wednesday and Friday only. • Tuesday, Thursday and Saturday only

NOTE 1—T O F C and Autos only.

Schedules Subject to Change Without Notice

(above) Rounding a curve between Wise and Norlina, N.C., is TT-23, *The Razorback*, in April 1963. The two GP30s and one GP9 will have no difficulty maintaining schedule with this 46-car train.
(Curt Tillotson, Jr.)

(facing page, bottom) Sprinting through Carolina with a 65-car TT-23 on a July afternoon in 1962 are three E7As. The train is at Gill, N.C., just about to pass under U.S. Route 1. Photographer Tillotson felt that the E-units looked as if they were designed for the TT-23.
(Curt Tillotson, Jr.)

(below) GP9 No. 1968 leads a northbound "Piggyback" train near Lawtey, Florida, on March 25, 1965.
(David W. Salter)

Chapter 7

Freight Equipment

(facing page, top) SAL automobile-furniture AF-1 class 40-foot boxcar No. 11353 was built by Pullman in 1940. It featured a rounded roof and "Route of the Orange Blossom Special" slogan.

(below) The hand brake end of SAL B-6 class 40-foot boxcar No. 18647.

(right) H-6 class 70-ton hopper car No. 37100 was built for SAL by Bethlehem Steel in 1941.

(All, W. E. Griffin, Jr. Collection)

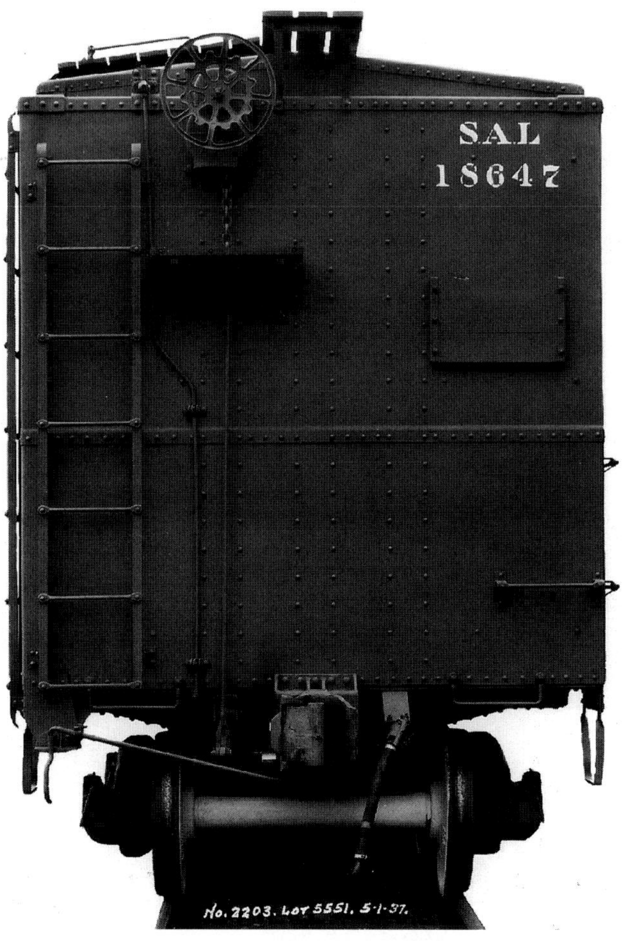

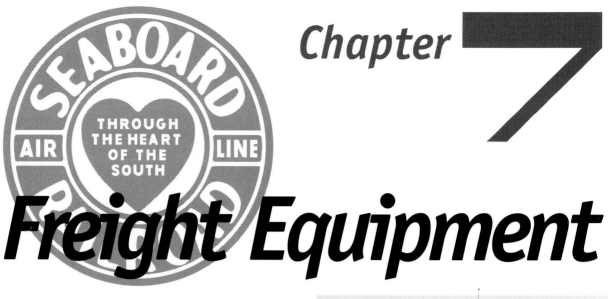

AUTOMOBILE — FURNITURE
SEABOARD AIR LINE RAILWAY
IL 40-6
IW 9-2
IH 10-0
CU.FT. 3713
BLT-3-40
AF-1
S.A.L.
S.A.L.
ROUTE OF THE
"Orange Blossom Special"
SEABOARD
11353
CAPY 100000
LD LMT 120700
LT WT 48300
NEW-3-40
No. 2714. Lot 5617 3-17-40.

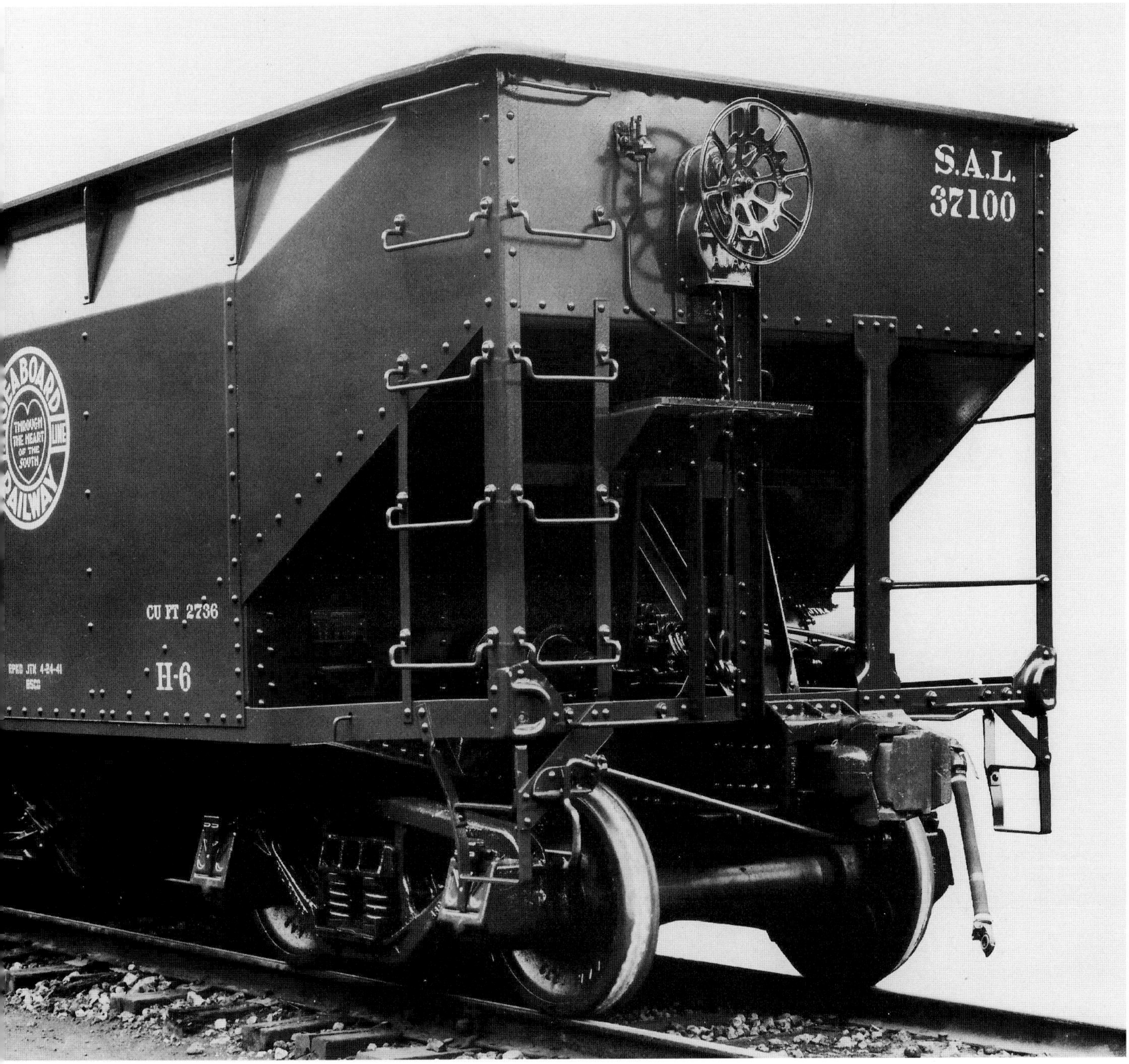
S.A.L.
37100
SEABOARD AIR LINE RAILWAY
THROUGH THE HEART OF THE SOUTH
CU FT 2736
H-6

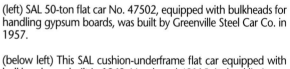

(top) 50-foot 70-ton SAL wood rack car No. 45688 was built by Thrall in March 1963.

(above) SAL 61-foot bulkhead flat car No. 48135 is shown with a load of steel plates at the Republic Steel Corp. in Alabama in 1964.

(left) SAL 50-ton flat car No. 47502, equipped with bulkheads for handling gypsum boards, was built by Greenville Steel Car Co. in 1957.

(below left) This SAL cushion-underframe flat car equipped with bulkheads was built in 1962. Numbered 48115, its load limit was 142,800 lbs.

(bottom left) SAL pulpwood car No. 46244 was specially designed and constructed at the company shops in Portsmouth. The car had a capacity of 13 cords. It is shown at Portsmouth in November 1937.

(All, W. E. Griffin, Jr. Collection)

(right) SAL Trailer Train auto rack car No. BTTX 913684 is loaded with new Ford Mustangs at Acca Yard in Richmond, Virginia.
(W. E. Griffin, Jr.)

(below) American Car and Foundry built gondola No. 91257 for the SAL in 1949.
(W. E. Griffin, Jr. Collection)

(second from bottom) SAL 50-ton low side gondola No. 93250 was built by Bethlehem Steel.
(C. L. Goolsby Collection)

(bottom) SAL mill-type gondola No. 6502 was photographed at Macon, Georgia, in 1968.
(C. L. Goolsby Collection)

(top) SAL 70-ton triple hopper No. 40496 was built by ACF in 1960.
(H. K. Vollrath Collection)

(above) SAL H-1 class composite hopper car No. 30403 was built by ACF in 1905.
(C. L. Goolsby Collection)

(below) SAL H-7 class 70-ton hopper car No. 37550 was built by Pullman-Standard in 1944.
(W. E. Griffin, Jr. Collection)

(above) 70-ton drop-bottom hopper car No. 36381 was used to haul wood chips.

(right) SAL H-3 class hopper car No. 36117 has had its sides raised to serve in wood chip service.

(Two Photos, Bob's Photo Collection)

(right) SAL 50-ton phosphate (wet rock) hopper car class P-5 was built by Magor in 1922.

(H. K. Vollrath Collection)

(below) Closed-top 70-ton phosphate (dry rock) hopper car class P-9 No. 58102 was built by Pullman-Standard in 1936.

(W. E. Griffin, Jr. Collection)

(above) SAL 70-ton covered hopper car class C-1 No. 8049 was built by Pullman-Standard in 1940 and was used to transport cement.

(left) SAL 70-ton covered hopper car No. 59584 was built by ACF in 1962 and is shown at Tampa, Florida.

(below) 100-ton aluminum covered hopper car No. 35018 is posed with 70-ton C-3 class covered hopper No. 8453.

(All, W. E. Griffin, Jr. Collection)

(above) SAL 100-ton aluminum covered hopper car No. 35034 has been spotted for loading.
(W. E. Griffin, Jr. Collection)

(left) SAL 70-ton covered hopper No. 31745 was built in 1967.
(Bob's Photo Collection)

(below) SAL Airslide™ covered hopper No. 7143 was built by General American Transportation Corporation in 1964.

(bottom) ACF built Center Flow™ covered hopper No. 35802 for the SAL in 1962.
(Two Photos, W. E. Griffin, Jr. Collection)

(above) SAL 36-foot, 40-ton V-9 class wooden ventilated boxcar was built by Chicasaw in 1922 for the perishable traffic.
(Jay Williams Collection)

(left) SAL 36-foot 40-ton V-10 class wooden ventilated boxcar No. 79269 at Sarasota, Florida, in 1952.
(Howard W. Ameling Collection)

(below left) SAL wooden boxcar No. 13040 was built in 1897, weighed 32,500 lbs. and had a capacity of 60,000 lbs.
(SAL Photo/CSX Transportation)

(below) Forty-foot, 40-ton B-3 class composite boxcar No. 12611 was one of 901 such cars built for the SAL by Pullman-Standard in 1926.
(Jay Williams Collection)

(facing page, top left) The hand brake end of SAL boxcar No. 19799.

(facing page, top right) SAL B-6 class 40-foot boxcar No. 17438 was built by Pullman in 1934.

(facing page, middle) SAL B-9 class 40-foot boxcar No. 19799 was built by Pullman in 1944.

(facing page, bottom) Automobile-furniture AF-1 class 40-foot boxcar No. 22109 was built for the SAL by Pullman in 1942. It carried the slogan for *The Robert E. Lee.*
(Four Photos, W. E. Griffin, Jr. Collection)

S.A.L.
19799

SEABOARD
17438
SEABOARD AIR LINE RAILWAY
B6
No. 2308. Lot 5502.

THE ROUTE OF COURTEOUS SERVICE
SEABOARD
19799
CAPY 100000
LD LMT 123900
LT WT 45100
NEW 9-45
S.A.L.
SEABOARD AIR LINE RAILWAY
THROUGH THE HEART OF THE SOUTH
EXW 10-5 H 13-1
EW 9-5 H 13-11
IL 40-6
IW 9-2
IH 10-0
CU.FT. 3713
BLT. 9-45
B-9
S.A.L.
19799
No. 4689. Lot 5804 9-11-45.

AUTOMOBILE—FURNITURE
SEABOARD AIR LINE RAILWAY
EXW 10-6 H 12-5
EW 8-3 H 14-2
IL 40-6
IW 9-2
IH 10-0
CU.FT. 3713
BLT-4-42
AF-2
S.A.L.
S.A.L.
ROUTE OF
The Robert E Lee
SEABOARD
22109
CAPY. 100000
LD LMT 120700
LT WT 48300
NEW-4-42

The slogan "The Route of Courteous Service" appeared on the side of SAL 50-foot XM series boxcar No. 27225. This car was built by ACF in 1955.

(W. E. Griffin, Jr. Collection)

(below) SAL 50-foot XM series 26000-26974 series boxcars are represented by this view of No. 26025.

(W. E. Griffin, Jr. Collection)

(bottom) SAL boxcar No. 19135 was one of 493 cars in the 40-foot B-7 class. These cars were built by Pullman in 1941.

(Bob's Photo Collection)

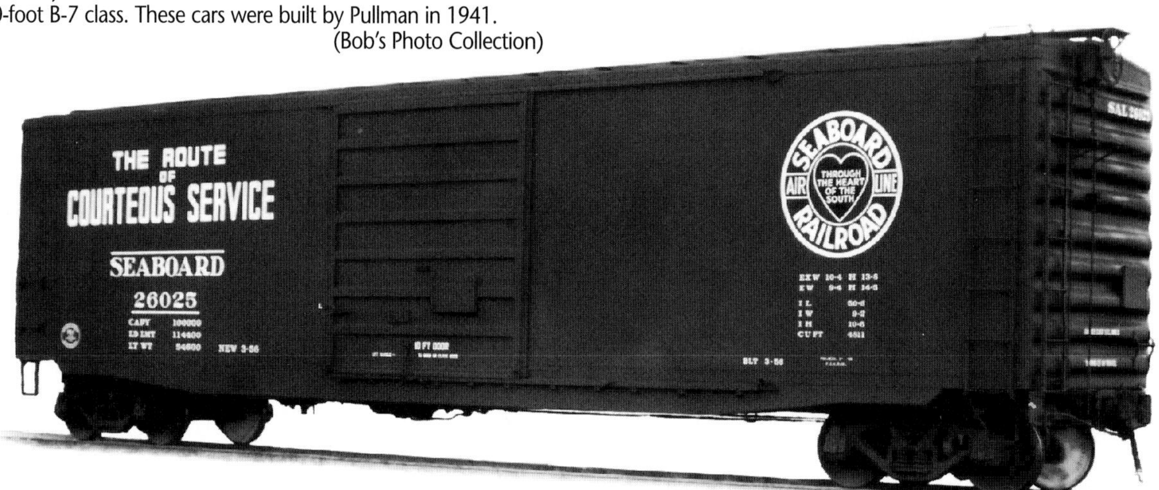

(top) No. 26991 is another of the SAL 50-foot XM series 26975-26999 series boxcars.

(C. L. Goolsby Collection)

(above) SAL 40-foot boxcar No. 20053 was one of three boxcars rebuilt in the Company's shops with two 10-foot sliding doors to provide for ease in the loading and unloading of lading.

(W. E. Griffin, Jr. Collection)

(below) SAL XM series 50-foot boxcar with a Superior Panel door was built in 1956.

(W. E. Griffin, Jr. Collection)

(top) The SAL XML 50-foot 16000-16299 boxcars were built in 1962 by Pullman-Standard with 10-foot door opening and cushion underframe. They were known as the "Green Hornets" because of their green paint scheme.

(above) No. 15000 was the first car in SAL 50-foot XML series 15000-15499 boxcars, built with 10-foot sliding door and cushion underframe.

(Both, W. E. Griffin, Jr. Collection)

(below) Automobile-furniture car No. 23315 carried the bold "Route of Courteous Service" slogan. It was one of 500 cars in the AF-5 class built by Pullman-Standard in 1948.

(W. E. Griffin, Jr. Collection)

Promoting the SILVER FLEET

(top) SAL B-5 class boxcar No. 14004 carried the slogan of the *Silver Meteor.*

(above right) No. 10127 was one of 199 cars in the SAL AF class 10000-10199 series automobile-furniture boxcars that were built in 1938 by Pullman. The 10127 had been rebuilt in the Jacksonville shops in 1960, and also carries the *Silver Meteor* script.
(Two Photos, H. K. Vollrath Collection)

(right) SAL XM series boxcar No. 25413 was photographed at Athens, Georgia, in 1972 with a slogan for *The Silver Star.*

(below) The slogan for *The Silver Comet* was carried on the side of XM series boxcar No. 24338, shown here at Manchester, Georgia, in 1964.
(Two Photos, C. L. Goolsby Collection)

(above) Wooden 1CC class SAL caboose No. 49658 was built by the Mt. Vernon Car Co. in 1912. It was still in service when photographed at Atlanta in 1967.
(O. W. Kimsey, Jr. Photo/John C. La Rue, Jr. Collection)

(below) SAL wooden caboose No. 49503 was photographed at Tampa in 1949. This 3CC class caboose was built by SSC Co. in 1916.
(John C. La Rue, Jr. Collection)

Virginia Division caboose No. 79445 was converted from a ventilated boxcar by SAL shop forces. Photographed here at Boykins, Va., in 1946, the caboose was used regularly on the Lewiston Branch.
(John C. La Rue, Jr. Collection)

(above) Georgia Division caboose No. 5445 was built by SAL in 1925. The caboose was photographed at Cartersville, Ga., in 1968.

(O. W. Kimsey, Jr. Photo/John C. La Rue, Jr. Collection)

(right) Wooden caboose No. 5231 is shown at Franklin, Virginia, in 1964. Assigned to the Virginia Division, this 5CC class caboose was built by Magor in 1923.

(John C. La Rue, Jr. Collection)

(below) SAL wooden 5CC class caboose No. 5248 is stenciled for the North Florida Division and is seen at Wildwood, Florida, in 1964. The caboose was built by Magor in 1924.

(F. Brunot Photo/John C. La Rue, Jr. Collection)

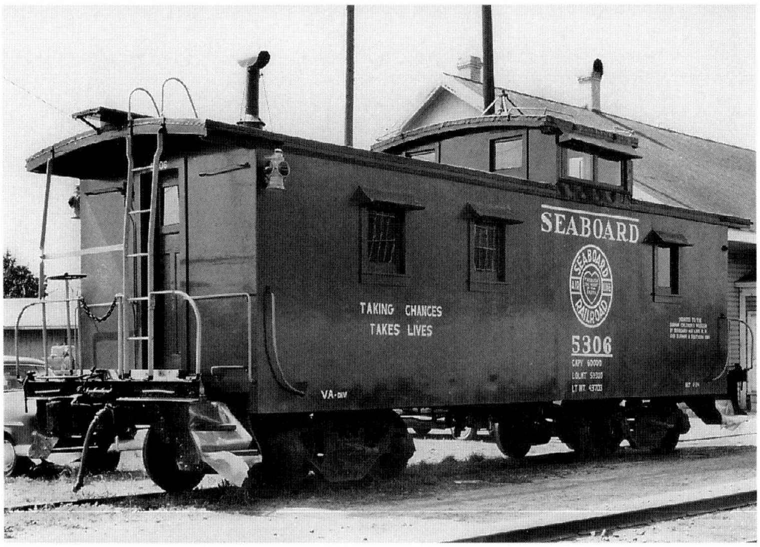

(above) Wooden caboose No. 5407 was built by the SAL in 1925. Assigned to the North Florida Division, the caboose is at Fort Lauderdale, Florida, in 1966.

(Howard W. Ameling)

(left) Virginia Division caboose No. 5306, built by AC&F in 1926, is seen at Dunn, N.C., in 1966.

(John C. La Rue, Jr. Collection)

(below) Bearing the safety slogan "Taking Chances Takes Lives," Carolina Division caboose No. 5226 awaits its next call to service.

(Bob's Photo Collection)

(above) Another North Florida Division caboose No. 5619 was built by IRC&EMF Co. in 1949 and is seen at Hialeah, Florida, in 1968.

(Howard W. Ameling)

(right) SAL caboose No. 5661 was built by the SAL in 1952. The caboose is stenciled for the Carolina Division but was photographed at Claxton, Georgia, in 1965.

(C. L. Goolsby Collection)

(below) The most modern SAL cabooses were the series 5700-5759 cabs built by International in 1963. The 5702 was photographed at Columbus, Georgia, in 1967.

(O. W. Kimsey, Jr./John C. La Rue, Jr. Collection)

SEABOARD AIR LINE RAILROAD COMPANY.

FREIGHT EQUIPMENT.

The freight cars of this Company are marked "Seaboard" and "Ga., Fla. & Ala." and numbered and classified as follows:

Item Number.	A. A. R. Mech. Designation.	Markings and Kind of Cars.	Numbers.	Dimensions. Inside. Length (ft. in.)	Inside. Width (ft. in.)	Inside. Height (ft. in.)	Outside. Length (ft. in.)	Outside. Width. At Eaves or Top of Sides or Platform (ft. in.)	Outside. Width. Extreme Width. (ft. in.)	Outside. Height from Rail. To Extreme Width. (ft. in.)	Height from Rail. To Eaves or Top of Sides or Platform (ft. in.)	Height from Rail. To Top of Running Board. (ft. in.)	Height from Rail. To Extreme Height. (ft. in.)	Doors. Side. Width of Open'g (ft. in.)	Doors. Side. Height of Open'g (ft. in.)	Doors. End. Width of Open'g (ft. in.)	Doors. End. Height of Open'g (ft. in.)	Capacity. Cubic Feet Level Full.	Capacity. Pounds or Gallons.	Number of Cars.
1	TM	Tank.....Note H	3000																8000 gal. 80000 lb.	1
2	TM	" .....Note H	3002 to 3010																10000 gal. 100000 lb.	9
3	XM	Box, Closed	4001 to 4279	40 6	8 6	8 7	42 6	9 7	10 1	12	12 9	13 3	14	6	7 11			2926	80000 lb.	275
4	RB	Refrigerator, Steel CenterSills, Note D	4400 to 4404	39 2	8 4	7 1	40 11¼	9 8⅜			12 5	13 0¼	14 4½	4	6 4			2312	80000 lb.	3
5	SM	Stock............	7900 to 7949	40 6	8 6	8 6	41 9	9	9 9	12	12 11	13 5	13 5	6	8 1			2926	80000 lb.	49
6	LO	Cement, Closed Top, Hopper Bot., Hatchway Roof	8000 to 8099	29 3	9 6		35 3	9 10	10 2	11 9	12 6	12 10	13 2					1958	140000 lb.	100
7	XAR	Automobile, Staggered Doors....Note C	9001 to 9010	40 6	9	10 2 / 9 5	41 9	8 2	10 3	13 6	14 6	15	15 1	12 ...	9 7			3721 / 3447	80000 lb.	10
11	XAR	Automobile, Staggered Doors....Note C	9011 to 9060	40 6	9	10 2 / 9 5	43 1	8 4	10 4	13 5	14 4	14 11	15	12 6	9 7			3721 / 3447	100000 lb.	50
12	XM	Auto., Furniture, Staggered Doors.	10000 to 10199	50	9 2	10 1	51 9	8 9	10 8	5 7	14 2	14 9	14 10	12 6	9 5			4629	100000 lb.	199
13	XM	Auto., Furniture, Staggered Doors......	11000 to 11999	40 6	9 2	10	41 11	8 3	10 6 / 10 8	12 5 / 4 2	14 2	14 7	14 8	12 6	8 8			3713	100000 lb.	977
14	XAP	" " Note M	" "	"	"	"	"	"	10 6 / 10 8	12 5 / 4 2	"	"	"	"	"			"	"	15
15	XM	Auto., Furniture, Staggered Doors......	22000 to 22199	40 6	9 2	10	41 11	8 3	10 6 / 10 8	12 5 / 4 2	14 2	14 7	14 8	12 6	8 8			3713	100000 lb.	200
16	XM	Auto., Furniture, Staggered Doors......	22200 to 22499	40 6	9 2	10	41 11	9 5	10 5 / 10 8	13 1 / 3 4	13 11	14 6	14 7	12 6	9 4			3713	100000 lb.	250
17	XM	Box, Closed. Note B	12000 to 12999	40 6	8 6	8 6	41 9	9	9 9	12	12 11	13 5	14	6	8 1	1 9	0 7	2926	80000 lb	904
21	XM	" " Note B	13001 to 13965	40 6	8 6	8 7	42 3	8 11	9 9	12	12 11	13 4	13 11	6	8 1	1 9	0 7	2965	80000 lb.	649
22	XM	" "	15000 to 16999	40 6	8 6	8 7	42 3	8 11	9 8	12 2	12 11	13 4	13 5	6	8 1			2965	100000 lb.	1962
23	XM	" "	17000 to 18999	40 6	8 9	9 4	42 4	8 5	10	12 5	13 6	13 11	14 1	6	8 8			3311	100000 lb.	1927
24	XM	" "	19000 to 19499	40 6	9 2	10	41 11	8 4	10 5 / 10 8	12 4 / 5 7	14 4	14 7	14 8	6	8 8			3713	100000 lb	496
25	XM	" "	19500 to 19999	40 6	9 2	10	41 11	9 4	10 5 / 10 8	13 1 / 4 9	13 11	14 6	14 7	6	9 4			3713	100000 lb.	499
27	VM	" Ventilated..	28000 to 29249	35 9	8 6	7 6	37 8	9 6	10 1	11 3	12 2	12 11	13 7	6	7	Note A	Note A	2280	80000 lb.	1196
31	VM	" "	79000 to 79999	36 1	8 6	7 6	37 11	9 6	9 10	11 3	12 2	12 11	13 7	6	7	Note A	Note A	2295	80000 lb.	949
32	VM	" "	89000 to 89899	35 9	8 6	7 6	37 8	9 6	10 1	11 3	12 2	12 11	13 7	6	7	Note A	Note A	2280	80000 lb.	857
33	HM	Coal, Hopper. Note F(1)	36000 to 36249	30	9 5		31 8	10			10 6		11 5					1834	100000 lb.	22
34	HM	" "	36250 to 36449	30	9 5		31 8	10			10		10 9					1670	100000 lb	196
35	HM	" "	36500 to 36699	30 6	9 5		31 11	10 3⅜			10 3⅜		10 8					1880	100000 lb.	195
36	HM	" "	36950 to 36989	30 6	9 5		31 11	10 1			10 8		11 5					1880	80000 lb.	5
37	HM	" "	37000 to 37399	40 8	10 4		41 8	10 5			10 8		10 8					2736	140000 lb.	398
41	HM	" "	37400 to 37599	40 8	10 4		41 8	10 5			10 8		10 8					2773	140000 lb.	200
42	GB	Gondola, Fixed Ends, Solid Bottom.	91000 to 91049	41 5	9 5	4 4	43 1	10 3	10 3	8 6			8 6					1695	100000 lb.	49
43	GA	Gondola, Drop Bottom, WoodFloor. Note J	92000 to 93274	37 6	8 7	4	39 4	9 1			8 1		8 8					1288	80000 lb.	15
44	GA	Gondola, Drop Bottom, WoodFloor. Note J	93277 to 94773	40 6	8 7	3 3	42 4	9 1			7 4		8 8					1130	80000 lb.	22
45	GB	Gondola, Fixed Ends, Solid Bottom, Wood Floor..........	95000 to 95099	41 5	9 1	3 11	43	9 6	10 2	6 8	7 8		7 8					1460	100000 lb	97
46	GB	Gon., Fixed Ends, Solid Wood Floor., Bottom	96000 to 97599	41 5	9 1	2 11	43 1	10 2			6 8		7 5					1107	100000 lb.	915
47	GB	Gondola, Fixed Ends, Solid Bottom, Wood Floor..........	98000 to 98099	41 5	9 1	3 11	43 1	9 6	10 2	6 8	7 8		7 8					1460	100000 lb.	95
51	GS	Gondola, Drop Bottom, Wood Floor......	98100 to 98999	41 5	9 1	3 11	43 1	9 6	10 2	6 8	7 8		7 8					1460	100000 lb.	842
52	GB	Gon., Fixed Ends. Solid Bottom, Wood Floor.	99000 to 99999	41 6	9 1	2 11	43 1	10 2			6 8		7 5					1107	100000 lb	576
53	LP	Flat, Wood Rack.	40000 to 40449	39 10⅛	9 5⅛		43 0½	8 6⅝	9 5⅛	3 8½	10 1½		10 1½						100000 lb.	378
54	LP	" Solid End, Wood Rack.	41300 to 41599	37 10	9		41 9	9	10 1	3 9	4 1								80000 lb.	176
55	FM	" ......Note K	" "	41	9 1		"	9 1	"	"	4								"	86
56	FM	"	46000 to 46931	41	9 1		41 9	9 1	10 1	3 9	4								80000 lb.	172
57	LP	" Bent Rail Wood Rack..Note G	" "	37 10	"		"	"	"	"	4 1								"	436
61	LP	" Solid End Wood Rack..Note L	" "	37 10	9			9	"	"	4 1								"	224
62	FM	"	47000 to 47199	49 11	9 4		50 9	9 4	10 3	3 5	3 9								100000 lb.	200
63	FM	"	47200 to 47499	49 11	9 4		50 9	9 4	10 2	3 5	3 9								100000 lb.	300
64	LO	Phosphate, Closed Top, Note F(2)	55001 to 55088	33 2	9 1		35 9	9 6			8 10	9 10	10 5					1547	80000 lb.	48
65	LO	" Closed Top, Note F(3)	55090 to 55148	33	9 1		36 9	9 9			9 1	9 10	10 6					1400	80000 lb.	26
66	LO	" Closed Top	55500 to 55599	33 ...	9 1		36 9	9 9			9 1	9 10	10 6					1400	100000 lb	88
67	LO	" " ..	56600 to 56799	34	9 1		37 2	9 9			9 9	10 5	11 1					1600	100000 lb	198
		Forward....																		17536

▲ Denotes additions. ◆ Denotes increase. ♦ Denotes reduction. (See Page xviii.)

FREIGHT EQUIPMENT—Continued.

Item Number	A.A.R. Mech. Designation	Markings and Kind of Cars	Numbers	Dimensions: Inside Length (ft. in.)	Inside Width (ft. in.)	Inside Height (ft. in.)	Outside Length (ft. in.)	Outside Width at Eaves or Top of Sides or Platform (ft. in.)	Outside Extreme Width (ft. in.)	Height from Rail: To Extreme Width (ft. in.)	To Eaves or Top of Sides or Platform (ft. in.)	To Top of Running Board (ft. in.)	To Extreme Height (ft. in.)	Doors Side: Width of Open'g (ft. in.)	Side: Height of Open'g (ft. in.)	End: Width of Open'g (ft. in.)	End: Height of Open'g (ft. in.)	Capacity: Cubic Feet Level Full	Pounds or Gallons	Number of Cars
		Brought forward																		17536
1	HT	Phosphate, Open Top...	57200 to 57399	34	9 1	......	37 2	9 9			9 9	10 6	11 1					1615	100000 lb.	200
2	LO	" Closed Top	57400 to 57599	34	9 1	......	37 2	9 9			9 9	10 6	11 1					1615	100000 lb.	197
3	HT	" Open Top..	57900 to 57999	34	9 1	......	37 2	9 9			9 7	......	10 4					1600	100000 lb.	97
4	LO	" Closed Top	58000 to 58199	34 10	10 2	......	36 6	9 9	10 3	9 9	10	10 10	10 11					1912	140000 lb.	200
5	MWB	Ballast, Roadway..	31250 to 31274																	24
6	...	Work Equip.....	601, 602																	2
7	...	" "	70000 to 72399																	982
11	...	" " Tanks.	73000 to 73042																	43
12	NE	Caboose.........	5211 to 5549																	226
13	NE	"	49500 to 49699																	52
14	XM	G.F.&A. Box.......	4001 to 4279	40 6	8 6	8 7	42 6	9 7	10 1	12	12 9	13 3	14	6	7 11			2926	80000 lb.	2
		Total........																		19561

PASSENGER REFRIGERATOR CARS.

Item Number	A.A.R. Mech. Designation	Markings and Kind of Cars	Numbers	Inside Length: Between Ice Tanks—Bulkheads in place (ft. in.)	Inside Length: Between Linings Clear (Bulkheads Collapsed) (ft. in.)	Width, Inside (ft. in.)	Height, Inside (ft. in.)	Outside Length (ft. in.)	Width at Eaves (ft. in.)	Extreme Width (ft. in.)	Height from Rail: To Extreme Width (ft. in.)	To Eaves (ft. in.)	To Top of Running Board (ft. in.)	To Extreme Height (ft. in.)	Side Doors: Width (ft. in.)	Side Doors: Height (ft. in.)	Capacity of Ice Tanks: Total Capacity for Crushed Ice (lbs.)	Total Capacity for Coarse Ice (lbs.)	Total Capacity for Chunk Ice (lbs.)	Capacity Measure: Cubic Feet	Capacity Measure: Depth (ft. in.)	Capacity of Car: Cubic Feet Level Full: Between Ice Boxes—Bulkheads in Place	Clear Capacity (Bulkheads Collapsed)	Pounds	Number of Cars
15	BR	PASSENGER. Refrigerator Express..	3600 to 3641	40 10	48 6	8 6	7 1	50 1	10 ...	10 4	4 6	12 4	13 10	13 10	5 ...	6 ...	12900	.....	11700	317	5 8	2383	2700	84000	18
		Total Passenger Refrigerators....																							18

RECAPITULATION OF CAR EQUIPMENT.

Class X—Box Car Type.

AGGREGATE AND AVERAGE.

A.A.R. Mech. Desig.	Inside Length ft. in.	Number of Cars	Capacity Cubic Feet	Aggregate Capacity Cubic Feet	Marked Capacity (Pounds)
XM	40 6	1,181	2926	3,455,606	80,000
XM	40 6	649	2965	1,924,285	80,000
XM	40 6	1,962	2965	5,817,330	100,000
XM	40 6	1,927	3311	6,380,297	100,000
XM	40 6	2,422	3713	8,992,886	100,000
XM	50 ..	199	4629	921,171	100,000
XAP	40 6	15	3713	55,695	100,000
XAR	40 6	10	3447	34,470	80,000
XAR	40 6	50	3447	172,350	100,000
	Total	8,415		27,754,090	

Average cubical capacity per car (for Commodity Loading)... 3298

Cars Equipped with Auto Loaders (Included in above)

A.A.R. Mech. Desig.	Inside Length ft. in.	Number of Cars	Capacity Cubic Feet	Aggregate Capacity Cubic Feet	Marked Capacity (Pounds)
XAR	*40 6*	*10*	*3721*	*37,210*	*80,000*
XAR	*40 6*	*50*	*3721*	*186,050*	*100,000*
	Total	*60*		*223,260*	

Average cubical capacity per car (for Automobile Loading)... *3721*

Class V—Ventilator Car Type.

A.A.R. Mech. Desig.	Inside Length ft. in.	Number of Cars	Capacity Cubic Feet	Aggregate Capacity Cubic Feet	Marked Capacity (Pounds)
VM	35 9	2,053	2280	4,680,840	80,000
VM	36 1	949	2295	2,177,955	80,000
	Total	3,002		6,858,795	

Average cubical capacity per car (for Commodity Loading)... 2285

Plain Box (XM)—	
Cars of 80,000 lbs. capacity	1,830
Cars of 100,000 lbs. "	6,510
Automobile (XAP)—	
Cars of 100,000 lbs. capacity	15
Automobile (XAR)—	
Cars of 80,000 lbs. capacity	10
Cars of 100,000 lbs. "	50
Ventilator Box (VM)—	
Cars of 80,000 lbs. capacity	3,002
TOTAL BOX CARS (Includes all class X and V cars)..	11,417

Class S—Stock Car Type.

A.A.R. Mech. Desig.	Inside Length ft. in.	Number of Cars	Capacity (Pounds)
SM	40 6	49	80,000
Total		49	

Class G—Gondola Car Type.

A.A.R. Mech. Desig.	Inside Length ft. in.	Number of Cars	Capacity Cubic Feet	Marked Capacity (Pounds)
GA	37 6	15	1288	80,000
GA	40 6	22	1130	80,000
GB	41 5	915	1107	100,000
GB	41 5	192	1460	100,000
GB	41 5	49	1695	100,000
GB	41 6	576	1107	100,000
GS	41 5	842	1460	100,000
Total....		2,611		

Gondola, Dump between rails (GA)—	
Cars of 80,000 lbs. capacity..	37
Gondola, Solid Bottom (GB)—	
Cars of 100,000 lbs. capacity..	1,732
Gondola, Dump outside of rails (GS)—	
Cars of 100,000 lbs. capacity..	842
Total	2,611

Class F—Flat Car Type.

A.A.R. Mech. Desig.	Inside Length ft. in.	Number of Cars	Marked Capacity (Pounds)
FM	41 ..	258	80,000
FM	49 11	500	100,000
Total.........		758	

Flat (All Class F cars except FB and FL)—	
Cars of 80,000 lbs. capacity..	258
Cars of 100,000 lbs. " ..	500
Total	758

OTHER REVENUE CARS.

Hopper (All Class H cars)—(Except Coke)	1,313
Refrigerator (All class R cars)..	3
Wood Rack (LP)	1,214
Tank, Oil (TM) General Service	10
Phosphate (LO)	757
Cement (LO)	100
TOTAL REVENUE FREIGHT EQUIPMENT	18,232
Non-Revenue Freight Equipment—	
Caboose	278
Ballast	24
Other freight Cars, including Miscellaneous Maintenance of Way	1,027
TOTAL FREIGHT EQUIPMENT CARS	19,561

Note A—Cars in this series are equipped with Wine ventilators.

Note B—Lumber door "A" end only.

Note C—Cars in series 9001 to 9060 are equipped with special automobile loading devices and cars stencilled "Auto Racks". Inside height and cubical capacity as follows:

With Loading Devices in position for loading automobiles—Inside height 10 ft. 2 in. Capacity 3,721 cu. ft.

With Loading Devices raised in stored position against roof of car for loading other commodities—Inside height 9 ft. 5 in. Capacity 3,447 cu. ft.

Note D—Refrigerator cars in series 4400 to 4404 are used in local service.

Note F—Individual numbers of cars in series 36000 to 36249, 55001 to 55088 and 55090 to 55148 that are assigned to cinder service:

F①	F②				F③		
		55020	55046	55064	55087	55101	55130
		55024	55049	55069		55107	55137
36002	55005	55028	55051	55084		55112	55144
36077	55007					55120	55145
36088	55009	55036	55052	55085	55091	55121	55146
36183	55012	55038	55060	55086	55099	55124	55148

▲ Denotes additions. ◆ Denotes increase. ↓ Denotes reduction. (See Page xviii.)

Chapter 8

Seaboard E4 No. 3005 heads into a passing siding near Savannah, Georgia, in anticipation of a meet with an opposing train.
(SAL Photo)

Seaboard Color Album

(above) GP7 No. 1760 is shown with a special passenger movement near Aberdeen, N.C., on March 5, 1966.

(W. E. Griffin, Jr. Collection)

(left) Southbound passenger train No. 3 is shown departing Petersburg, Virginia, behind E7 No. 3029 on August 16, 1963. With its heavy load of mail and baggage, No. 3 is just coming out of the curve south of the station and in a moment will pass under the main line of the Atlantic Coast Line.

(Ralph Coleman)

(facing page, top) Looking north from the Virginian Railway overpass, Wiley M. Bryan photographed SAL Mail and Express Train No. 4 departing Alberta, Virginia, in October 1959.

(W. M. Bryan Photo/W. E. Griffin, Jr. Collection)

(facing page, bottom) This SAL southbound freight is departing Hermitage Yard in Richmond, Virginia, on September 7, 1957. Motive power is provided by E7 No. 3045, E7 No. 3020 (still in the "citrus" paint scheme), and GP9 Nos. 1965, 1962, and 1912.

(Ralph Coleman)

SEABOARD

2701
F

Trains passing in the night. An SAL local passenger train behind Baldwin DRS6-4-1500 No. 2700 has taken the side track to allow for the passage of Seaboard's crack New York-Florida *Silver Comet*. (SAL Photo)

(above) SAL Baldwin DR12-8-3000 No. 4500 was the first of the company's fleet of fourteen "Centipedes." Painted in a modified version of the "citrus" paint scheme, the 4500 was initially placed in passenger service between Jacksonville and Tampa. It is shown on a Jacksonville-Tampa passenger run in 1946.

(SAL Photo)

(left) This original watercolor painting of SAL Q-3 class 2-8-2 No. 357 marching a northbound merchandise freight under the tracks of the Virginian Railway and past the Alberta, Virginia, combination freight and passenger station was commissioned by the author for the dust jacket of his book *All Lines North of Raleigh*, a history of the SAL's Virginia Division. It was painted by noted Virginia artist Casey Holtzinger and perfectly captures the essence of the era of SAL steam operation.

(Casey Holtzinger Painting/W. E. Griffin, Jr. Collection)

(facing page) Inside the SAL shop at West Jacksonville, two of the company's shop craft employees work on a traction motor, flanked by two Baldwin "Centipedes" wearing the freight color scheme.

(SAL Photo)

4506
SEABOARD
AIR
LINE
THROUGH THE HEART OF THE SOUTH
RAILROAD

(above) Railcar No. 2028 at Venice, Florida, in April 1967.
(Richard S. Short Photo/Ray Sturges Collection)

(below) On the occasion of a Washington Chapter, NRHS excursion on October 12, 1958, a classic portrait was staged at Richmond, Virginia's famous triple crossing. In this view, officials line up the portrait with Chesapeake & Ohio GP9 No. 6086, SAL GP9 No. 1913, and Southern RS3 No. 2032.
(John P. Stith)

(above) In a motive power lashup that is typical for SAL freight trains in the 1960s, GP9s Nos. 1922 and 1912 and four FTs roll a manifest train at Moncure, N.C., in July 1962.
(Ray Sturges)

(right) Alco RS11 No. 104 at Baldwin, Florida, in December 1965.
(Ray Sturges)

(below right) GP7 No. 1778 and GP30 No. 518 were at Charlotte, N.C., in April 1967.
(Richard S. Short Photo/Ray Sturges Collection)

(above) Three GP40 "Jolly Green Giants," led by No. 605, guide their southbound freight train out of Raleigh and toward Cary, N.C., on November 4, 1966.

(W. E. Griffin, Jr. Collection)

(left) SAL No. 1770 was one of six GP7s that received the light green paint scheme that was applied to the Seaboard's GP40s and U30Bs in 1966. The locomotive is at Hermitage Yard in June, 1967.

(W. E. Griffin, Jr.)

(below) SAL GP9 No. 1911 heads up a motive power consist that includes a GP30, three GP7s, and an F3. The train is shown rolling past the Aberdeen, N.C., station on March 5, 1966.

(W. E. Griffin, Jr. Collection)

(above) Baldwin S12 switcher No. 1481 at Baldwin, Florida, in April 1967.
(Richard S. Short Photo/Ray Sturges Collection)

(right) Baldwin RS12 No. 1469 sports the paint scheme of red and black carbody with silver/aluminum lettering that was applied to SAL switchers. The unit is in service at Richmond's Hermitage Yard in November 1966.
(W. E. Griffin, Jr.)

(below) One of the SAL's 5700-series cabooses brings up the rear of a southbound TOFC train, shown departing Richmond, Virginia, on August 16, 1963.
(Ralph Coleman)

BIBLIOGRAPHY

BOOKS

Calloway, Warren L. and Withers, Paul K., *Seaboard Air Line Railway Company Motive Power*, Halifax, Pennsylvania: Withers Publishing, 1988.

Griffin, William E., Jr., *All Lines North of Raleigh: History of the Seaboard Air Line Railway's Virginia Division*, Richmond, VA: William E. Griffin, Jr., 1991.

Griffin, William E., Jr., *The Richmond, Fredericksburg and Potomac Railroad Company: The Capital Cities Route*, Lynchburg, VA: TLC Publishing, 1994.

Johnson, Robert Wayne, *Through the Heart of the South: The Seaboard Air Line Railroad Story*, Erin, Ontario: Boston Mills Press, 1995.

Langley, Albert M., Jr.;Beckum, W. Forrest, Jr.;Tidwell, C. Ronnie, *Seaboard Air Line Railway Album*, North Augusta, S.C.: Union Station Publishing, 1988.

Mann, Robert W., *Rails 'Neath the Palms*, Burbank, CA: Darwin Publications, 1983.

Mordecai, John B., *A Brief History of the RF&P Railroad*, Richmond, VA: Old Dominion Press, 1940.

Mordecai, John B., *The RF&P Railroad in the Second World War*, Richmond, VA: Whittet and Shepperson, 1948.

Patterson, William H., "Through the Heart of the South: History of the Seaboard Air Line Railway 1832-1950," PhD Dissertation (Unpublished), University of South Carolina, 1951

Prince, Richard E., *Atlantic Coast Line Railroad Steam Locomotives, Ships and History*, Green River, Wyoming: Richard E. Prince, 1966.

Prince, Richard E., *Seaboard Air Line Railway Steam Boats, Locomotives and History*, Green River, Wyoming: Richard E. Prince, 1969.

Shrady, Theodore; Waldrop, Arthur M., *Orange Blossom Special: Florida's Distinguished Winter Train*, Valrico, FL: ACL and SAL Historical Society, 1996.

Stover, John F., *The Railroads of the South 1865-1900*, Chapel Hill, NC: The University of North Carolina Press, 1955

Wertenbaker, Thomas J., *Norfolk: Historic Southern Port*, Durham, NC: Duke University Press, 1931.

REPORTS AND PERIODICALS

Poor's Manual of the Railroads of the Unites States, various years.

Seaboard Air Line Railway Company, 35 I.C.C. Valuation Reports, 337.

MAGAZINE ARTICLES

Appleby, Sam, Jr., "Through the Heart of the South," *Trains* Magazine, February 1949.

Bryan, Wiley M., "Twin Stacks," *Trains* Magazine, August 1979.

Calloway, Warren L., "Seaboard Air Line E7s," *Prototype Modeler*, Nov/Dec 1984.

Lamb, J. P., Jr., "A Tale of Two Trains," *Trains* Magazine, May 1963.

Lamb, J. P., Jr., "ACL + SAL = SCL," *Trains* Magazine, October 1964.

"Locomotives of the Seaboard Air Line Railway," *Railroad* Magazine, September 1948.

"Locomotives of the Seaboard Air Line Railway," *Railroad* Magazine, June 1959.

McBride, H.A., "The Seaboard Railroad," *Railroad* Magazine, April 1953.

Pearce, T. H., "First Train to the Capital," *The State*, November 1976.

Pinkepank, Jerry A., "Wet Rock, Dry Rock and the Seaboard," *Trains* Magazine, October 1984.

"Seaboard Air Line Engines," *Locomotive Quarterly*, Spring 1990.

"Seaboard Air Line Railroad," *Virginia and the Virginia County*, October 1951.

Smiley, Tom, "Seaboard Air Line F3s," *Prototype Modeler*, May/June 1989.

Stewart, Peter C., "Railroads and Urban Rivalries in Antebellum Eastern Virginia," *The Virginia Magazine of History and Biography*, Janaury 1973.

COMPANY DOCUMENTS

A Brief History of the Seaboard Air Line Railway.

Brief History of the Seaboard Air Line Railway in Florida.

Davis, C. McD., "An Informal Look At Atlantic Coast Line," Address to New York Society of Security Analysts, 1951

Seaboard Air Line, Annual Reports, 1900-1967; Public Timetables, various years.

Seaboard Air Line Passenger Trains in Florida.

Smith, John W., "Building a Railroad (1832-1952)." Newcomen Society in North America, 1952.

Teamwork in Scheduled Transportation, SAL Manual of Information, 1944.